FOCUSSING ON REAL ESTATE

Englisch für die Immobilienwirtschaft

EPHREM WELLENBROCK
NORBERT J. HEIKAMP

FOCUSSING ON REAL ESTATE

Englisch für die Immobilienwirtschaft
Band 1

Herausgegeben von

ANNEGRET BUCH
WILMA ELSING
LIESELOTTE STEVELING

Hammonia

Die Autorinnen:

- Annegret Buch, StD i.E.
  Schulleiterin am Berufskolleg Immobilienwirtschaft im EBZ,
  Koordinatorin für den Fachbereich Englisch
- Wilma Elsing, M.A.
- Dr. Lieselotte Steveling
  Leiterin Fachbereich Studien – Führungsakademie im EBZ

Bearbeitet von:

- Norbert J. Heikamp, StR iH a.D.
  Dolmetscher / Übersetzer in Köln - Engelskirchen
- Ephrem Wellenbrock, OStR
  Englischlehrer am Berufskolleg
  Unterrichtseinsatz Berufsschulunterricht Englisch in der Immobilienwirtschaft,
  Lehreinsatz für Englisch in Studiengängen der Führungsakademie im EBZ

Tangstedter Landstr. 83
22415 Hamburg
Tel: 040-520103-0
Fax: 040-520103-30
www.hammonia.de

Redaktionsschluss: Juni 2007

Abbildungen, soweit nicht anders vermerkt:
Allgemeine Deutsche Schiffszimmerer-Genossenschaft Hamburg,
Bergbaumuseum Bochum, Eisenbahnmuseum in Bochum-Dahlhausen
Archiv Hammonia-Verlag (E. Czerny, Ch. Walter)

Gestaltung und Satz: Christiane Walter, Hammonia Verlag GmbH
Lektorat: Andrew Rylands
Druck: Dobler, Alfeld

Das Buch wurde gedruckt auf 115 g/m² maxibulk 1.1

ISBN
978-3-87292-254-0

Vorwort

Anlass für die Entwicklung des vorliegenden Lehrwerks ist insbesondere die Novelle des Berufsbildes Immobilienkaufmann / Immobilienkauffrau, in dem der Erwerb branchenbezogener Fremdsprachenkompetenz ab dem 01. August 2006 obligatorisch wird.

Generell werden berufsbezogene Fremdsprachenkenntnisse – insbesondere immobilienwirtschaftliches Englisch – im Berufsalltag verstärkt nachgefragt. Deshalb stellt das vorliegende Lehrwerk die Gestaltung kommunikativer Kompetenz in internationaler werdenden beruflichen Handlungssituationen in den Mittelpunkt. Das Anforderungsprofil der Mitarbeiterinnen und Mitarbeiter der Immobilienwirtschaft beinhaltet zunehmend Kenntnisse unterschiedlicher Sprachen sowie interkulturelle Kompetenz.

Aufbau, Inhalt und methodischer Ansatz dieses Lehrbuchs, das sich gleichermaßen in der Aus-, Fort- und Weiterbildung der gesamten Branche nutzen lässt, sind durchgängig dem Konzept handlungsorientierten Unterrichts verpflichtet. Anhand eines Modellunternehmens werden zentrale Geschäftsfelder der Immobilienwirtschaft mehrperspektivisch behandelt. Vielfältige aus beruflicher Praxis entwickelte Lernsituationen bieten dem Nutzer dieses Arbeitsbuches die Möglichkeit, auf unterschiedlichen Niveaustufen kommunikative Kompetenz in der Fremdsprache zu erwerben. Neben den fachlichen Kompetenzen werden in der Arbeitswelt zunehmend kommunikative Fähigkeiten gefordert. Durch die Nutzung dieses Lehrwerks bereitet sich der Lernende auf diese sich verändernden Anforderungen der Branche vor.

Bochum, Juni 2007

Annegret Buch
Schulleiterin am
Berufskolleg im EBZ

Wilma Elsing, M. A.

Dr. Lieselotte Steveling
Leiterin Fachbereich Studien
Führungsakademie im EBZ

Grußwort

Aufgrund der zunehmenden Internationalisierung der Immobilienmärkte und der Multinationalität von Kunden und Geschäftspartnern kommt der fremdsprachlichen Kommunikation eine immer größer werdende Bedeutung zu. Im novellierten Berufsbild „Immobilienkaufmann/-frau" sind diese neuen Anforderungen aufgegriffen und die berufsbezogenen Fremdsprachenqualifikationen als neuer Bestandteil der Ausbildung aufgenommen worden.

Hinzu kommt: Die vielfältigen Veränderungen in der Branche erfordern eine deutliche Dienstleistungsorientierung aller Mitarbeiter und Mitarbeiterinnen. In diesem Zusammenhang kommt der Förderung kommunikativer Kompetenzen – auch durch die Beherrschung von Fremdsprachen – eine wesentliche Bedeutung bei der Personalentwicklung und -förderung auf allen Hierarchiestufen der Unternehmen zu.

Mit dem vorliegenden Lehrbuch wird eine Arbeitshilfe zur Verfügung gestellt, die in der Ausbildung wie auch für die individuelle Weiterbildung in den Unternehmen eingesetzt werden kann. Damit liegt erstmals ein branchenspezifisches Fremdsprachenlehrwerk vor, das sowohl im strukturierten Unterricht als auch zum individuellen Selbststudium genutzt werden kann.

Wir begrüßen es sehr, dass der Impuls für das vorliegende Lehrbuch und die Entwicklung der Inhalte im EBZ Europäisches Bildungszentrum der Wohnungs- und Immobilienwirtschaft in Bochum, dem größten Bildungsdienstleister der Immobilenbranche, entstanden ist. Zur erfolgreichen Bewältigung der zunehmenden englischsprachigen Kommunikation ist es hervorragend geeignet.

Lutz Freitag
Präsident des GdW
Bundesverband deutscher
Wohnungs- und Immobilienunternehmen

Burghard Schneider
Verbandsdirektor
VdW Rheinland Westfalen

Inhaltsverzeichnis / Table of contents

Anmerkungen zum Umgang mit FOCUSSING ON REAL ESTATE – Englisch für die Immobilienwirtschaft

Die Herausgeberinnen und Autoren beabsichtigen mit der Vorlage dieses Lehrwerks ein Lehr- und Lernbuch „Englisch für die Immobilienwirtschaft" zu präsentieren, das sich gleichermaßen für den Unterricht im Klassenverband und das autodidaktische Lernen eignet. Dieser Grundidee tragen sowohl das Buch als auch die jedem Exemplar beigefügte Audio-CD in besonderer Weise Rechnung. Somit können die Lernenden besonders eine der Kernkompetenzen, das Hörverstehen, als Grundvoraussetzung für eine erfolg-reiche Interaktion und Rezeption in eigenem Lerntempo am selbst gewählten Lernort erarbeiten. Auch der jedem Kapitel nachgestellte Evaluationsbogen soll eine kritische Auseinandersetzung mit dem eigenen Lernprozess und dem Lernerfolg fördern.

Der Kernansatz des vorliegenden Buches ist die Steigerung der kommunikativen Kompetenz in beruflichen Handlungssituationen im Berufsfeld der Immobilienwirtschaft. Diese können äußerst vielfältig sein.
FOCUSSING ON REAL ESTATE versteht sich nicht als bilinguales Fachbuch, sondern durch die Vielzahl von beruflichen Kommunikationsanlässen als Anreiz für exemplarisches Lernen, aus dem sich dann Rückschlüsse für die Erweiterung und Festigung der beruflichen Handlungskompetenz in anderen beruflichen Handlungssituationen ergeben.

Deshalb ist das Buch nicht instruktionistisch angelegt. Anstelle einer Vermittlungsdidaktik stehen hier Lernprozesse im Vordergrund, die von den Lernenden eine sprachhandelnde Auseinandersetzung und Evaluation eines fachlichen Wissenszuwachses in beruflichen Handlungsituationen fordern. Kognitive Prozesse sind – genau wie die berufliche Realität – nicht auf Stillstand, ihr eigenes Ende und eine Abgeschlossenheit angelegt. Das genaue Gegenteil ist der Fall: Jede Antwort auf eine Frage wirft neue Fragen auf. Die Dinge, Begriffe, Sprachwirklichkeiten entwickeln sich. „To live is to know" (Maturana): Leben bedeutet Wissenserwerb, nicht Wissen allein.

Gemäß der Einteilung des Europäischen Referenzrahmens für Sprache bietet dieses Lehrwerk Aufgaben- und Übungsformen, die die Kernkompetenzbereiche der **Rezeption** (hörendes und lesendes Erfassen der wesentlichen Aussagen fremdsprachlicher Texte), der **Produktion** (Erstellen von mündlichen und schriftlichen Mitteilungen in der Fremdsprache), der **Mediation** (Übertragungen von Texten, Sachverhalten und Problemstellungen von einer Sprache in die andere) und der **Interaktion** (Führen von Gesprächen und Austausch schriftlicher Mitteilungen in der Fremdsprache) in besonderer Weise fördern. Zur besseren Orientierung sind Aufgaben und Übungen mit Symbolen versehen, die die hier besonders geförderte Kompetenz bezeichnen.

Aufgrund seiner Materialfülle bietet das Buch zweierlei: Zum einen hält es für die Lernenden eine große Auswahl an Texten, Wortschatzübungen, Hörverstehensübungen, Diskussions- und Präsentationsanlässen bereit. Zum anderen fordert es die aktive, engagierte Auseinandersetzung mit den präsentierten Inhalten im Abgleich mit der jeweils zugrunde liegenden Situation im realen Berufsleben.

Die vorgestellten Materialien eignen sich gleichermaßen für Einzel- und differenzierte Gruppen- und Projektarbeiten. Die Entscheidung, in welcher Tiefe und Breite z. B. die Projektideen im Unterricht oder in der individuellen Arbeit umgesetzt werden, kann variieren. Nicht alles muss im Klassenverband in der im Buch präsentierten Reihenfolge „abgearbeitet" werden, selbstständiges Lernen bedeutet auch die eigene Entscheidung über die Gestaltung des Prozesses „Lernen".

Das vorliegende Buch versteht sich gleichermaßen als Lehr- und als Arbeitsbuch. Verschiedene Wortschatzübungen (z. B. Lückentexte oder Kreuzworträtsel, Puzzles etc.) können direkt im Buch ausgefüllt werden, andere Vorgaben (z. B. Mindmaps) sollten besser in den eigenen Arbeitsunterlagen vervollständigt werden.

Die Steigerung der fremdsprachlichen kommunikativen Kompetenz in der Immobilienwirtschaft bedeutet, dass die Lernenden ihre eigenen Sachkenntnisse und ihren eigenen Erfahrungsschatz in den Lernprozess einbringen und systematisch durch Wortschatzarbeit, das Kennenlernen anderer Denk- und Organisationskonzepte sowie die Erarbeitung eigener Präsentationstexte erweitern. Grammatikkenntnisse bzw. die Bereitschaft, festgestellte Mängel in diesem Bereich selbstständig aufzuarbeiten, werden dabei vorausgesetzt. Insofern versteht sich dieses Lehrwerk auch nicht als Universalwerkzeug, das jede Art von Lücke in der Sprachbeherrschung des Englischen schließt – vielmehr soll es die Lernenden dazu motivieren, sich vor dem festgestellten Zuwachs einer beruflichen Handlungskompetenz in eigener Steuerung und Verantwortung mit individuellen Defiziten auseinander zu setzen und diesen zu begegnen.

Größtmögliche Selbstständigkeit, aktive Beteiligung am eigenen Lernerfolg und Arbeit im Team entsprechen in der Unterrichts- bzw. Lernsituation den unverzichtbaren Voraussetzungen für den Erfolg in der beruflichen Realität.

Erklärung der Symbole

Diagramme & Statistiken

revision unit

discuss in class

Rollenspiel

giving a talk

schriftl. Geschäfts-kommunikation

Hörverstehen

Simulation

Information

Telefonieren

Lernstrategien

Textarbeit

Lernzielbeschreibung

Wortschatzarbeit

Mediation

www more info

UNIT 1 Working in real estate, housing and the property market - Getting to know the business

Was Sie in diesem Kapitel lernen:

- wie man sich und andere vorstellt
- wie man den deutschen Wohnungsmarkt beschreibt
- wie man die Immobilienbranche und die Aktivitäten des eigenen Unternehmens beschreibt
- wie man den eigenen Arbeitsablauf beschreibt
- wie man das eigene Unternehmen vorstellt (Aktivitäten, Belegschaft, Struktur)
- wie man den europäischen Wohnungsmarkt beschreibt
- wie man eine Hotelunterkunft bucht
- wie man seine eigene Wortschatzarbeit organisiert
- wie man mit der Methode des Clustering thematisch zusammenhängenden Wortschatz lernt

Living in Germany – Partner interview

Have a look at the map below. Tell your partner about the town and the region you live in. Include information such as

- its population
- the population density
- its infrastructure and economy
- its number of dwellings
- the main employers and industries in the area
- its cultural highlights
- larger cities in the area
- what you like and do not like about the town

What is your favourite city in Germany?
Do you prefer a rural or an urban atmosphere?
Where were you born?
Where or in what kind of town would you like to live in 20 years time?

Present your partner and his or her answers to the rest of the class.

Here are some phrases you can use to introduce somebody:

This is…
I´d like to introduce
I´d like you to meet…
S/he comes from…
S/he lives in…
S/he works for…

Manners that sell....

When dealing with colleagues and customers, you are expected to behave in a professional way. Complete the following table with tips you believe are essential.

Manners that sell...	
when talking to colleagues ...	when dealing with customers ...

Discuss your lists in class and agree on a ranking for each category.

PRE-READING...

Have you got a dress code in your company?
Can you wear whatever you want to wear?
Are you expected to dress differently when you meet customers?
Does a company-style exist?
Do you find differences in the way the managers and the office staff dress?

QUESTIONS ON THE TEXT

What – according to the text – are the reasons that justify dress codes?

"When personal appearance diktats appear too rigid, staff will feel disengaged from an organisation". Explain this statement in your own words.

What do customers in your line of business expect from business people in terms of business dress?

theguardian

Do dress codes still matter?

Matt Keating
Saturday December10, 2005 Guardian

Dress codes are about conformity. Dressing in a particular way identifies an individual with a particular group or function. Nowhere is this more obvious than in the workplace. But just because civil servants or the new Tory leader, David Cameron, no longer have to wear ties while on the job does not mean the starched-collar rigidity of the past has been consigned to the Pathé newsreels.

This week, the Commonwealth Bank of Australia apologised after criticism that a "grooming guide" it issued to its staff was too prescriptive. The booklet included advice on how often staff should cut their hair, what underwear was best and the length at which ties should be worn. The Finance Sector Union of Australia worries the bank's employees could face disciplinary action if the guidelines became company policy and were breached.

When personal appearance diktats appear too rigid, staff will feel disengaged from an organisation, says Dianah Worman, diversity adviser for the Chartered Institute of Personnel and Development. "However, dress codes are part and parcel of how a business communicates. They help an organisation say what it is about and the specific role and contribution its staff are expected to make."

Corporate Britain is rediscovering this after a decade of increasingly lax interpretations of appropriate work attire by employees who have been spurred on by dress-down Fridays and the ambiguity of "smart casual". In September, it was reported that Barclays Bank had sent its staff a memo stipulating that jeans, shorts, flip-flops, strapless tops, sportswear, T-shirts or trainers would not be tolerated in the workplace.

"That went down fantastically well with the public, because in such situations you want people to conform to certain standards," says Dylan Jones, the sartorially elegant editor of GQ magazine. "It is like going into a police station and finding police officers wearing jeans and trainers instead of uniforms."

"It's not just about instant identification. People respond to uniforms in a very positive way. Postal workers no longer have to adhere to a strict uniform code as they did in the past, and I think that has helped foster a negative image of the Post Office."

Dress, grooming and personal hygiene affect the public's impression of a business. Despite the desire for greater diversity in the workplace, we still resort to stereotypes when it comes to how we expect people to dress. [...]

Holiday Office Party

What do you think?

Do you have to go?
Who should I talk to?
Must I talk to the boss?
How long do I have to stay?
When can I start with the food?
What are common mistakes?
Can I have alcohol?

"When the boss isn't around to watch us he loads up this screen saver."

Now listen to the recording. Lydia Ramsey, a business etiquette expert, talks about what we should and should not do at an office party. Compare your ideas with what she says.

Discuss her answers with your neighbour.

Word search: Find the terms hidden in the following word search.

C	B	C	S	E	E	Y	O	L	P	M	E	V	I	L
U	L	O	D	M	E	Y	V	Q	O	C	R	D	P	A
S	O	L	E	T	R	I	K	S	L	H	E	A	E	U
T	U	L	P	O	V	O	C	O	I	N	P	R	K	S
O	S	E	A	W	P	W	F	C	T	P	R	L	A	A
M	E	A	R	N	P	K	P	I	E	Y	E	B	H	C
E	C	G	T	D	O	M	F	A	N	N	S	E	S	G
R	A	U	M	F	A	I	R	L	E	U	E	H	D	U
G	L	E	E	N	C	A	S	I	S	A	T	A	N	I
B	P	S	N	A	N	U	G	S	S	H	A	V	A	D
W	K	E	T	C	O	Y	O	I	E	T	T	I	H	E
D	R	I	E	I	H	B	I	N	R	F	I	O	T	L
S	O	T	R	V	M	T	J	G	D	O	O	U	L	I
N	W	E	T	I	Q	U	E	T	T	E	N	R	S	N
L	S	U	E	I	S	T	E	R	E	O	T	Y	P	E

Another day at the office...

When you come into your office, you find the following email which your boss sent you.

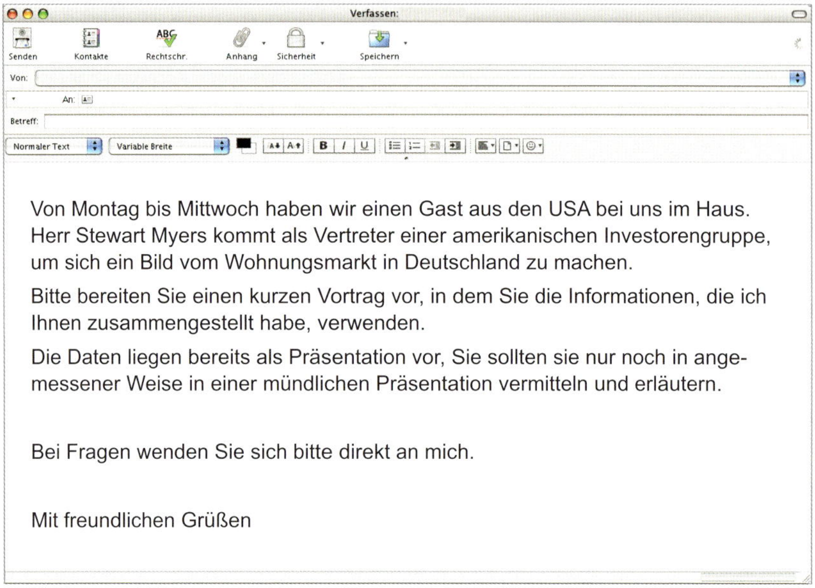
Verfassen:
Senden Kontakte Rechtschr. Anhang Sicherheit Speichern
Von:
An:
Betreff:
Normaler Text Variable Breite

Von Montag bis Mittwoch haben wir einen Gast aus den USA bei uns im Haus. Herr Stewart Myers kommt als Vertreter einer amerikanischen Investorengruppe, um sich ein Bild vom Wohnungsmarkt in Deutschland zu machen.

Bitte bereiten Sie einen kurzen Vortrag vor, in dem Sie die Informationen, die ich Ihnen zusammengestellt habe, verwenden.

Die Daten liegen bereits als Präsentation vor, Sie sollten sie nur noch in angemessener Weise in einer mündlichen Präsentation vermitteln und erläutern.

Bei Fragen wenden Sie sich bitte direkt an mich.

Mit freundlichen Grüßen

Work through the information provided. Then decide in which order you would like to present the information. Make notes that will help you give the talk.

Information provided

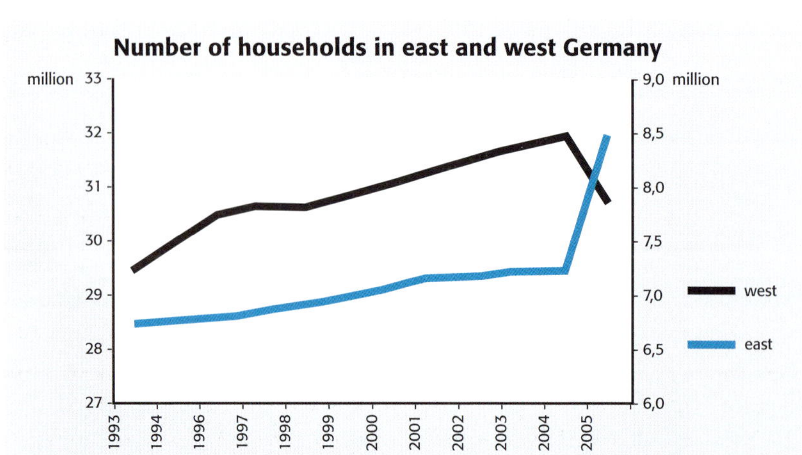

Source: Statistische Jahrbücher für die Bundesrepublik Deutschland

Number of households rising

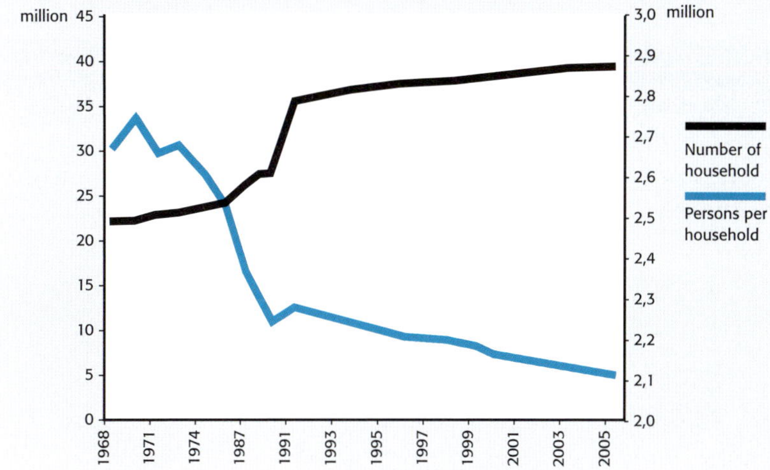

Source: Statistische Jahrbücher für die Bundesrepublik Deutschland

Wohnfläche je Einwohner
Deutschland und Bundesländer 2004

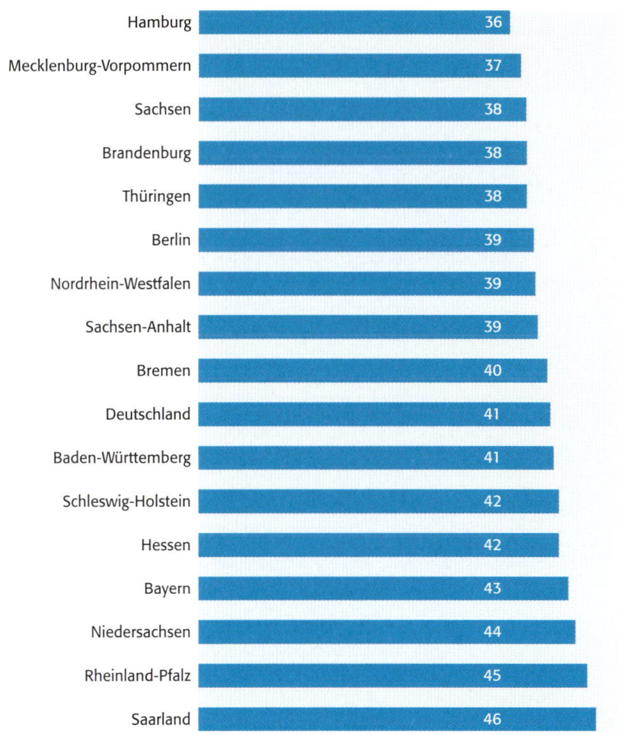

Source: Statistisches Jahrbuch für die Bundesrepublik Deutschland 2006, S. 282

Dwelling stock

Specification	Unit	2002	2003	2004
			Germany	
Dwelling stock				
Dwellings (residential and non-residential buildings)	1 000	38 924.8	39 141.5	39 362.9
Of which with ... rooms				
1	1 000	841.3	843.4	844.0
2	1 000	2 418.4	2 423.7	2 428.9
3	1 000	8 500.2	8 515.0	8 526.2
4	1 000	11 608.0	11 635.4	11 663.0
5	1 000	7 529.8	7 589.6	7 651.8
6	1 000	4 081.5	4 134.4	4 190.8
7 and over	1 000	3 945.6	4 000.0	4 058.3
Rooms, total	1 000	170 507.5	171 725.0	172 992.4
Living floor space, total	mn m^2	3 310.9	3 339.2	3 369.0
Structural data on the dwelling stock				
Dwellings per 1000 inhabitants	Number	472	474	477
Living floor space per dwelling	m^2	85.1	85.3	85.6
Living floor space per inhabitant	m^2	40.1	40.5	40.8
Rooms per dwelling	Number	4.4	4.4	4.4

Last updated on 29 July 2005

There are about 39 million households in Germany today, roughly as many as there are housing units. So on the national level at least the housing market is balanced.

There are very distinct regional differences in household sizes. The lowest level is recorded in Munich (1.7 persons), the highest in the borough of Cloppenburg (approx. 3 persons).

Age of residential property
excluding hostels

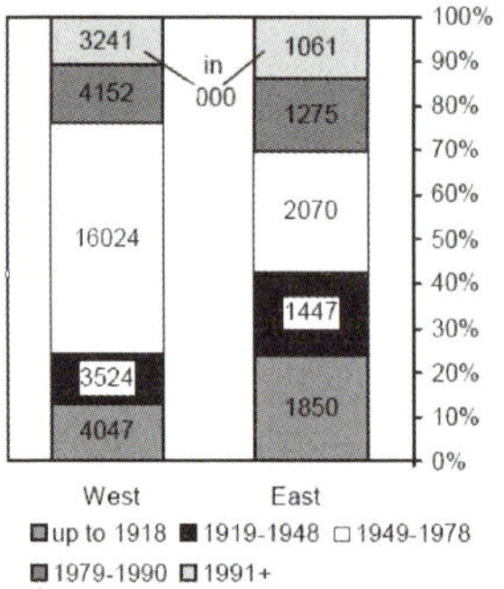

Source: Federal Statistical Office, microcensus

Occupied housing by building sizes 2002

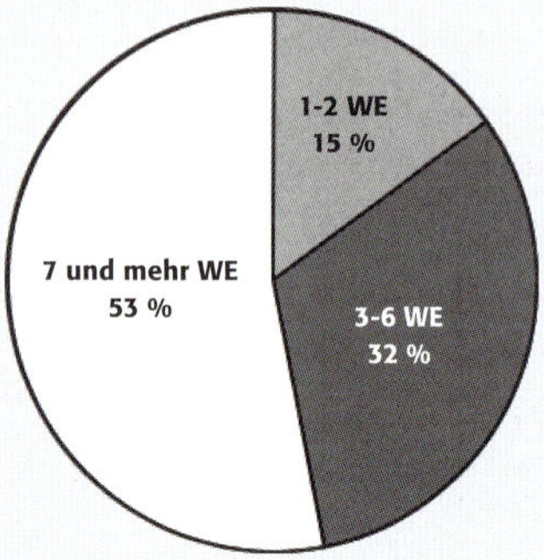

Source: Statistisches Jahrbuch 2006

Households

Specification	Unit	2002[1]	2003[1]	2004[1]
Households [1]	1 000	38 720	38 944	39 122
1-person households	1 000	14 225	14 426	14 566
2-person households	1 000	13 060	13 169	13 335
3-person households	1 000	5 487	5 462	5 413
4-person households	1 000	4 315	4 268	4 218
Households with 5 or more persons	1 000	1 633	1 618	1 590

[1] Microcensus results: 2002 in April; 2003 in May; 2004 in March.
Last updated on 22 March 2005

Who are homeowners?

% of household type in owner occupation 2002

	Germany	West only
Household size		
1 person	25	27
2 persons	49	52
3 or more	56	57
Age of head		
Under 30	7	8
30-59	43	44
60 and more		
Monthly net income (euro)		
less than 500	16	18
500 - 1.300	24	26
1.300 - 3.200	43	45
3.200 and more	68	69

Source: Federal Statistical Office

Of the almost 10 million units managed by professional providers a very large part is owned by public-sector corporations (more than 3 million units) and housing cooperatives (2.3 million apartments).

Private housing companies own only 2.6 million apartments, just 7 % of the total housing supply.

Slightly more than half the housing is in apartment blocks, with only one out of every ten apartments located in buildings containing more than 13 units. The other not quite half is made up of owner-occupied houses, i.e. single- and two-family houses. In this segment single-family houses occupy a more prominent position, with nearly 10 million units, than two-family houses, of which there are roughly 6.5 million units.

Housing stock in Germany (2003)

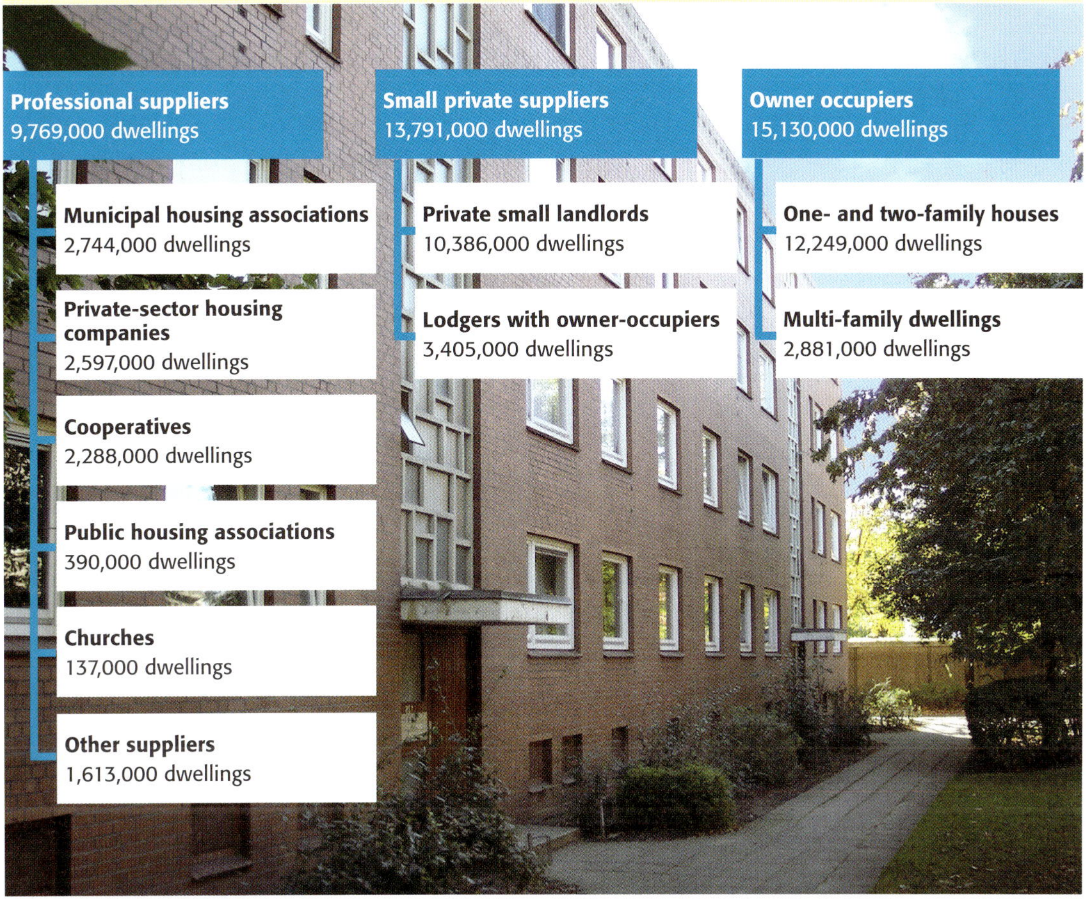

The housing market – working with words

Once again, go through your notes and the information provided and complete the following table.

Talking about people	Talking about buildings	Talking about companies	other words you consider important
inhabitant ...	dwelling unit ...	public-sector corporations private housing companies	average reunification ...

Lernen Sie Vokabeln in Sinn- und thematischen Zusammenhängen. Nutzen Sie beispielsweise die Methode des Clustering: Sie schreiben einen Fachbegriff in die Mitte auf einen Zettel oder eine Karteikarte und vervollständigen möglichst viele „Arme" mit thematisch relevanten Begriffen.

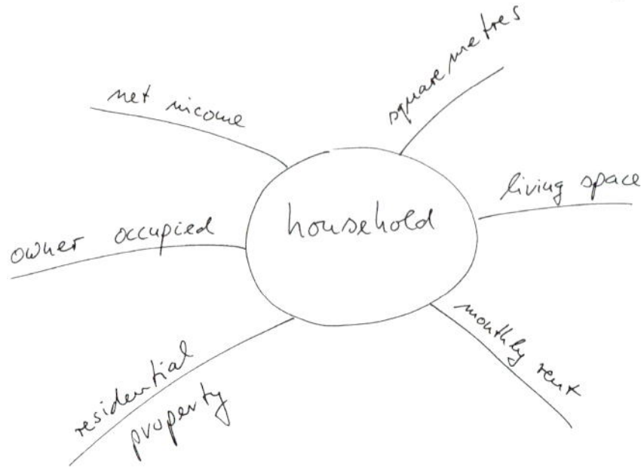

Diese Methode eignet sich auch zum Wiederholen von Themenblöcken oder Kapiteln. Nehmen Sie ein Blatt und schreiben – je nach Zeit oder Motivation – einzelne Wörter des Themenzusammenhangs in je einen Kreis. Ergänzen Sie nun weitere bekannte Begriffe in der oben beschriebenen Weise.

Innerhalb kurzer Zeit haben Sie den relevanten Wortschatz angewandt und eingeübt. Anschließend können Sie nun noch versuchen, alle auf dem Zettel befindlichen Wörter in einem zusammenhängenden Text strukturiert anzuwenden.

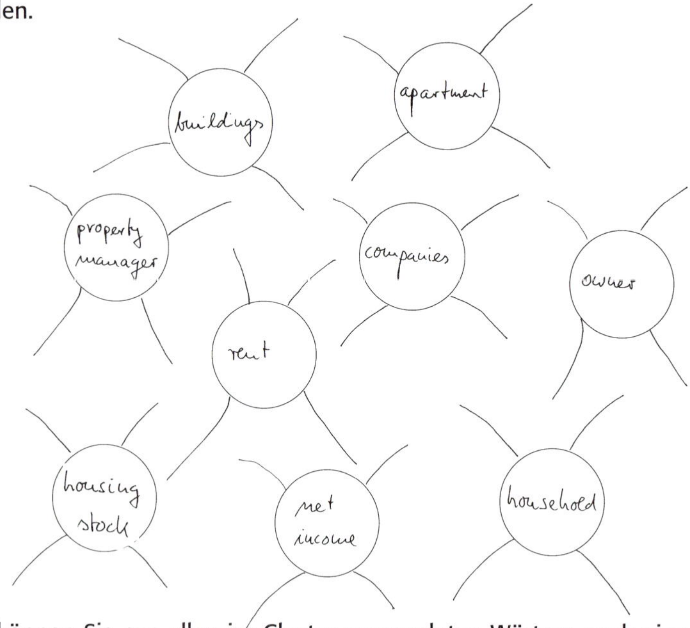

Nun können Sie aus allen im Cluster verwendeten Wörtern noch einen Satz oder einen kurzen Text erstellen.

"The living space which a household can afford often depends on the monthly net income. The more square metres you occupy, the higher the rent you will have to pay. Of course you do not have to pay a landlord, if your residential property is owner occupied and belongs to you. Very often in this case, however, people have to pay for their mortgages."

Talking about the real estate industry and about your job

1. Have a look at the four short German texts. Read the text that best describes your company's activities on the real estate market. Summarise the main aspects in English. You do not have to translate the entire text, however, you should try and cover its key aspects.

Wohnungsbaugesellschaften sind in privatwirtschaftlicher, kommunaler, industrieverbundener oder kirchlicher Trägerschaft tätig. Neben der Wohnraumversorgung sind sie maßgebliche Partner bei der städtebaulichen Betreuung und erfüllen eine wichtige Funktion für den sozialen Frieden in den Kommunen. Die professionelle Dienstleistung rund um die Immobilie reicht von der Finanzierung bis zum Gebäudemanagement und zur Mieterbetreuung. Wohnungsbaugesellschaften verfügen in der Regel über große Wohnungsbestände und müssen sich daher aufgrund der Marktentwicklung und unterschiedlichen Zielgruppen immer neuen Herausforderungen stellen. Der Unterhaltung und Entwicklung von Immobilien kommt dabei besondere Bedeutung zu.

Immobilienmakler handeln mit Grundstücken, Miet- und Eigentumswohnungen sowie ganzen Wohngebäuden oder Gewerbeobjekten. Dazu bedarf es kompetenter Fachleute, die mit großer Sachkenntnis und Kundenorientierung kaufen, verkaufen und vermitteln können. Die Akquisition und Beratung von Kunden, Objektbesichtigungen und die erforderliche Recherche machen den beruflichen Alltag abwechslungsreich. Verhandlungen mit Banken und Versicherungen, Kalkulationen und Durchführung von Verwaltungsarbeiten erfordern ein hohes Maß an Verantwortung. Selbstständiges Arbeiten und der souveräne Umgang mit modernen Medien sind unabdingbare Voraussetzungen für die erfolgreiche Arbeit im Maklerbereich.

Die Verwaltung von Wohneigentum bzw. die Betreuung von Wohnungseigentümergemeinschaften hat sich zu einem eigenständigen Geschäftsfeld entwickelt. Gute Kenntnisse des Wohnungseigentumsrechts und ein noch besseres Verhandlungsgeschick im Umgang mit Eigentümern erfordern eine qualifizierte Persönlichkeit, die sich auf neue Situationen schnell einstellen kann. Der Verwalter hat eine Vielzahl von Aufgaben zu bewältigen. Er leitet Wohnungseigentümerversammlungen, ist Moderator und setzt die Beschlüsse der Gemeinschaft durch. Die Vielfalt dieser Aufgaben erfordert Qualifikation und Sachkenntnis. Das reicht von rechtlichen bis zu technischen Fragen (z. B. Veranlassen von Instandhaltungs- und Instandsetzungsmaßnahmen). Psychologisches Einfühlungsvermögen und Verhandlungsgeschick sind wichtige Voraussetzungen zur Erfüllung der Aufgaben im kaufmännischen, technischen und allgemeinen Verwaltungsbereich.

Wohnungsgenossenschaften gelten als dritter Weg zwischen Wohneigentum und Miete. Sie nutzen privates Kapital für gemeinschaftliche Projekte und sind für ihre Mitglieder tätig. Die genossenschaftlichen Prinzipien Selbsthilfe, Selbstverwaltung und Selbstverantwortung charakterisieren diese interessante und erfolgreiche Unternehmensform. Im Unterschied zu den Wohnungsbaugesellschaften gehören die meisten der rund 2.000 Wohnungsgenossenschaften zu den mittleren und kleineren Unternehmen. Zusätzliche Herausforderungen und vielseitige Aufgaben ergeben sich durch die stärkere Mitgliederbindung und die erforderliche effektive Kommunikation mit den Wohnungsnutzern.

2. Now have a look at the list which contains common activities people working in the real estate business have to carry out.

3. Tick the boxes which best describe your daily responsibilities. Of course, you can add activities which might be missing.

- ❑ ...maintain and increase the value of real estate investments.
- ❑ ...oversee the performance of income-producing commercial or residential properties.
- ❑ ...ensure that real estate investments achieve their expected revenues.
- ❑ ...manage the common property and services of condominiums and cooperatives.
- ❑ ...handle the financial operations of the property.
- ❑ ...find tenants for existing property.
- ❑ ...find buyers for properties to be sold.
- ❑ ...provide advice to those wanting to buy property.
- ❑ ...provide advice on questions of financing.
- ❑ ...plan the tenants' move-in and move-out procedures.
- ❑ ...ensure that mortgages, taxes, insurance premiums, payroll and maintenance bills are paid on time.
- ❑ ...supervise the preparation of financial statements and periodically report to the owners on the status of the property, occupancy rates, dates of lease expirations and other matters.
- ❑ ...negotiate contracts for janitorial, security, groundskeeping, trash removal and other services.
- ❑ ...assist home-sellers in finding buyers for their property.
- ❑ ...solicit bids from several contractors.
- ❑ ...talk to local authorities to identify plots for building.
- ❑ ...assist home-builders in the steps necessary to build their houses.
- ❑ ...recommend which contractor's bid to accept.
- ❑ ...monitor the performance of contractors.
- ❑ ...investigate and resolve complaints from residents and tenants when services are not properly provided.
- ❑ ...provide low-income housing.
- ❑ ...purchase supplies and equipment for the property.
- ❑ ...make arrangements with specialists for repairs that cannot be handled by regular property maintenance staff.
- ❑ ...are responsible for day-to-day operations for one piece of property, such as an office building, shopping centre, community association, or apartment complex.
- ❑ ...routinely inspect the grounds, facilities and equipment to determine if repairs or maintenance are needed.
- ❑ ...meet with current residents when handling requests for repairs or trying to resolve complaints.
- ❑ ...carry out necessary steps in eviction procedures.
- ❑ ...meet with prospective residents or tenants to show vacant apartments or office space.

- ❑ …are responsible for enforcing the terms of rental or lease agreements, such as rent collection, parking and pet restrictions, and termination-of-lease procedures.
- ❑ …keep accurate, up-to-date records of income and expenditures from property operations.
- ❑ …submit regular expense reports.
- ❑ …market vacant space to prospective tenants through the use of a leasing agent, advertising, or by other means.
- ❑ …plan the refurbishment of existing properties.
- ❑ …prepare vacant properties for letting.
- ❑ …act as the property owners' agent and adviser for the property.
- ❑ …plan and direct the purchase, development and disposition of real estate on behalf of the business and investors.
- ❑ …focus on long-term strategic financial planning.
- ❑ …manage the day-to-day operations of the property.
- ❑ …negotiate contracts for the purchase or lease of the property.
- ❑ …periodically review their company's real estate holdings.
- ❑ …identify properties that are no longer financially profitable.
- ❑ …negotiate the sale or termination of the lease of such properties.
- ❑ …acquire land and plan construction of shopping centres, houses, apartments, office buildings, or industrial parks.
- ❑ …negotiate with representatives of local governments, other businesses, community and public interest groups.
- ❑ …explain aspects of the tenancy agreement.
- ❑ …help to negotiate short-term loans to finance the construction of the project.
- ❑ …later negotiate long-term permanent mortgage loans.
- ❑ …help choose, assist, and advise the architectural firms that draw up detailed plans and the construction companies that build the project.
- ❑ …interact on a daily basis with homeowners and other residents.
- ❑ …are responsible for the operation of community pools, golf courses, and community centres, and for the maintenance of landscaping and parking areas.
- ❑ …________________________________
- ❑ …________________________________
- ❑ …________________________________
- ❑ …________________________________
- ❑ …________________________________
- ❑ …________________________________

4. Using your results of 1-3, now prepare a short talk in which you explain to your classmates what you typically do in your company.

Here are some phrases you might use:

Our company's main activities are…

We mainly … commercial/residential property …

One of the typical activities in my job is to…

Very often I have to…

At the moment I mostly have to …

However, I never have to…

5. Now listen to the short statements your classmates give and ask them questions.

Here are some phrases you might use:

Did I understand you correctly when you said that …

Do you never…

Which are the things you find most rewarding?

Which are the things you find most interesting?

Which are the things you find most boring?

Talking about the real estate industry and about your job:

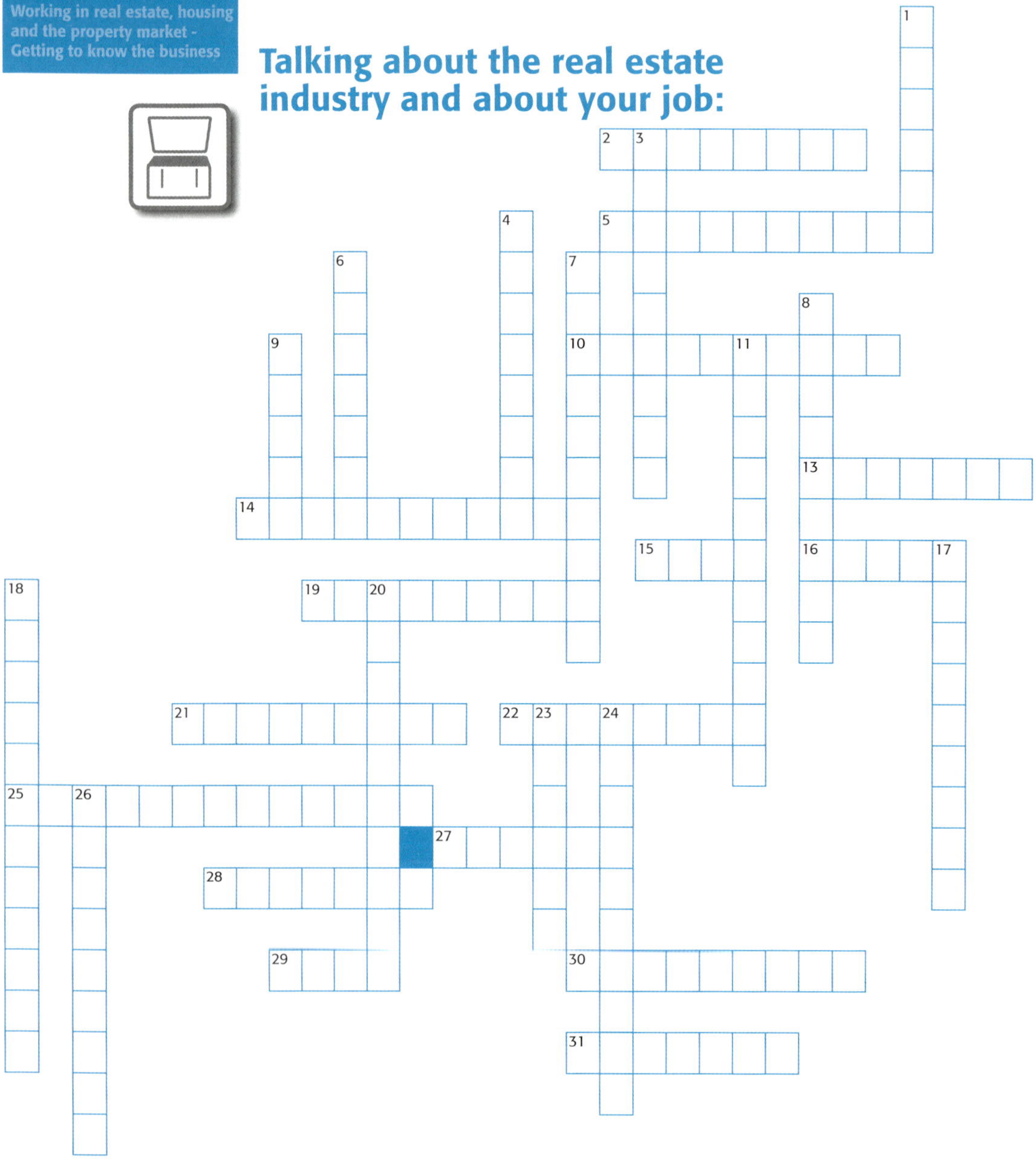

Down		Across	
1. verwalten	18. Errichtung, Bau	2. Vermieter	27. Mieter
3. Vertrag	20. Regierung	5. profitabel	28. Büros
4. Hypotheken-darlehen	23. leer stehend	10. Beschwerden	29. Grundstück
6. kaufen, erwerben	24. Vertragsfirma	13. Dienstleistung	30. Belegung
7. Sicherheiten	26. Finanzierung	14. Erschließung	31. Einzug
8. Investoren		15. Miete	
9. Wert		16. Eigentümer	
11. Werbung		19. verhandeln	
17. Anwohner		21. Architekt	
		22. Zwangsräumung	
		25. Sanierung	

(Begriffe aus zwei Wörtern mit Bindestrich eintragen)

Introducing your Company „Gut und sicher wohnen" in Bochum at GW BO

Listen to the first part of the interview with Jürgen Witt, commercial manager at GW BO, and collect as much information as possible. While listening to the interview, please try and complete the following mind map to gather as much relevant information as possible.

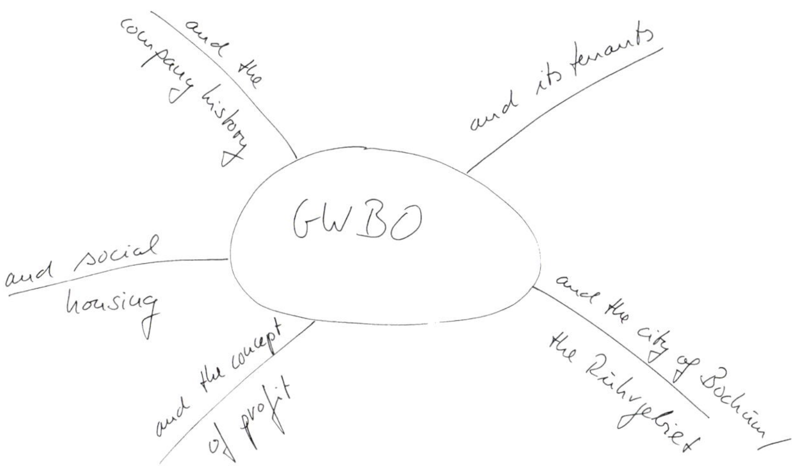

Interview with the Commercial Manager of GW BO, Mr. Jürgen Witt:

Journalist Mr. Frank Lüttke: Mr. Witt, you are the Commercial Manager of our local housing enterprise GW BO, known by most of the people living in this city. Lots of them are your tenants or they live in owner-occupied homes you are managing on their behalf. But do we really know GW BO?

Mr. Witt: Well, GW BO is a very old company, founded in 1892, and has undergone numerous changes during the last century. We have always been and still are a community-owned housing enterprise with a distinct social commitment, as we act on behalf of our shareholder. We implement the social and urban development in this city. But nowadays, we are also very much market-driven.

Traditionally, we used to offer housing with affordable rents for low-income groups. This was very important in our area, the industrialised North Rhine-Westphalia until the early 70s of the last century.

But we are, let me say, no more limited to that category of the population, for the times they are a-changing, as I already said. The former German Housing Act of 1956, which was in force until the year 2002, clearly stipulated that "large sections of the population" had to be the target group of publicly funded housing.

That was in view of the tremendous housing need after World War II and the progressive industrialisation of North Rhine-Westphalia.

Although public housing in those days was subject to a certain number of conditions, notably regarding the income limits of our tenants, nearly 40 percent of the entire population used to be eligible for social housing in the late 70s, early 80s.

J.: What has actually changed for your enterprise, Mr. Witt?

W.: Change is a very complex issue, Mr. Lüttke, and it needs a thorough management. When I scan the various fields of our activities, I'd say that the groundbreaking change for our sector was the abolition of the German non-profit housing act, the WGG at the end of 1989. From January 1st, 1990 on, the former German non-profit housing associations started to be fully exposed to the free market. With all the potentials but also risks involved.

J.: Please tell us first about the new potentials. We can perhaps revert to the risks later.

W.: The abolition of the non-profit housing act in Germany gave us much more freedom to manoeuvre and also new business opportunities. The old limit of a maximum of 4 percent profit was finally given up, because our shareholders expected us to be more performing, they wanted to cash in more profit eagerly needed for their local budgets.

Most of the housing enterprises added new business activities to their traditional product portfolio, which was mainly rental and a few affiliated services. They started developing and to compete with the private sector. Some of them were quite lucky.

Hence, the major impact did not result from the individual detailed aspects of the legal change. The former non-profit housing sector experienced, let me call it, a new spirit. In spite of our voluntary social commitment which was renewed immediately after the abolition of the old status by most of the municipal housing enterprises, we had to mutate from a more administration-type and easy-going structure to a straight and tough entrepreneurial positioning and attitude. That meant, above all, absolute cost control and the implementation of the appropriate future-oriented tools and processes such as corporate vision, good governance, cost and risk management, business scorecards, benchmarking, control and transparency, certification, etc.

And the second great challenge was the new housing market situation. You see, until early in the 90s, we had an offer-driven market. That was in line with our business practice. We had the flats, the tenants queued to get them. Since the 90s, the situation switched to a demand-driven market. This applies particularly to East Germany, where the Kohl government tremendously promoted the new construction of housing after the reunification of Germany, for both rental housing and owner-occupation.

Nowadays, we have an oversupply of housing of about one and a half million dwelling units in Germany. Often you put an ad in the newspaper for the same flat twice or three times. We simply had to learn what it takes to be successful in a demand-driven market.

When you come into your office the next morning, you receive the following email which your boss sent you referring to the scheduled visit of Stewart Myers.

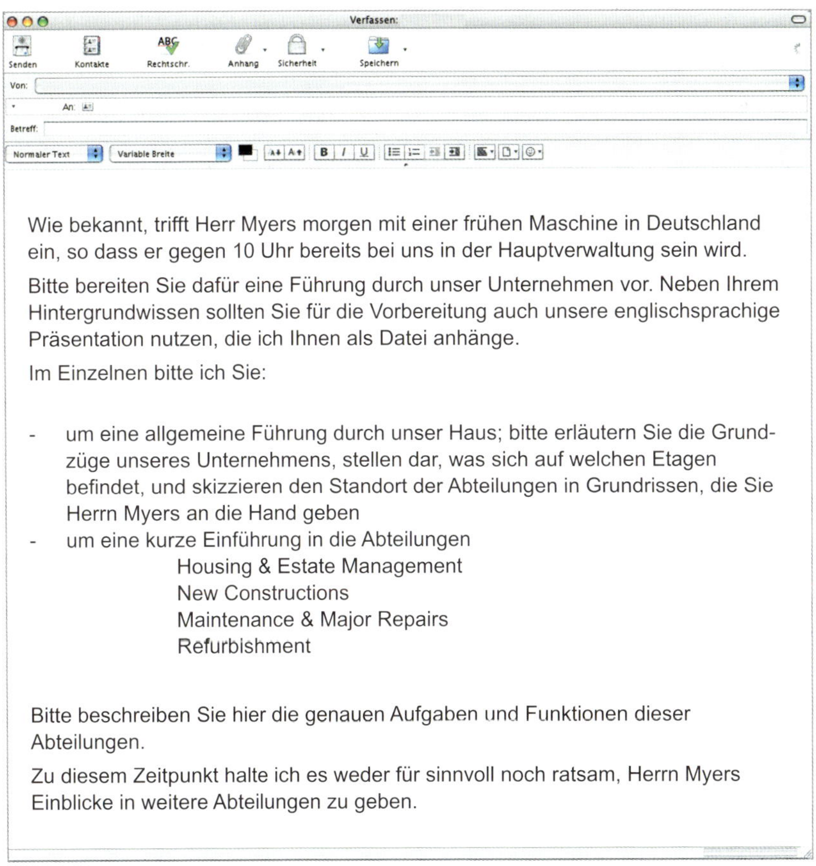

Wie bekannt, trifft Herr Myers morgen mit einer frühen Maschine in Deutschland ein, so dass er gegen 10 Uhr bereits bei uns in der Hauptverwaltung sein wird.

Bitte bereiten Sie dafür eine Führung durch unser Unternehmen vor. Neben Ihrem Hintergrundwissen sollten Sie für die Vorbereitung auch unsere englischsprachige Präsentation nutzen, die ich Ihnen als Datei anhänge.

Im Einzelnen bitte ich Sie:

- um eine allgemeine Führung durch unser Haus; bitte erläutern Sie die Grundzüge unseres Unternehmens, stellen dar, was sich auf welchen Etagen befindet, und skizzieren den Standort der Abteilungen in Grundrissen, die Sie Herrn Myers an die Hand geben
- um eine kurze Einführung in die Abteilungen
  - Housing & Estate Management
  - New Constructions
  - Maintenance & Major Repairs
  - Refurbishment

Bitte beschreiben Sie hier die genauen Aufgaben und Funktionen dieser Abteilungen.

Zu diesem Zeitpunkt halte ich es weder für sinnvoll noch ratsam, Herrn Myers Einblicke in weitere Abteilungen zu geben.

Material provided:

Introducing your company "Gut und sicher wohnen" at GW BO

GW BO is a German medium-sized housing enterprise located in the city of Bochum in North Rhine-Westphalia.

As many housing associations in Germany, **GW BO** is a limited liability company. The only shareholder is the City of Bochum.

The City of Bochum has about 382,000 inhabitants living in about 186,300 dwellings. **GW BO** is one of the larger landlords in the city and has about 16,224 clients living in the company's 7,725 dwellings. Thus, **GW BO** has an influence on the local housing market.

Our core business is the management and letting of commercial and residential property. In addition to that, we are continuously privatising parts of our dwelling stock for owner-occupation and to private investors. Last but not least, we act as privileged partner of the City Council in view of the sustainable urban renewal of the City and its outskirts. We constantly refurbish our own stock, we invest in the construction of new housing and we support specific community development projects.

We wish to consolidate our traditionally strong market position in the city by constantly improving our products and services, by offering excellent and affordable housing to the quite demanding urban population and by remaining a reliable partner for a sustainable urban, economic and social development.

Involving our tenants in helping us to improve our services has always been a major priority for **GW BO**.

Organisation chart of GW BO

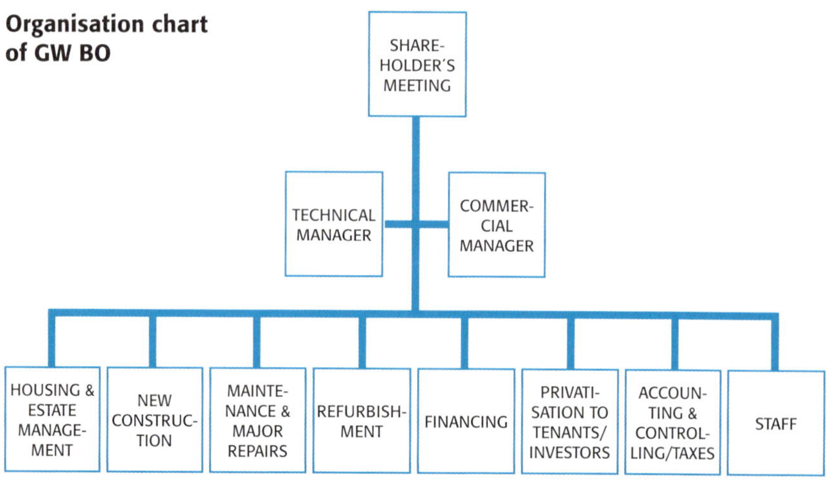

Key facts and figures:

N° of dwellings	built before 1920	built between 1920 and 1945	built between 1946 and 1970	built between 1971 and 2005
total 7,725	2,535	1,715	1,858	1,617
refurbished in:	1984	1992	1998 / 2005	
./. social housing (i. e. built with public funding not yet fully amortised)	----	---	1,858	772
social housing in % of total stock: 34%			abt. 24%	abt. 10%
dwellings in:	1-family houses	2-family houses	building up to 4 floors	buildings with 4 to 6 floors
	77	112	2,159	5,377
types of dwelling (Bedsits)	1-bed flats	2-bed flats	3-bed flats	4-bed flats
	141	3,399	3,170	1,015
staff	2002	2003	2004	2005
total	117	108	99	103
./. commercial	56	51	48	50
./. technical	52	50	45	46
./. social care professionals	9	7	6	7

The development of new homes and services and our ability to meet the needs of new and existing residents in the years to come is critical for **GW BO**'s future.

Thus, our department "Housing & Estate Management" is constantly comparing the development of the demand with our offer in order to avoid mismatches and costly vacancies. This strategy applies for both our commercial and residential property. In close cooperation with the local authorities, the department **"New construction"** completed 52 new homes this year, including 27 in a mixed scheme for affordable rent (social housing) and owner-occupation in the city-centre. This scheme particularly underpins our commitment to the economic, social, ethnic and cultural mix in a modern urban reality.

The company refurbished a total of 117 dwelling units over the year, mainly in multi-storey buildings of the early 70s. The departments **"Maintenance & Repair"** and **"Refurbishment"** cooperate in order to ensure that our homes are always a little bit more attractive than the rest of the city's dwellings. We added balconies, wherever possible, renewed the wall cladding with an additional thermal insulation in order to keep heating costs as low as possible and built in new bathrooms. In addition to that, we are proud to continue our strategic partnership in the community broadband project, so that we can offer broadband internet and phone to members of the community who otherwise might have no access to it.

Given the present opportunity of historically low interest rates, our department **"Privatisation to tenants/investors"** still continued to sell dwellings to our tenants. Thanks to the creativity of our department **"Financing"**, we are able to offer very attractive conditions to our tenants who are glad and proud to remain in their traditional neighbourhood and to own their flats.

Planning a business trip to Lithuania

Your boss has been invited to take part in a conference "The housing market in the new EU member states" which is to be held in Vilnius, Lithuania.

He asks you to prepare a short German text for him in which you summarise both the diagrams provided and an interview he was sent to prepare for the conference.

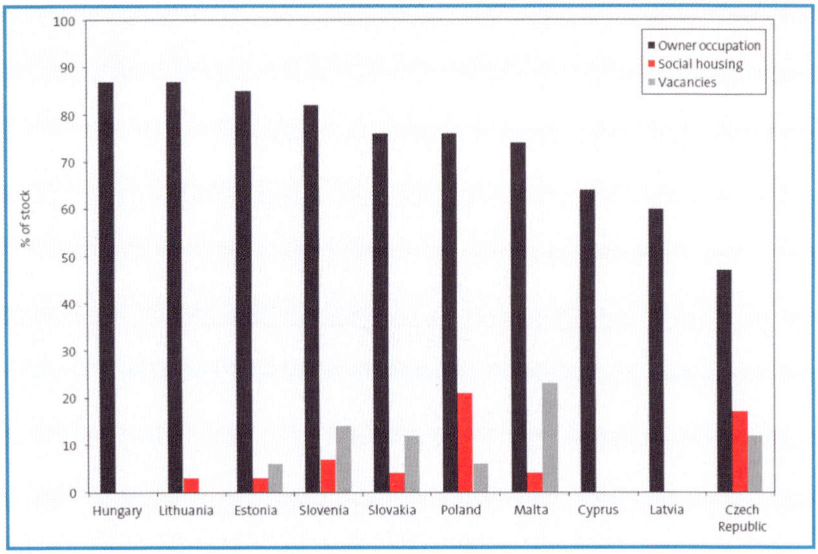

Number of dwellings built per 1.000 inhabitants, EU countries compared

Latvia	**0.4**
Lithuania	**1.1**
Hungary	**2.2**
Poland	**2.3**
Slovak Republik	**2.4**
Czech Republik	**2.5**
Slovenia	**3.1**
Cyprus	**7.6**
France	**5.1**
Germany	**3.5**
UK	**3.1**
Ireland	**14.1**
Spain	**13.8**

Notes: 2000-2002 depending on latest available figures, data unavailable for Estonia & Malta

Source: Housing Developments in European Countries

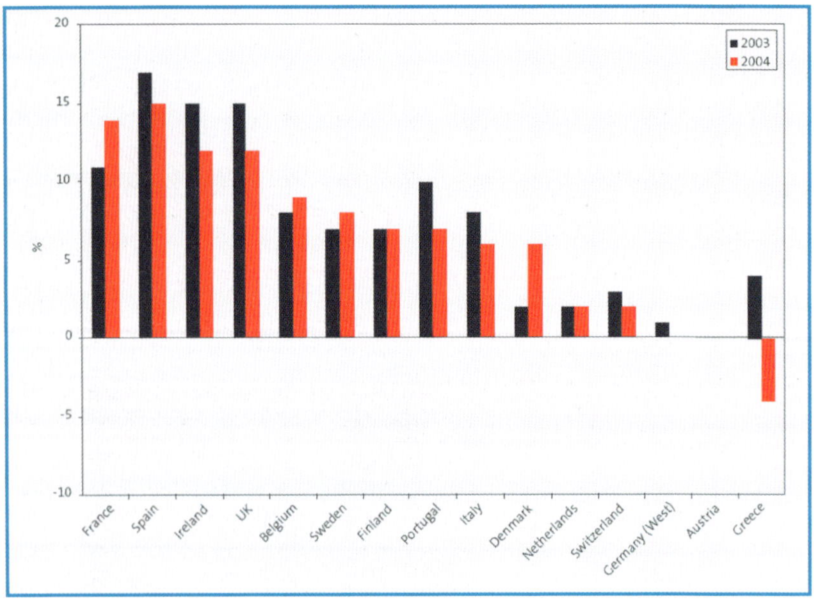

Listen to the following interview in which journalist Pete Russ (European Real Estate Journal EREJ) and Albertas Vignorius (president of the Lithuanian Real Estate Association) talk about the situation of housing in the new EU countries. In order to write the short German text your boss asks you to produce, first complete the following table:

general standard of housing	supply of housing	quality of housing stock	living space	prospects for the future
...	...	...	...	...

Pete Russ, EREJ: Mr Vignorius, in May, 2004, an additional 10 countries joined the EU –Cyprus, the Czech Republic, Estonia, Hungary, Latvia, Lithuania, Malta, Poland, the Slovak Republic and Slovenia. Could you as the president of the Lithuanian Real Estate Association and the host of the conference "The housing market in the new EU member states", please tell us in general about the living standards and housing in these countries?

Albertas Vignorius: All these new member states have lower standards of living than we would consider usual in Western Europe but surely hope and plan to catch up with the rest of the EU. As they tend to have lower living standards and as housing is an important element in characterising these living standards, it can generally be said that their housing volumes and qualities are far lower than in Western Europe.

Pete Russ, EREJ: Do you see any signs of a stronger investment in the housing sector?

Albertas Vignorius: Along with these good basic consumption characteristics go high levels of national investment on housing. Moreover, faster-growing countries also tend to invest proportionately more in housing. This is usually seen as necessary in a rising consumption if they are to meet the needs of expanding workforces in the major growth regions. Over the past decade, these characteristics could strongly be seen in such European countries as Greece, Ireland, Portugal and Spain.

Furthermore, the past histories of Central and Eastern European countries (the CEE8) made housing investment especially important within them. Housing played particular roles in CPE frameworks. They tended to build lots of dwellings, especially during the 1970s and 1980s.

Pete Russ, EREJ: Talking about buildings in these countries, what sort of dwellings were mostly put up in that time?

Albertas Vignorius: What was constructed were generally standardised, industrialised building apartment blocks containing dwellings of limited quality and size. Housebuilding became as much a component of the command economy, with five year plan targets to be met, as being aimed at satisfying consumer needs.

Pete Russ, EREJ: Does that mean that there was hardly any building activity by private owners?

Albertas Vignorius: No, saying that would not be correct, either. Dwellings were built in rural areas and small towns by owners in piecemeal ways using the available building materials, which were not always the most appropriate or of good quality. This rural housing stock that has a relatively high absence of basic amenities and generally shows poor building quality.

Pete Russ, EREJ: Generally speaking, would you say that today there are enough new dwellings in the new EU member states?

Albertas Vignorius: In Poland, overall housebuilding did not manage to keep up with rising household numbers, so that it has faced an absolute shortage of about 1 to 1.5 million dwellings for a long time, despite relatively high building rates during the

1970s and 1980s. The Slovak Republic and Lithuania also face shortages. Overall, this pre-1990 housebuilding legacy has left unique housing stocks in the CEE8 of relatively young, but often rundown, homes - with limited internal and neighbourhood amenities and poor insulation.

Pete Russ, EREJ: So this would mean a need for new buildings and refurbishments on existing ones?

Albertas Vignorius: Yes, that's how we see it today. In many of the CEE8 countries the issue is as much about the quality of the existing stock as its general availability. Moreover, these dwellings are often not physically adaptable for serious upgrading to provide better sizes, nor is it often worthwhile modernising them. This suggests the need for very high levels of dwelling replacement over the long-term.

Pete Russ, EREJ: The average living space per inhabitant in Germany is slightly more than 40 square metres. What is the situation like in the new member states?

Albertas Vignorius: Dwellings sizes are also notably smaller than in Western Europe. In the old EU15, dwellings have an average of 4.4 rooms and 84 square metres of living space whereas in the new CEE8 members, they have only 3.2 rooms and 58 square metres of living space.

Pete Russ, EREJ: To Germans, the Southern European countries traditionally have been more interesting than others because of e. g. tourism. What does housing look like in Cyprus and Malta for example?

Albertas Vignorius: Within the more southern economies, housing has also been traditionally favoured. The built form is obviously different. It usually consists of simply-equipped one or two-storey dwellings developed by their owners in a piecemeal, haphazard fashion, using traditional or simple concrete frame and block methods. Cyprus has the largest recorded average dwelling size in the EU15, at 145 square metres and 5.8 rooms; in Malta, the average is five rooms. This high level of building investment reflects the strong family and financial motives associated with housing in these countries and the importance of tourism.

Pete Russ, EREJ: If you look into the future, what kind of development do you expect in terms of urban planning?

Albertas Vignorius: As the land market takes on a greater role in these countries in the future, it is likely that the cities of many other new accession countries will develop widely decentralised, spread-out urban structures, more in keeping with US models than the planning-induced emphasis on high density and historic city centres more common in Western Europe. Activities will search out the cheaper locations, lower congestion and higher amenities of the fringe without the same strong pull of city centres on them as in the west.

Pete Russ, EREJ: Mr Vignorius, thank you very much for this interview.

Bitte fragen Sie per Mail beim litauischen Fremdenverkehrsamt nach einer Hotelunterkunft im Zentrum von Vilnius für die Woche 04. Februar bis 09. Februar an.

Die E-Mail-Adresse lautet:

turizm.info@vilnius.lt

- **Make sure that you give your reader a meaningful subject line.**
- **When replying, quote the email you are referring to.**
- **Pay attention to the layout of your email:**
  - **use short paragraphs**
  - **stick to plain text, do not use smileys, creative punctuation, abbreviations etc.**
  - **keep your message short (maximum one computer screen)**
  - **write one email for each topic you wish to talk about**
- **Make sure that your mail corresponds with your company style:**
  - **be formal and polite**
  - **check grammar, punctuation and spelling**
  - **include signatures, position in the company and your full name**
  - **keep in mind that emails are part of official business communications and can be stored for future reference**

Step A: What do these symbols stand for? Match them with the words you find below.

television in the rooms	air-conditioned rooms	telephone in the rooms
green surrounding	restaurant	mini-bar service in the rooms
outdoor swimming pool (heated)	sauna	lift
dry cleaning and/ or laundry service	radio in the rooms	medical service available
centrally heated rooms	mini golf	indoor swimming pool
outdoor swimming pool	squash	car park available
water sports at or near hotel establishment	conference room	tennis
facilities for disabled	room service	baby sitting service available
seafront location	hair dressing salon	fitness room
satellite TV in the rooms	bar service	live entertainment

Step B: The more facilities a hotel offers, the higher the rates you have to pay. Discuss which facilities business people definitely need. Which ones could be done without? Are any facilities missing?

Discuss in class.

Vilnius Tourist Information

letter head

Gemeinnützige Wohnungsbau-
gesellschaft Bochum
Kellerstraße 35-39
48456 Bochum
Germany

receiver's address or inside address

March 25, 200

date

Dear Sir or Madam,

salutation

Your enquiry for hotel accommodation in Vilnius

subject line

Thank you very much for your email which we received today.

We are pleased to inform you that we indeed have a number of excellent hotels in our capital.
I enclose a brochure which should give you some information about the hotels, the location and their facilities. The Narutis Hotel is one of the best-known business hotels in our city. People from all parts of the business world come and stay here. The staff all speak English.
Should you decide to book a room in this or any of the other hotels, you can directly contact these hotels. Of course, we would also be pleased to do this on your behalf. In that case, please do not hesitate and contact us again with all the information we might require.

Thank you once again for your interest in our capital and our country. We are sure that a stay in Vilnius will be an unforgettable experience should this be the first time for you in our country.

Should you have any further questions or comments, please do not hesitate to contact us by email, phone or by fax.

We are looking forward to hearing from you soon.

body of the letter

Yours sincerely,

complimentary close

Stevenson

T. Stevenson
Bookings manager

signature block

enclosures
hotel brochures

UNIT 1

Working in real estate, housing and the property market - Getting to know the business

Vilnius hotels - from cheap to luxury Vilnius hotels

http://www.vilnius-hotels.1bigeurope.com/detail.aspx?id=456

zon eBay News ▾ Yahoo! Neuer Ordner ▾

VILNIUS HOTELS

HOME | ABOUT US | SECURITY&PRIVACY | CO-OPERATE WITH US | LINK PARTNERS | SEND US A FRIEND

Destination info | Why to book with us | How to book | FAQ | Contact us

» MORE COUNTRIES

Narutis Hotel *****
Pilies 24, Vilnius

Place specification: **center**
Type of facility: **hotel**

Location:
Hotel Narutis is located on the main artery of Vilnius Old Town.

Hotel:
This building is the architectural monument from 16th century that was specially built to a hotel. Windows of the Hotel face the square of St. John's Church of the University, which is the most beautiful square of the Old Town. Other windows have a view over a quiet courtyard of the former Botanical Gardens of the University. From the Hotel windows you can see a beautiful panorama of church and mansion towers, the Gediminas Castle and the Hill of Three Crosses.

Rooms:
The Hotel practically does not have two rooms that would be the same. Each room has its own face with unique frescoes, wall paintings, original 16th century beam ceilings, timber-framed floors or Gothic vaults. At the end of 2000 all rooms of the Hotel were redecorated under the supervision of the French architect and designer Anne Toulous. Each room has a mini bar, satellite TV with world channels, two Pay-TV channels broadcasting programmes all around the clock. The Hotel has a powerful air-conditioning system and autonomous (independent from the city) heating system, which also ensures constant supply of hot water. All bathrooms have modern equipment, including hairdryers and other conveniences.

Boarding:
The restaurant offers European cuisine, carefully selected and prepared by the chef of the international class.

Map with location | Seasons and prices

After studying the enclosed brochure and doing some internet research, you inform your boss about your research so far.

In the afternoon he sends you an email with the following particulars:

Verfassen:

Senden | Kontakte | Rechtschr. | Anhang | Sicherheit | Speichern

Von:

An:

Betreff:

Normaler Text | Variable Breite

Danke für die Liste mit den Hotels. Ich habe mich für das Narutis Hotel entschieden. Bitte buchen Sie für mich in dem bekannten Zeitraum ein Einzelzimmer, das die folgenden Kriterien erfüllt.

- Nichtraucherzimmer
- möglichst im zweiten Stock
- Zimmer in einem ruhigen Gebäudeteil
- Internetanschluss und Telefon sollten im Zimmer verfügbar sein

Bitte fragen Sie, wie weit es vom Hotel bis zum Konferenzzentrum ist.

Bitten Sie um Bestätigung per Mail oder Fax.

Write a letter to the hotel in which you include all relevant details. Follow the layout of a business letter, too.

TEROETICSINP

SEAF

PASTOPRS

ERKAYCD

ROMO-RIEVECS

NAMBIRI

SUANA

POORLLIHW

LITF

ORLOF

LOUEDB-BDE

REWSOH

RIA-CDIITNNOINOG

WETLOS

HOTTO-SEAPT

WAEK-PU LACL

SAKFEBRAT

RAET

Unscramble each of the clue words.

manage investors
residential housing cooperative
owner landlords
landlords density
rent sellers
purchase taxes
budget tenants
construction sewage
owner-occupied demand
stock purpose
commercial rent
repairs dwellings
self-help agents
stock limited liability company
company cooperatives
maintenance architects

Fill in the gaps!

When describing an economy's real estate market, we have a look at both ____________ and ____________ properties. These properties are either ____________ or they are let by ____________ .

The responsibility for owner-occupied properties of course is with the ____________. This means that, regardless of the ____________ of the building, after the ____________ or ____________ of the property the owners are responsible for ____________ and upkeep. They need to carry out necessary ____________ , replace faulty components and pay all fees and ____________ that local or national governments might claim.

____________ , however, who use these properties for commercial or residential reasons, just pay a monthly ____________ to the landlord to which they must add variable utility costs for the consumption and use of services such as among others water, electricity, ____________ or heating. Repairs, refurbishment and maintenance works are of course the responsibility of the landlords.

In a market economy, the letting of properties is driven by ____________. This demand has a great influence on the number of properties that are built and of course on the ____________ levels in the country. Housing enterprises in Germany own a large ____________ of ____________. They usually have the legal form of a ____________ or a ____________ or a ____________. Housing ____________ are an important factor in the

German housing market. With 2.1 million dwellings the cooperative housing stock totals about 10 percent of all rental dwellings. They have proven themselves as a form of organisation due to their organised __________. They ________________ and let their properties to residential tenants. Of course, they also build and sell properties for owner-occupation and to private ________________. Depending on their size, they often have their own ________________ . As the average household size in this country is changing, housing companies have to adapt to these changes as well. They need to provide flats for 1, 2 or three people if they want to be able to compete on a global market. Surely, these aspects are strongly influenced by regional factors such as population __________ and infrastructure.

Real estate __________ offer their services in selling or letting procedures. They find buyers and __________ for various properties and also help __________ find suitable tenants for their buildings. Property managers offer a variety of services that are needed to manage rental properties or condominiums. They control a __________ which is needed to finance properties, they coordinate necessary repairs work and of course report to the owners of the properties.

Prepare a 3-minute talk about "Housing in Germany" in which you include the following terms in any order of your choice.

Use your vocabulary list and refer to Unit 1 of this book whenever necessary. Prepare to present this talk to the class.

- **number of dwellings**
- **business communication**
- **housing stock in Germany**
- **at the office**
- **talking to tenants**
- **providing housing on a competitive market**
- **negotiating with contractors**
- **housing enterprises**
- **organisation chart**
- **living space**
- **business letters**
- **emails**

CECODHAS: THE EUROPEAN LIAISON COMMITTEE FOR SOCIAL HOUSING

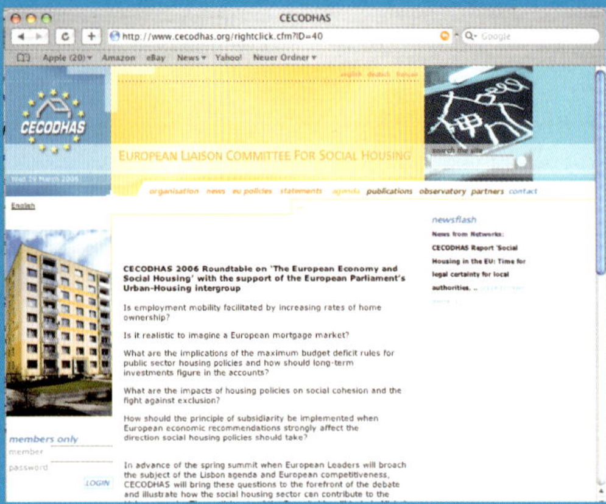

CECODHAS, established in 1988, is the European network for the promotion of the right to decent housing for all. In our membership we have 46 regional and national federations which together represent over 2,000 public, voluntary and cooperative social housing enterprises in 19 countries. All members are non-for-profit and non-governmental. Together they provide 21 million homes for rent or home ownership. CECODHAS is funded by membership fees.

TOGETHER WE ARE WORKING TO:

- reinforce the European social model and promote the values, successes and the vital future role of our members within that model;
- promote integrated approaches to sustainable urban development, stressing that the work of social housing providers is the backbone of social cohesion in European cities;
- protect fundamental rights and fight for quality social services, accessible to all.

ACTIVITIES

To fulfill our mission we:

REPRESENT AND NEGOTIATE for strategic common interests on issues such as:

- Structural Funds
- Services of General Interest and State Aid
- Public Procurement
- Social inclusion
- Energy efficiency
- Urban sustainable development

ESTABLISH ALLIANCES AND MAINTAIN CONTINUOUS DIALOGUE WITH:

- European Ministers responsible for housing
- European institutions
- The European Parliament, in particular the 'Urban-Housing' intergroup
- Social partners
- European networks of local authorities
- International institutions such as: UNECE, Council of Europe, European Investment Bank
- Cooperatives in Europe, European Housing Forum Social Platform of NGOs

With our partners we raise the profile of housing issues on the European agenda and develop projects and seminars to exchange best practices.

Vokabeln

A	abbreviate (verb)	abkürzen
	abbreviation	Abkürzung
	abolish (verb)	abschaffen
	abolition	Abschaffung
	accession countries	Beitrittsländer
	accounting	Buchhaltung, Bilanzbuchhaltung
	achieve (verb)	erreichen, erzielen
	acquire (verb)	erwerben
	acquisition	Erwerb
	advice	Beratung, Ratschlag
	affiliated service	mieternahe Dienstleistung
	affordable	erschwinglich, bezahlbar
	agreement	Einigung, Vertrag
	amenities	Vorzüge, Annehmlichkeiten, Ausstattungsmerkmale
	amortisation	Tilgung
	apartment complex	Wohnimmobilie, Geschosswohnungsbau
	apologise (verb)	entschuldigen
	appropriate	geeignet
	architect	Architekt
	arrangements	Arrangements
	attire	Kleidung
	authorities	Behörden
	availability	Verfügbarkeit
	available	verfügbar
	average	Durchschnitt, durchschnittlich
B	balanced market	ausgeglichener Markt
	be eligible for (verb)	einen Anspruch haben auf
	be subject to (verb)	Gegenstand von etw. sein
	bed-sit	Zimmer, möbliertes Zimmer
	benchmarking	Benchmarking, Maßstab, Bezugsgröße
	bid	Angebot
	borough	Bezirk, Gemeinde
	broadband internet	Breitband-Internetanschluss
	brochure	Broschüre, Prospekt
	budget	Budget, Haushalt
	business trip	Geschäftsreise
	buyer	Erwerber, Käufer
C	cash in (verb)	vereinnahmen
	centralised	zentralisiert
	century	Jahrhundert
	certification	Zertifizierung
	civil servant	Beamter, öffentlicher Angestellter
	civil service	öffentlicher Dienst
	colleague	Kollegin, Kollege
	command economy	Planwirtschaft
	commercial (real estate) property	Gewerbeimmobilie
	commercial manager	kaufmännischer Geschäftsführer
	common	gemeinschaftlich
	common property	Gemeinschaftseigentum
	community association	Eigentümergemeinschaft
	community development project	Quartiersentwicklungsprojekt
	community-owned	in Gemeinschaftsbesitz
	compete (verb)	konkurrieren
	competition	Wettbewerb, Konkurrenz
	complaint	Reklamation, Klage
	complimentary clause	Grußformel
	concrete	Beton
	congestion	Andrang, Verdichtung
	consist of (verb)	bestehen aus
	consolidate (verb)	konsolidieren
	construct (verb)	bauen
	construction	Bau
	consumption	Verbrauch
	consumption goods	Verbrauchsgüter
	contractor	Auftragnehmer
	cooperative	Genossenschaft
	core business	Kerngeschäft
	corporate	Unternehmens-
	cost control	Kostenmanagement
	costly	teuer
	current	gängig, aktuell
	customer	Kunde
D	day-to-day operation	Tagesgeschäft
	decade	Jahrzehnt
	decentralised	dezentralisiert
	demand-driven market	Nachfragemarkt
	determine (verb)	bestimmen, festlegen
	develop (verb)	entwickeln
	development	Entwicklung
	disabled	behindert
	disciplinary action	Disziplinarmaßnahme
	disposition	Veräußerung
	draw up (verb)	anfertigen, aufstellen, entwerfen
	dress code	Kleiderordnung
	dwelling	Wohnung
	dwelling stock	Wohnungsbestand
E	economy	Wirtschaft
	employee	Angestellter, Arbeitnehmer
	employer	Arbeitgeber
	enclose (verb)	beifügen
	enclosures	Anlagen
	enforce (verb)	in Kraft setzen, durchsetzen
	ensure (verb)	gewährleisten, sicherstellen
	enterprise	Unternehmen
	entire	gesamt
	entrepreneur	Unternehmer
	entrepreneurial	unternehmerisch
	equipment	Ausstattung, Ausrüstung
	essential	wichtig, wesentlich
	etiquette	Etikette, Benimmregeln
	EU member states	EU-Mitgliedsstaaten
	eviction	Räumung
	existing	bestehend
	expenditures	Ausgaben, Aufwand
	expense	Ausgabe, Kosten
F	facility	Facility, Einrichtung
	faulty	fehlerhaft, defekt
	financial operation	finanzielle Transaktion
	financial statement	Geschäftsbericht
	financing	Finanzierung

UNIT 1

Working in real estate, housing and the property market - Getting to know the business

	first-home buyer allowance	Eigenheimzulage
	floor	Stockwerk
	focus (verb)	Fokus, Hauptaugenmerk
	found (verb)	gründen, begründen
	fringe	Brache, Rand-
	funding	Finanzierung
G	gather (verb)	versammeln
	German housing act of 1956	II. Deutsches Wohnungsbaugesetz von 1956
	German non-profit housing act	WGG, Wohnungsgemeinnützigkeitsgesetz
	governance	Führung, Steuerung
	grooming guide	Knigge
	grounds	(Außen-)Anlagen
	groundskeeping	Reinigung und Pflege von Außenanlagen
	growth	Wachstum
H	half	halb
	handle (verb)	handhaben
	haphazard	wahllos, willkürlich
	head of	Chef, Leiter
	heating	Heizung
	heating costs	Heizkosten
	hesitate (verb)	zögern
	hold a conference (verb)	eine Konferenz abhalten
	home-builder	Bauherr, Häuslebauer
	homeowner	Hausbesitzer, Eigentümer
	home-seller	Hausverkäufer
	hostel	Wohnheim, Herberge
	household	Haushalt
	housing	Wohnungswesen
	housing association	gemeinnützige Wohnungsbaugesellschaft (britische Form)
	housing cooperative	Wohnungsbaugenossenschaft
	housing market	Wohnungsmarkt
	housing supply	Wohnversorgung
I	income limit	Einkommensgrenze
	income-producing	Einkommen schaffend
	increase (verb)	wachsen, anwachsen, steigern, ansteigen
	industrial park	Industriegebiet
	industrialized building / apartment block	Plattenbau
	infrastructure	Infrastruktur
	inhabitant	Einwohner
L	line of business	Geschäftsaktivität, Geschäftssegment
	living space	Wohnraum
	living standard	Lebensstandard
	loan	Darlehen, Baudarlehen
	local authority	Kommunalbehörde
	local budget	kommunaler Haushalt
	local government	Stadt-, Gemeinderat
	located	gelegen
	lodger	(Unter-)Mieter
	long-term strategic financial planning	langfristige, strategische Finanzplanung
	low-income housing	Sozialwohnungsbau
M	maintain (verb)	unterhalten, beibehalten, instand halten, warten
	maintenance	Wartung, Instandhaltung
	maintenance bill	Rechnung für Wartung / Instandhaltung
	manage (verb)	managen, Geschäft führen
	manners	Betragen, Benimm, Verhaltensweisen
	means	Mittel (um etwas zu tun)
	medium-sized	mittelgroß
	mismatch (verb)	nicht zusammenpassen
	monitor (verb)	überprüfen, nachverfolgen
	mortgage	Hypothek
	move-in and move-out procedure	Verfahren bei Auszug / Einzug
	multi-family	Mehrfamilien-
	multi-storey	mehrgeschossig
	municipal	kommunal
	municipality	Kommunalverwaltung
N	negotiate (verb)	verhandeln
	negotiation	Verhandlung
	neighbourhood	Nachbarschaft, Quartier
	net income	Nettoeinkommen
O	occupancy	Belegung
	occupancy rate	Belegungsrate
	occupied	belegt, genutzt
	offer-driven market	Angebotsmarkt
	on time	pünktlich
	operation	Transaktion, Operation
	outskirt	Stadtrand
	oversee (verb)	überblicken
	oversupply	Überangebot
	own (verb)	besitzen
	owner-occupied house	selbst genutztes Wohneigentum
P	paragraph	Absatz
	parking	Pkw-Stellplatz
	payroll	Gehaltsliste
	performance	Leistung
	periodical report	Monats- / Quartalsbericht
	periodically	periodisch
	periphery	Peripherie, Stadtrand
	pets	Haustiere
	piecemeal	stückchenweise, allmählich, nach und nach
	plot	Grundstück
	population	Bevölkerung
	population density	Bevölkerungsdichte
	portfolio	Produktpalette, Bestand, Portfolio
	postal worker	Postangestellter
	premium	Prämie
	private housing company	privates Wohnungsunternehmen
	privatisation	Privatisierung
	privatise	privatisieren
	professional housing provider	Wohnungsunternehmen
	profitable	einträglich, profitabel
	promote (verb)	fördern
	proportionate	proportional
	prospective tenant	möglicher Mieter
	provide (verb)	Versorgen, bereitstellen
	public interest group	Öffentliche Interessengruppen

	public-sector corporation	öffentliches Unternehmen
	punctuation	Interpunktion
	purchase (verb)	kaufen, erwerben
R	ranking	Klassifizierung
	real estate industry	Immobiliensektor
	real estate investment	Immobilieninvestition
	receiver	Empfänger (bei Geschäftskorrespondenz)
	refurbishment	Modernisierung
	reliability	Zuverlässigkeit
	reliable	zuverlässig
	rent	Miete
	rent collection	Vereinnahmung der Miete
	rental	Miet-
	repair	Instandsetzung
	representative	repräsentativ
	request (verb)	nachfragen, fordern
	resident	Anwohner
	residential (real-estate) property	Wohnimmobilie
	resolve (verb)	lösen, beschließen
	responsibility	Verantwortung
	restrictions	Beschränkungen
	revenue	Einkommen, Ertrag
	rigid	steif, starr
	roughly	ungefähr
	routine	Routine
	routinely	routinemäßig
	rundown	verwohnt, abgewirtschaftet, heruntergekommen
	rural	ländlich
S	salutation	Begrüßung
	scorecard	Berichtsbogen, Scorecard
	seafront	an der Küste
	security	Sicherheit
	segment	Segment, Abschnitt
	service of condominium	WEG-Verwaltung
	sewage	Abwasser
	shareholder	Aktionär
	shopping centre	Einkaufszentrum
	shortage	Not, Mangel
	short-term	kurzfristig
	signature	Unterschrift
	size	Größe
	slightly	ein wenig
	social commitment	Sozialengagement
	social, cultural, economic, ethnic mix	soziale, kulturelle, wirtschaftliche, ethnische Durchmischung
	solicit	jmd. bitten, auffordern
	specialist	Fachmann, -frau, Spezialist
	square metre	Quadratmeter
	staff	Personal
	starched collar	gestärkter Kragen
	stipulate (verb)	festsetzen, niederlegen, vereinbaren, vorschreiben
	stock	Bestand
	storey	Stockwerk, Geschoss
	subject line	Betreffzeile
	submit (verb)	vorlegen
	supervise (verb)	überwachen, überprüfen
	supplier	Lieferant
	supplies	Lieferungen, Zubehör, Betriebsstoffe
	supply	liefern
	supply (and demand)	Angebot (und Nachfrage)
	sustainable	nachhaltig
	sustainable urban development	nachhaltige Stadtentwicklung, Stadtumbau
T	target	Ziel
	target group	Zielgruppe
	tax	Steuern, Abgaben
	tenancy agreement	Mietvertrag
	tenant	Mieter
	tenants' involvement	Mieterbeteiligung
	terminate (verb)	beenden, abschließen
	termination-of-lease procedure	Beendigung des Mietvertrags
	terms and conditions	Geschäftsbedingungen AGB
	thermal insulation	Wärmeisolierung
	thorough	sorgfältig
	tie (verb)	(fest-)binden, festzurren
	tool	Werkzeug
	trash removal	Müllabfuhr
U	unit	Einheit
	urban	städtisch, urban
V	vacancy	Wohnungsleerstand
	vacant apartment, flat, dwelling	leer stehende Wohnung
	value	Wert
	voluntary social commitment	freiwillige Sozialverpflichtung
W	wall cladding	Fassade
	waste disposal	Abfallentsorgung
	workforce	Arbeitskraft

SELF-ASSESSMENT GRID AFTER UNIT 1

Gehen Sie die einzelnen Abschnitte des gerade abgeschlossenen Kapitels noch einmal durch und überprüfen Sie sich selbstkritisch. Was haben Sie gelernt? Was sollten Sie wiederholen bzw. vertiefen? Was bereitet Ihnen Schwierigkeiten? Schreiben Sie kurze Kommentare in die Kästchen, die Ihren Lernzuwachs für Sie selbst erläutern. Arbeiten Sie nach eigenen Prioritäten Unterpunkte nach, wenn Sie mehrheitlich Ihre Kommentare in der rechten Spalte gesetzt haben.

Was ich in diesem Kapitel gelernt habe...	**Wie ich meinen Fortschritt einschätze**		
	Ich fühle mich beim Sprechen/Schreiben und beim Hören bzw. Lesen zu diesem Aspekt insgesamt sicher und verstehe einen Großteil der Informationen bzw. kann einen Großteil der Informationen wie beabsichtigt weitergeben; auch wenn ich Fehler mache, habe ich insgesamt Vertrauen in meine Sprachbeherrschung.	Ich kann vieles von dem, was für diesen Aspekt wichtig ist, mündlich und schriftlich ausdrücken bzw. beim Hören und Lesen verstehen; allerdings fehlen mir einige Fachvokabeln und auch die grundsätzliche Sicherheit, mich frei über diesen Aspekt auszutauschen.	Ich habe zu diesem Aspekt einige Fachbegriffe und Redewendungen gelernt und verstehe auch Informationen; jedoch erschließen sich mir noch nicht alle Zusammenhänge; sowohl die Textrezeption (Hören und Lesen) als auch das Sprechen und Schreiben bereiten mir noch Probleme; ich weiß, dass ich einige Aspekte nacharbeiten sollte.
mich selbst und andere vorzustellen.			
den deutschen Wohnungsmarkt zu beschreiben.			
die Immobilienbranche und die Aktivitäten des eigenen Unternehmens zu beschreiben.			
meinen eigenen Arbeitsablauf zu beschreiben.			
mein eigenes Unternehmen vorzustellen.			
den europäischen Wohnungsmarkt zu beschreiben.			
eine Hotelunterkunft zu finden.			

UNIT 2 Describing properties

In dieser Unit lernen Sie:

- den Fachwortschatz zur Beschreibung von gewerblichen und Wohnimmobilien in ihrer Funktion und gemäß ihren Eigenschaften
- Einzelheiten zur Beschreibung unterschiedlicher Arten von Wohnimmobilien
- Grundaspekte zur Sicherheit und zur Vorbeugung von Einbrüchen
- Anforderungen an moderne Mietwohnungen zu reflektieren und darzustellen
- Grundlagen des Telefonierens in der englischen Sprache
- wie man ein kurzes englischsprachiges Exposé schreibt
- wie man eine Diagrammbeschreibung anfertigt
- wie man das Erlernte in einer **WEB UNIT** anwendet
- wie man sich sprachlich in einer Diskussion behauptet und seine Meinung vertritt
- Tipps und Anregungen zum eigenen Umgang mit englischen Hörtexten – wie man zu schreibende Texte im Vorfeld strukturieren kann

UNIT 2

Describing properties

Talking about various types of properties

Have a look at the properties listed below.

1. **Decide if the property is commercial or residential and tick the appropriate box.**
2. **Find the correct term to name this property in the list of terms below.**
3. **Find a suitable definition for this property. Fill in the appropriate number from the list below.**

residential ❑ commercial ❑

term: ____________________

definition: ____________________

residential ❑ commercial ❑

term: ____________________

definition: ____________________

residential ❑ commercial ❑

term: ____________________

definition: ____________________

residential ❑ commercial ❑

term: ____________________

definition: ____________________

residential ❑ commercial ❑

term: ____________________

definition: ____________________

residential ❑ commercial ❑

term: ____________________

definition: ____________________

residential ❑ commercial ❑

term: ____________________

definition: ____________________

residential ❑ commercial ❑

term: ____________________

definition: ____________________

residential ❑ commercial ❑

term: ____________________

definition: ____________________

residential ☐ commercial ☐
term:
definition:

residential ☐ commercial ☐
term:
definition:

residential ☐ commercial ☐
term:
definition:

residential ☐ commercial ☐
term:
definition:

residential ☐ commercial ☐
term:
definition:

residential ☐ commercial ☐
term:
definition:

residential ☐ commercial ☐
term:
definition:

residential ☐ commercial ☐
term:
definition:

residential ☐ commercial ☐
term:
definition:

residential ☐ commercial ☐
term:
definition:

residential ☐ commercial ☐
term:
definition:

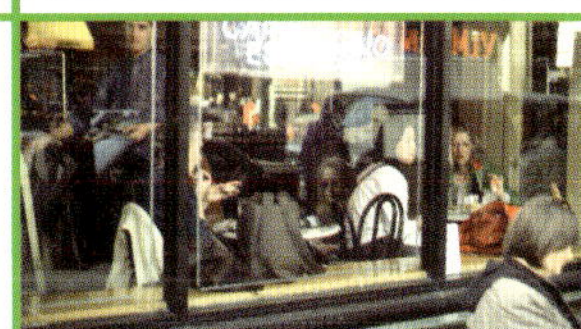

residential ☐ commercial ☐
term:
definition:

residential ☐ commercial ☐

term: ______________________

definition: ______________________

residential ☐ commercial ☐

term: ______________________

definition: ______________________

residential ☐ commercial ☐

term: ______________________

definition: ______________________

residential ☐ commercial ☐

term: ______________________

definition: ______________________

residential ☐ commercial ☐

term: ______________________

definition: ______________________

residential ☐ commercial ☐

term: ______________________

definition: ______________________

residential ☐ commercial ☐

term: ______________________

definition: ______________________

Terms and definitions (in jumbled order):

takeaway bar	a repair shop where cars and trucks are serviced and repaired	1
airport	an outbuilding (or part of a building) for housing automobiles	2
garage	a large structure at an airport where aircraft can be stored and maintained	3
garages	a building where people go to eat	4
corner shop	mercantile establishment consisting of a carefully landscaped complex of shops representing leading merchandisers; a modern version of the traditional marketplace;	5
hangar	a mercantile establishment for the retail sale of goods or services;	6
restaurant	a very tall building with many storeys	7
retail shop	an airfield equipped with control tower and hangars as well as accommodations for passengers and cargo	8
conference centre	a house that stands alone	9
mall, shopping centre	especially designed building in which a conference can be held	10
block of flats	a dwelling that is attached to something on only one side	11
skyscraper	a row of houses built in a similar style and having common dividing walls (or the street on which they face);	12
2-family house	pretentious and luxurious country residence with extensive grounds	13
villa	a storehouse for goods and merchandise	14
manor house	a large retail store organised into departments offering a variety of merchandise; commonly part of a retail chain	15
bungalow	a building where travellers can pay for lodging and meals and other services	16
detached house	a building containing offices where work is done	17
terraced house	a shop where food is prepared which is taken away to be eaten	18
semi-detached house	a house designed in such a way that two families can live in it	19
multi-family house	tall building with many storeys which offers living space for many people	20
multi-storey car park	a large and imposing house	21
warehouse	a small shop at the corner of a street traditionally selling stationery etc.	22
department store	a small house with a single story	23
hotel	a house designed in such a way that several families can live in it	24
office building	building containing a car park consisting of several storeys	25
holiday park	a room where a doctor or dentist can be consulted	26
campsite	an area of land which includes various facilities and buildings for holiday or leisure activities	27
surgery	a site where people on holiday can pitch a tent	28

Using the properties listed above, complete the following table. Of course you can add other types of properties as well.

RESIDENTIAL PROPERTIES	COMMERCIAL PROPERTIES

Measurement and Conversions

from	to	multiply by
inch	centimetre	2.54
centimetre	inch	0.39
square feet	square metres	0.0929
square metres(m^2)	square feet	10.764
square yards(yd^2)	square metres	0.83612
square metres	square yards	1.196
cubic inches (cu in; in^3)	cubic centimetres	16.387
cubic centimetres (cc; cm^3)	cubic inches	0.061
cubic feet	cubic metres	0.0283
cubic metres	cubic feet	35.315
cubic yards	cubic metres	0.7646
cubic metres	cubic yards	1.308

Abbreviations

ac	acre
a/c	air conditioning
APT	apartment
ba	bath
Balc	balcony
bd; br	bedroom
bkporch	backporch
Bkyd	fenced backyard
blt	built-in
Bsmt	basement
Bung	bungalow
3	3 bedrooms
4/3	4 bedrooms/ 3 bathrooms
1C, 2C	1 or 2 car garage
1 LV, 2 LV	1 or 2 living levels
cac	central air conditioning
CFan	ceiling fan
Cldsc	cul-de-sac
Crwl	crawl space
Cth	cathedral ceiling
CVAC	central vacuum
crprt	carport
Dk	deck
dbl	double
d/w	dishwasher
Dr	dining room
Dry	clothes dryer
Dsp	garbage disposal
ELE	electric
ELV	elevator
END	end unit
Exr	exercise room
Ffbr	first floor bedroom
fncd yd	fenced yard
Fp, Fpl	fireplace
gar	garage
garb	garbage
GAROP	garage door opener
HW	hot water

INT	intercom
LFT	loft
lrg	large
liv rm or lr	living room
MAR	marble
MBA	master bedroom w/bath
Meik	modern eat-in kitchen
Mk	modern kitchen
mo	month
Mstr	master bedroom
OFF	off street parking
PAT	patio
PERM	permanent attic stairs
PLAY	playground
PULL	pull-down attic stair
R/OPT	rent with option to buy
REF	refrigerator
rv prkg	RV parking
SAT	satellite dish
Scrnd porch	screened porch
SECSY, sec sys	security system
SEW,SWR	sewer
SKY	skylights
spklr	sprinkler system
sq ft	square feet
STOR	assigned storage
STR	on street parking
TOWN, Th	town house
Txs	taxes
UTRM	utility room
WHKP	washer hookup
WLKIN	walk-in closet
WTR	water
w/w cpt	wall to wall carpet
w/d	washer/dryer
w/d hkup, or w/d con	washer/dryer hookup
wtr pd	water paid
yd	yard

Source: Flavia Westerwelle, http://www.westerwelle.net

Now have a closer look at the four properties below. Which of the following amenities are necessary and common for which property? You may want to use some amenities more than once.

nearest airport 5 minutes	air conditioning	burglar alarm	intercom	lift
free car park for 25 vehicles	flexible partition walls	carpet flooring	biometric access control	tea kitchen
double glazed windows	central heating	refurbished in 2003	closest subway 5 minutes	large front window
busy main road	excellent traffic connections	toilets	further shops nearby	large rectangular ground floor
light	ground floor	flexible lighting system	storage facilities	staff toilets
rolling grill	sun-blinds	tiled kitchen	completely furnished	unfurnished
1st floor	garage	bedroom	living room	bathroom
built-in cupboards	noise protection	broadband internet	balcony	small garden
terrace	modern heating technology	insulation	quiet neighbourhood	playground nearby
potential for conversion	building permission	laundry room	guest toilet	fitted kitchen
low rent	residential area	walk-in cupboard	schools and public institutions within walking distance	utility costs included
fixed tenancy agreement	only one tenant using the property	first time use	deposit	cellar
7900 sq. ft.	skylights above	underground parking		

PROPERTY 1: OFFICE SPACE IN A MODERN OFFICE BUILDING

amenities...

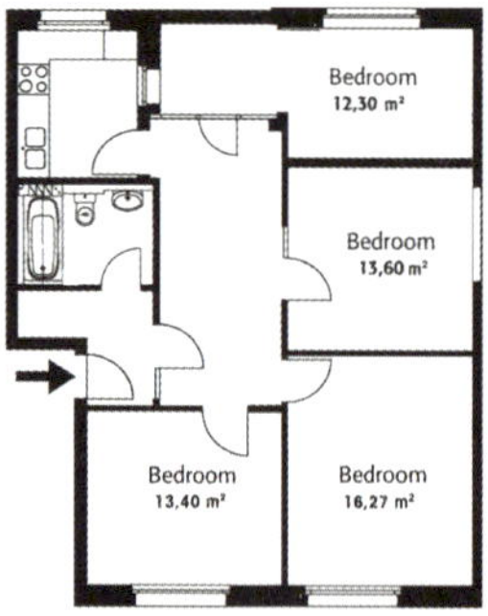

PROPERTY 3: 4-BEDROOM FLAT

amenities...

PROPERTY 2: A SEMI-DETACHED HOUSE

amenities...

PROPERTY 4: RETAIL SPACE

amenities...

1. Get together in groups. This group is your **home group**. Within your group, divide the four properties among you. (Person A works on property 1, person B on property 2 etc.)
2. Now all of you (from each of the home groups) working on the same property (e. g. office space) come together and work on their property in the new groups (group A, group B etc.). These four new groups are the **expert groups** for the respective property.

Your task: Prepare to introduce this property to the others using all the information provided. Add any information you consider relevant when presenting this property. Of course you can make up details as long as they are realistic.

3. At the end of the time given, return to your **original home group**. Each member of the home group now presents the result of their work in the expert group (i. e. their property) to the rest of the home group. The others listen to the four presentations and make notes about the information they are given about the four properties.

Here are some phrases you can use to describe a property:

The ... is located in a ...road / neighbourhood/area.

It is located on the .. floor of a ...building.

It consists of ... rooms.

The property is equipped with ...

The total living space/floor space of this property is...

In ..., the ...... was /were modernised/ repaired/refurbished/ replaced.

Source: Freedomship, Florida, USA

Listening Comprehension Floating City

Pre-Listening Activity.

Imagine you had to design a ship which should attract wealthy people and motivate them to spend a certain time (from just one week to one year) on board. Which amenities would you include?

If you had the money to afford such a trip, would you spend some time on such a vessel? Why? Why not?

Now listen to the interview in which a radio journalist interviews Norman Nixon, the man who has plans to build the world's largest ocean-going vessel, a ship that's one mile long and 25 stories high.

Having a discussion: The hot seat

One or two of you take the role of Norman Nixon. Prepare to defend your idea to the questions and criticism from class.

The others work in pairs and prepare questions they are going to ask Norman Nixon.

When having the discussion, make sure that you follow the general rules:

- Always be polite!
- Look at the people you are talking to but don't stare at them.
- Don't interrupt unless you feel it is really necessary.
- Listen carefully to what other people are saying.
- Keep to the point.
- Don't talk too much.

Here are some phrases you might use in a discussion:

TO ASK FOR AN OPINION:

What do you think/feel about ...?

What is your view/opinion on/about ...?

What would you say?

TO INTERRUPT SOMEONE:

Sorry to interrupt, but could you please explain/repeat the point you just made.

Excuse me for interrupting, but I don't understand what you just said.

Sorry for interrupting but can I please say something/make a point?

TO GIVE AN OPINION:

As far as I'm concerned ...

I think/feel/believe/am of the opinion that ...

To my mind ...

In my opinion ... /In my view ...

TO RESPOND TO A SUGGESTION:

That's a good idea!/Fine!

OK/Yes, why not?

OK, if you want, I don't really mind.

I think it would be a better idea to talk about/consider ...

Couldn't we look at this/do this another way?
What about...?

I'm not sure ...
if that's such a good idea.
How about ...?

TO DISAGREE:

I disagree (entirely/with some of the things you said/etc.)

I'm sorry but I completely disagree.

Stop exaggerating!

I think you're oversimplifying things.

That's an interesting point, but

That's not the point.

You've missed the point (entirely).

TO SAY THAT A POINT HAS BEEN MISUNDERSTOOD:

I'm sorry but that's not what I meant to say (at all)!

I think you've got the wrong end of the stick!

You've got me (completely) wrong.

You've (completely) misunderstood me.

That's not what I was trying to say!

I didn't make myself clear.
I'll try and explain again.

TO CHANGE THE SUBJECT:

There is something else that I'd like to say ...

Have you ever thought of/considered ...

On the other hand ...

Try looking at things another way/from a different angle.

I'd like to bring up another point/point out something else.

TO ASK FOR FURTHER EXPLANATION:

Did I get that right?

Do you really mean that...?

Did /I understand correctly that you think...?

Could you explain what you just said/the point you just made/etc. again, please?

Could you give me/us a concrete example, please?

TO AGREE:

You are (quite/absolutely) right.

That's a very good point!

Absolutely! /Exactly!

I agree (with you/.../etc.).

You have a point.

You might/could be right.

/ think you're right to a certain extent/up to a point.

Now collect all the arguments for and against this floating city and decide whether you would advise your boss to invest some of your company's money into this project.

Englische Texte hören und verstehen

Nutzen Sie die zahlreichen Möglichkeiten, englischsprachige Texte zu hören. Ob im (digitalen) Radio, im Satelliten- bzw. Kabelfernsehen, im Internet oder auch auf englischsprachiger CD-Rom: Der Markt und die Verfügbarkeit von Hörtexten sind so groß wie unübersichtlich.

Hier einige grundsätzliche Regeln und Tipps:

- Je mehr „Weltwissen" Sie über ein bestimmtes Thema haben, umso leichter wird Ihnen das Verstehen des englischsprachigen Textes fallen. Beschäftigen Sie sich – wenn möglich – mit dem Thema des Hörtextes erst ausführlich im Vorfeld, so dass Sie eine konkrete Vorstellung davon haben, worum es gehen könnte. Dieses kann auch bedeuten, dass Sie z. B. erst Nachrichten in deutscher Sprache hören, bevor Sie dann die englischsprachigen Nachrichten verstehen wollen.
- Seien Sie geduldig mit sich: Das Ziel, einen muttersprachlichen Sprecher gleich beim ersten Mal zu 100 % zu verstehen, ist sehr ehrgeizig. Hören Sie sich den Hörtext mehrere Male an, machen Sie sich beim Hören Notizen, die Sie zunehmend ergänzen. Spielen Sie abschließend vor dem Hintergrund Ihrer Notizen den Text noch einmal und vergleichen Sie.
- Setzen Sie sich beim Hören realistische Ziele, die Sie nach und nach steigern: So kann es beim ersten Hören z. B. genug sein, dass Sie herausfinden, wie viele Sprecher es gibt, wie sie heißen und welche Funktion sie haben. Dieses Vorgehen, mit dem Sie einen ersten Gesamteindruck gewinnen, nennt man *listening for gist.*
- Erst der zweite oder dritte Hör-Schritt *(listening for detail)* führt Sie zu den Details des Hörtextes.
- Dosieren Sie die Länge der Hörtexte: Fangen Sie mit kürzeren Texten an (Spieldauer 2 – 5 Minuten), bevor Sie allmählich längere Passagen hören.

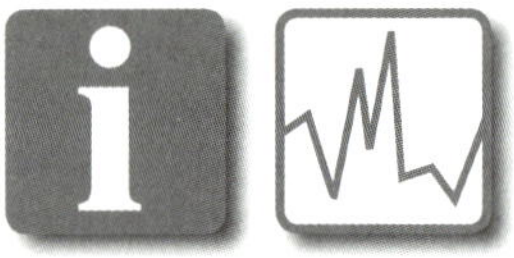

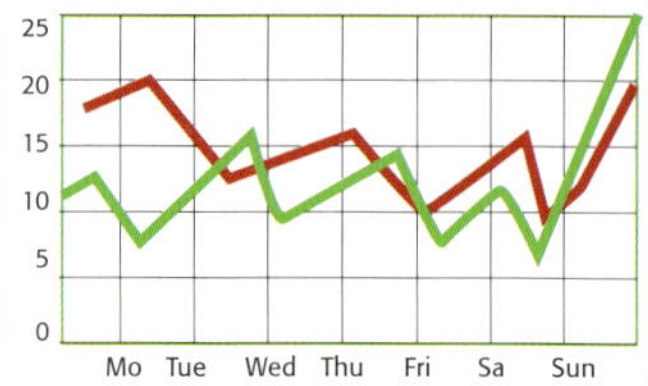

A LINE GRAPH

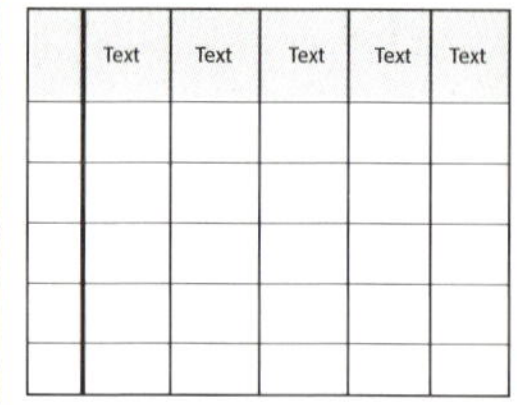

A TABLE

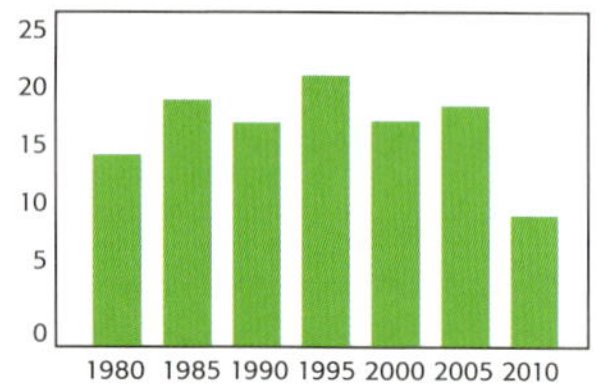

A BAR CHART

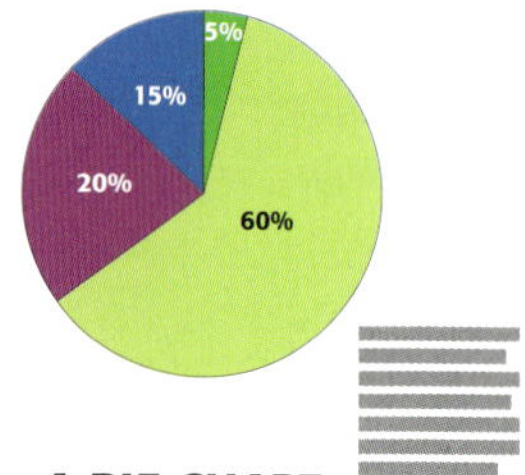

A PIE CHART

USEFUL ADJECTIVES AND ADVERBS
steady
slow
drastic
sudden
unexpected
all-time
dramatic
roughly
exactly
extreme/
extremely

UP
to rise
to grow
to increase
to climb
to become more
to explode
the rise
the growth
the increase
to double
twofold
threefold
sixfold

USEFUL NOUNS
half
third
fourth
fifth
sixth
fraction
percent
percentage
average

USEFUL NOUNS (DIAGRAMS)
x-axis
y-axis
column
unit
decade
bar
line
graph
chart

USEFUL NOUNS (DEVELOP-MENTS)
a change
a peak
a climax
a low
a high
turning point
a stop
an extreme

NO CHANGE
to remain unchanged
to stay the same
to stagnate
to remain constant
the stag-nation

DOWN
to fall
to sink
to decrease
to become less
to drop
to plummet
the fall
the decrease
the drop
to halve

Describing and analysing diagrams and statistics

1. Start your description with a short introduction:
   - Inform the readers about the kind of diagram.
   - What is the general topic?
   - How many categories, bars, columns, etc. does the diagram consist of?
   - What do they stand for?
2. The main part of your text should be the analysis:
   - What are the extremes? Talk about maximums, tops, peaks, extremes, lows, developments, averages.
   - Select and briefly describe examples and give further explanations, if necessary.
3. General summary: Summarise the main results in one or two sentences.

When describing graphs and diagrams, do not include your personal opinion. Make sure that you use the simple present tense (only exception: talking about past years *[In 1978 more houses were sold.]*). Do not include too many details, restrict your analysis to the most important aspects and results.

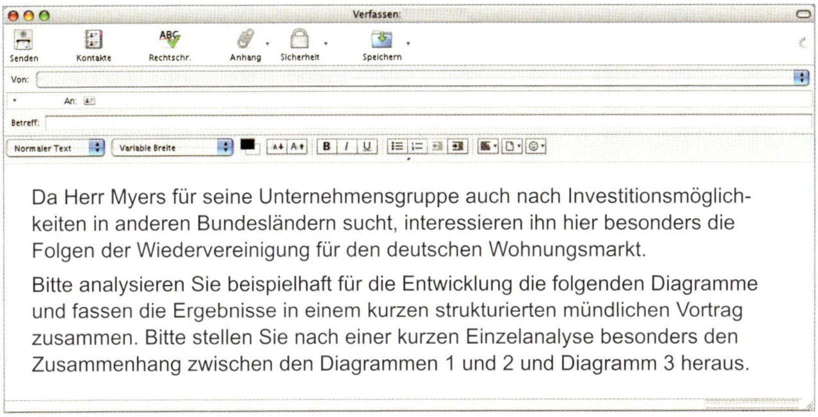

DIAGRAM 1: migrated population to Bavaria given in units and percentage

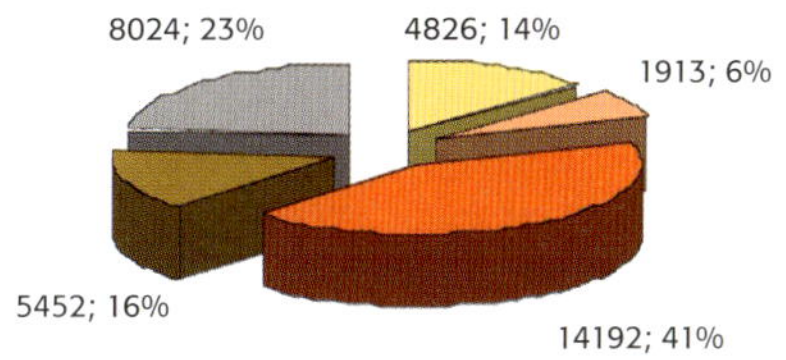

DIAGRAM 2: migrated population from Bavaria given in units and percentage

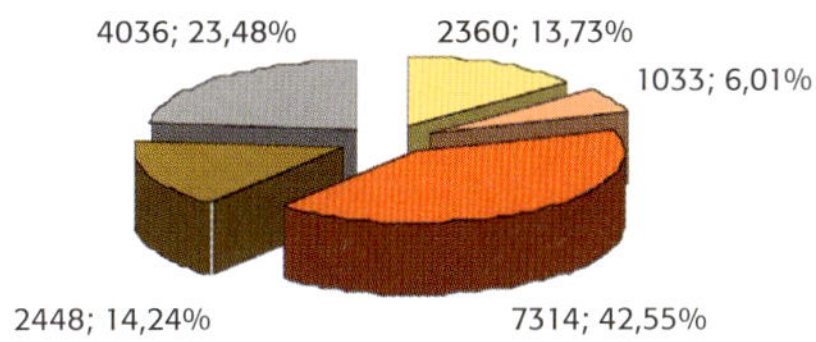

DIAGRAM 3: building permits in units

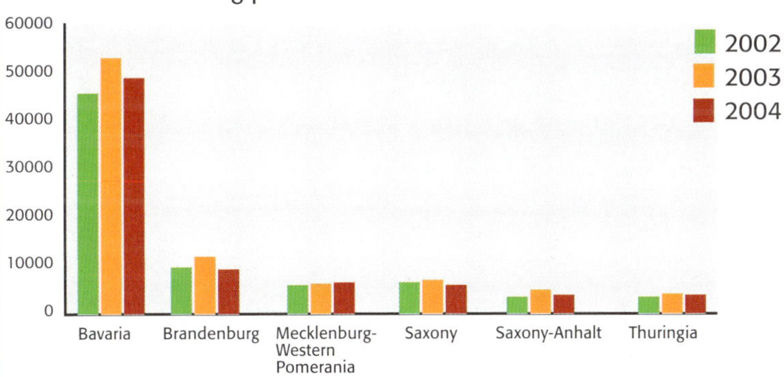

Population migration from the 5 New German Federal States to Bavaria

Pie diagram number 1 shows the phenomenon of population migration from the five new German Federal States to Bavaria in 2003. Each coloured sector of the pie represents one of the New German Federal States (see legend). The figures respectively indicate the absolute number of people who left their Federal State and the percentage of the entire population immigrating to Bavaria from each of the 5 New German Federal States. With 41% of the migrated population, the largest group came from Saxony, followed by 23% from Thuringia. Just under 5,500 people (16%) left Saxony-Anhalt, which is roughly two percent more than those who migrated from Brandenburg. The smallest group with under 2,000 migrants came to Bavaria from Mecklenburg-Western Pomerania.

UNIT 2
Describing properties

Diagrams and statistics

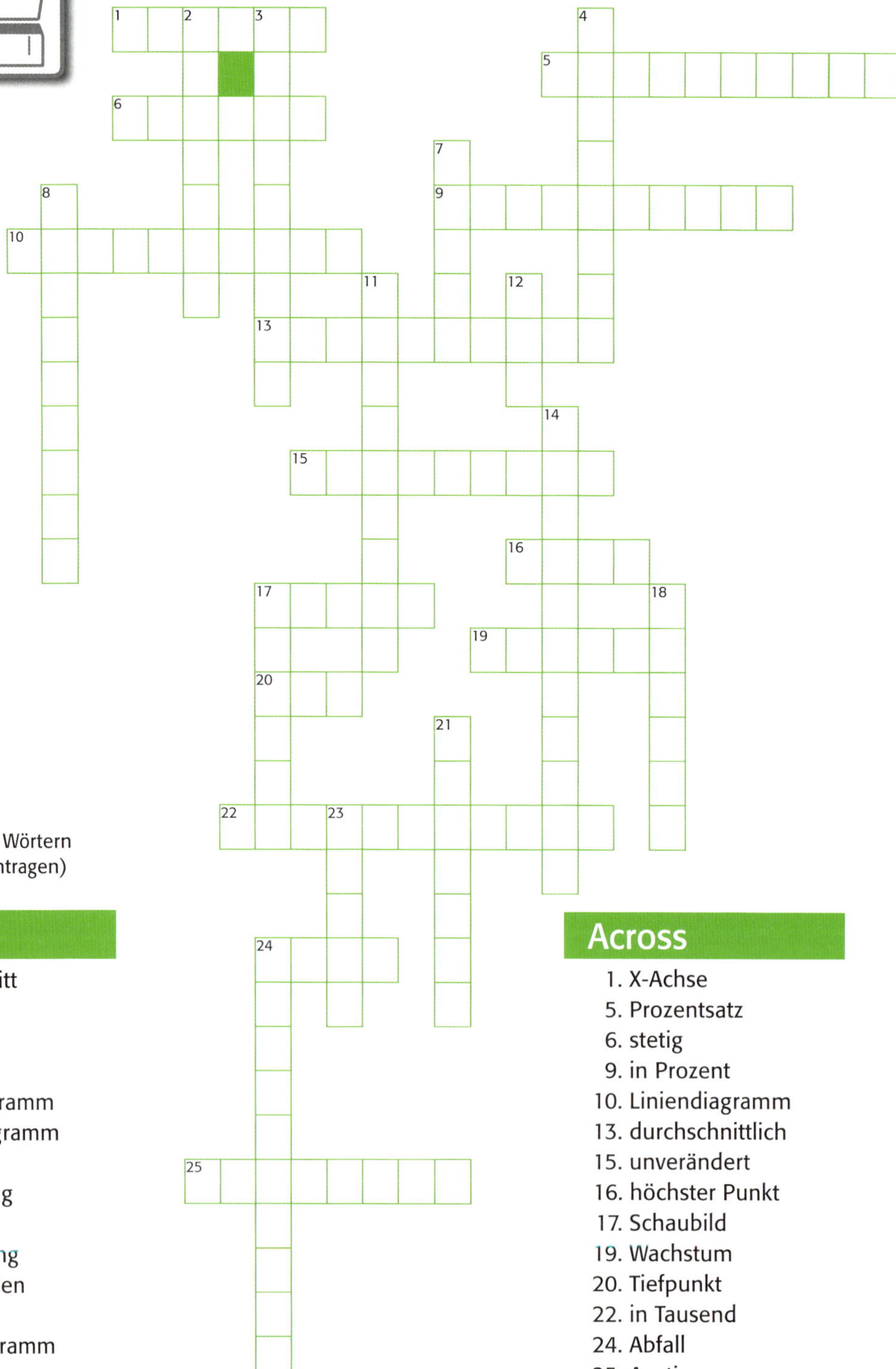

(Begriffe aus zwei Wörtern mit Bindestrich eintragen)

Down

2. Durchschnitt
3. Indikator
4. Rückgang
7. Titel
8. Tortendiagramm
11. Säulendiagramm
12. Säule
14. Entwicklung
17. Spalte
18. Veränderung
21. stark abfallen
23. Tabelle
24. Ablaufdiagramm

Across

1. X-Achse
5. Prozentsatz
6. stetig
9. in Prozent
10. Liniendiagramm
13. durchschnittlich
15. unverändert
16. höchster Punkt
17. Schaubild
19. Wachstum
20. Tiefpunkt
22. in Tausend
24. Abfall
25. Anstieg

Describing commercial properties

Work in pairs. One of you is the letting agent, the other one is the caller. With the help of the German role cards, prepare the following phone call. Use the telephone phrases given below if necessary.

Rollenkarte 1:

Sie arbeiten für einen gewerblichen Makler. In der Wochenendausgabe einer Frankfurter Zeitung haben Sie eine Anzeige für ein Café geschaltet, das Sie vermieten. Sie erhalten einen Anruf von einem Vertreter einer amerikanischen Restaurantkette, der ein Lokal für einen American Coffee Shop sucht. Beantworten Sie die Fragen des Anrufers und vereinbaren Sie zum Ende des Gesprächs einen Besichtigungstermin *(appointment to view the property)*.

Dieses sind die Informationen, die Ihnen zur Verfügung stehen:

- aufwändig saniertes Gebäude
- Café im Erdgeschoss *(on ground floor)* mit Kelleretage *(basement level)*
- 7 Meter breites Fenster
- an belebter Geschäftsstraße *(busy main road)* gelegen, in der Nähe zu vielen Büros und weiteren Geschäften
- insgesamt 65 qm Bewirtschaftungsfläche *(floor space)*
- Platz für ca 35 Gäste *(35 seater)*
- neuer Fliesenboden
- hohe Decken *(high ceiling)*
- indirekte Beleuchtung
- Spotstrahler *(spotlights)* über der Theke *(counter)*
- offene Kochecke *(open-plan cooking area)* im hinteren Bereich *(rear part)* mit Edelstahldunstabzugshaube *(stainless steel extractor hood)*
- 65 qm Kellerfläche (Lagerfläche) *(storage area)*
- 2 separate Lagerräume mit Regalen *(shelves)*
- Herren- und Damentoiletten
- Theke
- 6-flammiger Gasherd *(6-burner gas cooker)*
- Grill *(grill)*
- Kaffeemaschine
- 2 Mikrowellen
- Geschirrspülmaschine
- großer Kühlschank
- Getränkekühlschrank mit Sichttür *(drinks display fridge)*
- Computerkasse *(itemised electronic cash register)*
- monatliche Miete € 1450

Rollenkarte 2:

Sie sind Vertreter der amerikanischen Restaurantkette Starmugs. In der Wochenendausgabe einer Frankfurter Zeitung haben Sie eine Anzeige für ein Café gelesen, das Sie interessiert. Sie wissen nur, dass das Café in der Frankfurter Innenstadt liegt.

Sie rufen den Makler an und stellen Fragen zu dieser Immobilie. Besonders sind Sie an den folgenden Informationen interessiert:

- Einzelheiten zum Ladenlokal
- Lage des Ladenlokals
- Bodenbelag
- genaue Ausstattung *(equipment)*
- Kochmöglichkeiten *(cooking facilities)*
- Toiletten
- Lagerräume
- Miete

Geben Sie weitere Einzelheiten über Ihre Restaurantkette und vereinbaren Sie anschließend einen Besichtigungstermin *(appointment to view the property)*.

i

telephone phrases

STARTING THE CALL

Good morning/afternoon/evening..

This is..

My name is...

I'm calling to...

The reason I'm calling is...

OFFERING HELP/INFORMATION

What can I do for you, Mr /Mrs / Ms...

How can I help you?

ASKING FOR INFORMATION/HELP

Could you please...

I was wondering if you could..

I've got several questions and was wondering if you could...

SAYING THAT YOU DID NOT UNDERSTAND

Sorry, I did not get that.

Could you say that again, please?

I'm afraid I didn't get what you said.

Could you speak up please?

ENDING THE CALL

Thanks for your help.

Thanks for calling.

Is there anything else I can do for you? (person called)

SAYING GOOD-BYE

See you on/in...

Speak to you on.../later.

Bye for now.

Good-bye.

W.M.Smith Ltd
Letting agents – residential and commercial-
35 - 39 Hillsgate, Ipswich IP6 8UH
Directors M.Turner, M.Sc., Ch. Prescott, St. Parker
Telephone (0473) 567310 Fax (0473) 784235 email: info@wmsmith.co.uk

Your Ref.
Our Ref.: CP/JT

Mr. Werner Koch
Brabant OHG
Westring 201
44629 Herne
Germany

May 13, 200

Dear Mr. Koch,

Your enquiry for office space in Ipswich

Thank you very much for your fax which we received yesterday.

We are pleased to inform you that we indeed have a number of commercial properties in our listings which we could offer you.

However, in order to provide you with more detailed information, we would need to get some additional information to be able to answer your query. Therefore, we would like you to complete the attached form and return it to us either by fax or by letter.

In the meantime, you could as well have a look at some of the properties we offer which are described on our homepage www.wmsmith.co.uk.

Should you have any further questions or comments, please do not hesitate to contact us by phone or by fax.

We are looking forward to hearing from you soon.

Yours sincerely,

Stevenson

T. Stevenson
Commercial lettings

enclosures
questionnaire

Summarising an English business letter in German: an enquiry for office space

Have a look at the letter.

1. Name the parts of the business letter.
2. Write a short German text in which you summarise the main aspects of this letter (deutschsprachiger Vermerk)

Another day at the office...

In der morgendlichen Besprechung der Abteilungsleiter übergibt Ihnen Ihr Chef die Kopie der folgenden E-Mail:

Dear Sirs,

We kindly refer to our Mr. Myers´ visit to your company in early spring and the talks we had in Bochum.

To enable the correct assessment of the assets discussed and to prepare due diligence, we kindly ask you to confirm the visit of our delegation on Monday next week.

The delegation will be composed of Mr. Myers himself, our chief controller Mr. Donald, our tax adviser Mrs. Salantino, our director "Commercial Real Estate Properties" Mr. Vanderbuilt and our director "Residential Real Estate Properties", Mrs. Gonzales.

We kindly ask you to prepare a comprehensive presentation of your <u>two real estate properties in Bochum-Riemke and Bochum-Dahlhausen.</u>

We are particularly interested in looking at the substantial details of your investment in the Bochum-Riemke shopping mall you erected in 1998 and to visit the facilities.

Furthermore, we intend to proceed to a thorough visit of your housing estate in Bochum-Dahlhausen. As we remember, you there own 160 dwellings in 8 multi-storey buildings.

We would be grateful, if you prepared a documentation/guided tour for both containing, in particular:

- the description of the City of Bochum itself
- a brief description of the types of buildings and activities in the aforementioned properties
- some general remarks as to the general condition of the buildings (needs in terms of maintenance / repair)

Please confirm.

With best regards

Myers & Myers Real Estate Corp. Ing.

Emily Hilington

Projekt 1:

Allgemeine Präsentation der Stadt Bochum mit anschließender Stadtführung

What you see:
The German Mining Museum.
What you feel:
Changing times.
What you see:
A glimpse of the Historical Art Collection.
What you feel:
The presence of great art.

- **Bilden Sie eine Projektgruppe für die Erarbeitung dieser englischsprachigen Präsentation.**
- **Gehen Sie arbeitsteilig vor (Geschichte – Konversionsthematik, Sehenswürdigkeiten, Wirtschaft).**
- **Bereiten Sie die Führung der Delegation detailliert vor (Streckenführung, Zeitplanung usw.).**

MEMO

Informieren Sie sich auch über Wirtschaftsdaten. Nutzen Sie hierfür die verfügbaren englischsprachigen Publikationen wie z. B. auf der Homepage: http://www.bochum.de/english.

Projekt 2:

Beschreibung der Gewerbezeile in Bochum-Riemke

Der Stadtteil Riemke liegt nur unweit des Bochumer Stadtzentrums in dessen Norden und schaut auf eine jahrzehntealte Industriegeschichte zurück. Obwohl im Ruhrgebiet schon nach 1820 dank der Schaffung der nötigen Verkehrswege der Bergbau und die Industrialisierung eine rasante Entwicklung nahmen, kam es in Riemke erst im Jahre 1911 zur Abteufung der ersten Schachtanlage Constantin der Große. In den Zwanzigerjahren wurde dann eine Kokerei gebaut. Riemke wurde schon im April 1926 nach Bochum eingemeindet.

Riemke war seit jeher ein Arbeiterviertel und noch lange Zeit bis in die zweite Hälfte des 20. Jahrhunderts „Auffangbecken" für die benachteiligten Bevölkerungsgruppen der Stadt Bochum, die sich insbesondere östlich und westlich der Autobahn A 43 in den Sozialwohnungen der Zillertal- und der Herzogstraße fanden.

Schul- und Berufsausbildungschancen waren für die Kinder dieser Siedlungen oft nur in bescheidenem Umfang gegeben. Die Kinder besuchten zumeist die Sonderschule an der Riemker Straße 12.

Im Zuge der allgemeinen Konversionspolitik der Stadt Bochum und der damit verbundenen Steigerung der Attraktivität von Stadtquartieren mit besonderem Entwicklungsbedarf investierte die GW BO schon 1998 in die Errichtung und Verpachtung der Gewerbezeile Riemker Einkaufspark entlang der Herner Straße zwischen der Grummer und der Tippelsberger Straße.

Der Riemker Einkaufspark ist Einkaufsmittelpunkt in erster Linie für die Stadtteile Riemke, Hofstede, Hamme und Grumme. Er wurde im Jahr 1998 eröffnet und wird seither von einem Tochterunternehmen der GW BO, der GW Bochum City Management GmbH, erfolgreich bewirtschaftet.

Aufgrund seines attraktiven Branchen- und Mietermixes auf zwei Etagen (Kleingewerbe: Modeboutiquen, kleine Läden für Tabakwaren, Zeitungen und Zeitschriften, Lottoannahmestelle, Bäckereien, Fleischereien, Reinigung, Photogeschäft etc. – Gastronomie: ein Café / Konditorei mit ca. 80 Sitzplätzen, eine italienische Espressobar, ein Bistrorestaurant mit Außengastronomie, eine Nordseefiliale, ein Weinladen mit Ausschank) – einem großen Markt für Elektro- und Unterhaltungselektronik, einem für sein exklusives Warensortiment bekannten Premium-Supermarkt einer großen Handelskette und anderer Dienstleistungsbetriebe zieht der Riemker Einkaufspark aber auch Kundschaft aus den weiter entfernt liegenden Stadtteilen (Eickel, Hordel), der Innenstadt und den Nachbargemeinden Wanne-Eickel und Herne an.

An Verkaufsfläche stehen insgesamt ca. 30.000 qm zur Verfügung. Sämtliche Lokale sind zurzeit langfristig verpachtet. Die durchschnittliche Gewerbemiete beträgt hier 16,50 € / qm zzgl. Nebenkosten.

Der Riemker Einkaufspark ist verkehrstechnisch hervorragend über die A 43, die Dorstener und die Herner Straße angebunden. Besuchern steht ein unterirdisches Parkhaus mit 1.300 Einstellplätzen zur Verfügung.

MEMO

Bitte legen Sie einen Layoutplan des Riemker Einkaufsparks an und bereiten Sie eine englischsprachige Führung durch die gesamte Anlage vor.

Informieren Sie Ihre Gäste insbesondere über die genaue Zusammensetzung Ihrer gewerblichen Mieter, über deren Aktivitäten, Größe der Ladenlokale, Höhe der Pacht usw.

Projekt 3:

Beschreibung der Wohnanlage in Bochum-Dahlhausen

The Railway–Museum in Bochum-Dahlhausen

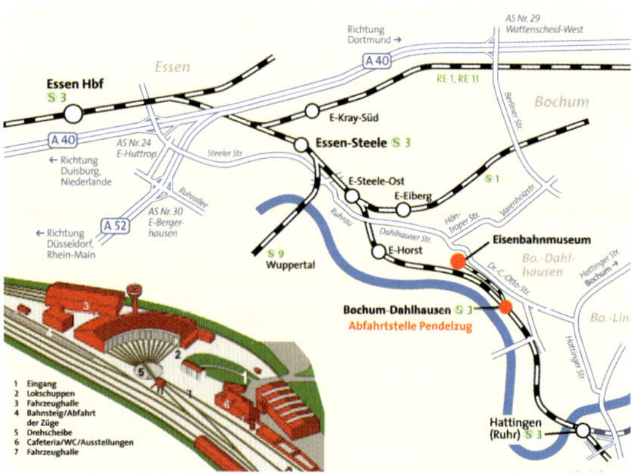

Wer Dahlhausen hört, denkt zumeist an die Geschichte der deutschen Eisenbahn und das heutige DGEG-Eisenbahnmuseum auf dem Gelände des ehemaligen, zwischen 1916 und 1918 errichteten Bahnbetriebswerkes.

Hier verfügt die Stadt über attraktive Grundstücksreserven in der Nähe und entlang der Ruhr.

1991 errichtete die GW BO eine Wohnanlage in der Willi-Geldmacher-Straße.

Bochum-Dahlhausen ist ein attraktives Wohnquartier mit hohem Freizeitwert. Die im Osten gelegenen, sanft geschwungenen Höhenzüge am Nord-West-Ufer der Ruhr, die Landschaft um Hattingen und Burg Blankenstein laden zu ausgiebigen Erkundungsfahrten und Waldspaziergängen ein. Die Ruhrgebietsmetropolen Bochum, Essen und Witten sind verkehrstechnisch gut zu erreichen. An bestimmten Stellen ist der Blick durch das Ruhrtal atemberaubend.

Dahlhausen verfügt über eine gute Infrastruktur: hochwertige Gewerbeeinheiten, Kindertagesstätten, Schulen, ein Einkaufszentrum, Wellness-Angebote und vieles andere mehr.

Die Wohnanlage der GW BO wurde auf der an der Südseite der Willi-Geldmacher-Straße gelegenen Brachfläche errichtet und umfasst 160 Wohneinheiten unterschiedlicher Größen und Typologien in der für Bochum klassischen Blockbebauung mit großzügigen Innenhöfen.

Angesichts des allgemein in Bochum zu beobachtenden Trends zu Single- bzw. Zweipersonenhaushalten wurde auf ein entsprechendes Angebot im Hinblick auf die nachhaltige Vermietbarkeit der Objekte Wert gelegt.

Im Einzelnen entstanden dort 160 Sozialwohnungen, und zwar:

- 16 Vierzimmerwohnungen mit umlaufendem Balkon an den Ecken der Blockbebauung,
- 36 Dreizimmerwohnungen mit Balkon,
- 84 Zweizimmerwohnungen mit Balkon,
- 16 Studentenapartments mit Balkon,
- 8 behindertengerecht ausgestattete Zweizimmerwohnungen.

Alle Wohneinheiten sind zurzeit mit unbefristeten Mietverträgen vermietet. Aufgrund der guten Ausstattung und der hervorragenden Lage ist mit Leerstand hier nicht zu rechnen.

Das Objekt verfügt über eine hochmoderne Gaszentralheizung mit Brennwerttechnologie. Die Wärmeisolierung der Gebäude entspricht dem neuesten technologischen Stand. Ein Energiepass ist zurzeit in Vorbereitung.

Alle Wohnungen verfügen über einen Multikabel-Anschluss für TV, Telefon und Internetzugang.

In den Außenbereichen befinden sich: zentral abgestellte Abfallbehälter und Fahrradständer.

Im Erdgeschoss ist eine Kindertagesstätte untergebracht.

Die Innenhöfe sind begrünt. In den Erdgeschossen verfügen die Wohnungen über kleine Mietergärten, die von den Mietern auch selbst gepflegt werden. In der Mitte des Innenhofes wurde ein Kinderspielplatz („Abenteuerspielplatz") angelegt. Der Außenraum ist mit Holzsitzbänken möbliert.

Gemäß den Förderbestimmungen der Wohnungsbauförderungsanstalt NRW *(WFA – vgl. auch http://www.nrwbank.de/pdf/dt/pdf_Wfa_EnglishSummary.pdf und http://www.nrwbank.de/de/wohnraumportal)* dürfen die Höchstdurchschnittsmieten im öffentlich geförderten Wohnungsbau nicht überschritten werden. Diese ergeben sich aus den spezifischen Darlehens- und Tilgungsbedingungen (Zinssatz, Bewirtschaftungs- und Instandhaltungspauschalen). Die Mieten dürfen in Bochum die Kostenmiete von ca. 4,66 € zzgl. Nebenkosten nicht überschreiten.

MEMO

Bitte bereiten Sie eine Präsentation der Wohnanlage in englischer Sprache vor. Zeichnen Sie einen Layoutplan und planen Sie den Rundgang mit Ihren amerikanischen Gästen.

Planen Sie Wohnungsbesichtigungen der unterschiedlichen Wohntypen ein. Dokumentieren Sie im Vorfeld Kurzinterviews mit den Mietern hinsichtlich Ihrer Zufriedenheit mit ihrer Wohnung und dem unmittelbaren Wohnumfeld.

Describing residential properties

Copy the following mind map into your exercise books and add as much information as possible. Present your mind map to another group and exchange your vocabulary lists.

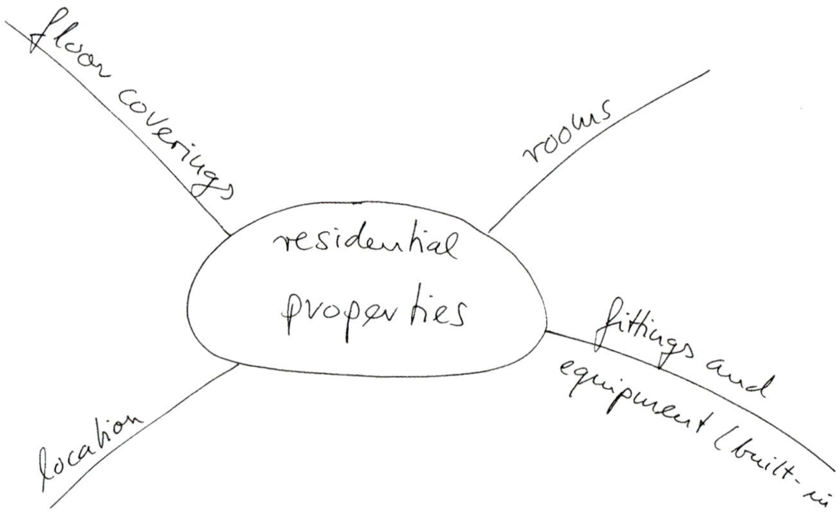

Representative art nouveau flat in Bochum: gap-filling exercise

Welcome to this representative flat in an art noveau building in a quiet suburb of Bochum.

Bu______ in 1902, th______ property of______ the ch_________ of a mo______ turn-of the-century b______.

The fl______ has go______ a sq______ footage of ov______ 230 square me______ and co______ of seven ro______. It is lo______ on the first fl______ of a 12-un______ property wh______ is cu______ used for bo______ co______ and re______ purposes. The pa______ floor and the high ce______ (3.2 metres) create a li______ and ai______ atmosphere.

In 2005, the flat was completely re______ and was eq______ with a new ki________ and new ba________. There is a fi________ kitchen which co______ a fr______, a fr______, a microwave, st______ and a dishwasher. The small ba________ faces a small park op______ the bu______. As you can see from the at______ fl______ plan, the flat can also be us________ for co______ purposes (lawyer's of________, surgery etc.)

The re__________ is € 1050 per mo__________, fu__________ there is a €180 adv__________ payment of ut_____________ costs p______ month. We ch______ a three mo________' rent se______ deposit pl_____________ a letting agent's f__________ of two month's rent.

Letter-writing exercise

Re-write the following text as a business letter by putting the sentences into a logical order. Then, arrange the different parts in the layout of a business letter.

shouldyouhaveanyfurtherquestionspleasedon'thesitatetocontactuseit-herbyphonefaxoremailgemeinnützigewohnugsbaugesellschaftbo-chumkellerstraße35-3948456bochumapril23,2006dearmrthomasbuilt in1910theflatwascompletelymodernisedin2005andhasgotnewwindo wsamodernheatingsystemandanewbathroom3bedroomflatbochumto wncentrethemonthlyrentforthisflatis€495towhichmustbeadded€95ut ilitycostsirefertoyesterday'sphonecallandwouldliketoofferyouthefollo-wing3-bedroomflatinbochumduetotherecentshortageinthisproperty-sectorwewouldadviseyoutocontactusassoonaspossiblesothatwecan-findadatetoviewthepropertytheflatconsistsofthreebedroomsonelarg eeat-inkitchenalivingroomandabathroomfurthermorethehardwood-floorswerecompletelyreplacedtheflatislocatedonthesecondfloorofa3-familyhouseinaquietsidestreetinbochumclosetobochumstadtgarteni-enclosethefloorplanandsomerecentpictureslookingforwardtohearing fromyousoonyourssincerelypeterweinbauerresidentiallettingsstewart thomas45norwichdrivenr324lalowestoftgreatbritain

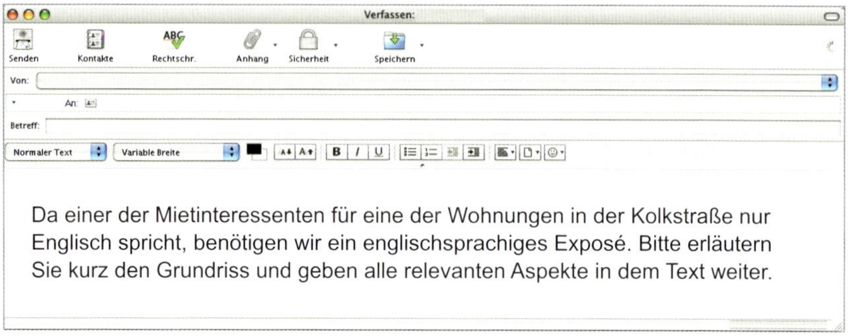

- **Wohnfläche:**
  ca. 94 qm
- **Zimmeraufteilung:**
  Wohn-/ Esszimmer, Schlafzimmer, Gäste-WC, Kinderzimmer, Küche, Badezimmer, Balkon mit herrlichem Ausblick;
- **Heizung:**
  Etagenheizung
- **Sonstiges:**
  Wohnhaus mit nur drei Wohneinheiten
- **Beziehbar:**
  sofort
- **Kaltmiete pro Monat:**
  415,- €
- **Garage/Stellplatz:**
  35,- €
- **Nebenkostenvorauszahlung:**
  25,- € pro Monat für Versicherung, Hauslicht, Grundsteuer, Schornsteinfeger;
- **Kaution:**
  900,- €
- **Gesamtprovision:**
  zwei Monatsmieten zzgl. ges. gült. MwSt. fällig bei Übergabe

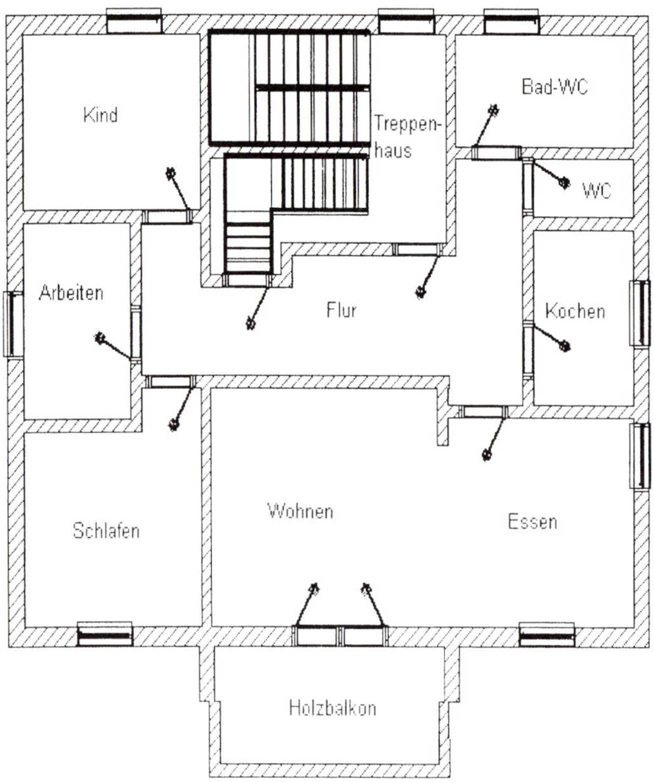

Pre-writing Activities zum Strukturieren eines zu schreibenden Textes

Strukturieren Sie den englischen Text, den Sie schreiben sollen, im Vorfeld. Wenn Sie sich vor dem Ausformulieren eine klare Struktur geben, können Sie mehr Sorgfalt auf Rechtschreibung und Grammatik legen.

Eine empfehlenswerte *Pre-writing Activity* ist das *Clustering*. Sie schreiben die groben Strukturelemente des Textes in entsprechend große Kreise. Alle sofort erkennbaren Unterpunkte, die sich auf das größere Strukturthema beziehen, werden um diesen Kreis in kleineren Kreisen gruppiert. Wenn sich nun an diese wiederum Unterpunkte anschließen, werden diese durch eine weitere Kreiseinheit dargestellt.

So bekommen Sie für jeden wesentlichen Gliederungspunkt ein Kreisgebilde (ein Cluster), das z. B. einen Abschnitt Ihres Textes darstellen könnte. Bringen Sie Ihre Abschnitte nun in eine sinnvolle Struktur und die Gliederung für Ihren Text ist fertig.

Für die oben verlangte Aufgabe könnte dieses *Clustering* so aussehen:

UNIT 2

Describing properties

(Begriffe aus zwei Wörtern mit Bindestrich eintragen)

Across

2. begehbar
3. Sanierung
6. Kaution
9. doppelt verglast
10. Einzug
15. Heizkörper
17. Zwangsräumung
18. gefliest
20. Reparaturarbeiten
25. sozialer Wohnungsbau

Down

1. Gasheizung
4. Einbauküche
5. Wohngeld
7. Mietvertrag
8. Mieter
11. Leerstand
12. Heizkosten
13. Miete
14. Decke
16. Vermieter
19. Teppichboden
21. Dach
22. Versicherung
23. Grundriss
24. Fußboden
26. Dusche

Types of Homes

Work in small groups. Decide for one type of home. Using the information provided below, write an interview between an estate agent and a potential buyer who first of all needs to be informed about characteristics, advantages and disadvantages of the properties. Present your interview to the class.

SINGLE FAMILY HOMES

Your ownership includes the house and extends to the limits of the property lines.

OURS

TOWNHOUSES

Your ownership includes the lot on which your house sits as well as the entire structure.

THEIRS OURS THEIRS THEIRS

CONDOMINIUMS

Your ownership is limited to a single unit and a shared interest in all of the common areas.

COMMON OWNERSHIP

Group A single family homes

By far the most common form of housing in North America is the single family detached home-ranging from 600 square foot bungalows to 6000 (or more) square foot sprawling mansions. The most important distinguishing factors that determine a single family dwelling are that it sits on its own piece of land (which is sold part and parcel with the home) and it is not attached to anyone else's residence. With single family homes, your home pretty much is your castle. Subject to neighborhood and subdivision regulations and ordinances, you can do with it as you wish. Want a different exterior color? Usually you can accomplish that (taking into account the fact that the neighbors may not be receptive to a purple house with ecru trim). Need more room and want to add on? Subject to the codes of your jurisdiction, you may be able to expand your living space.

OURS

You will probably have a yard of some sort – from "postage stamp" size up through multiple acres, and your ownership will include all of it. In effect, when you buy a single family home your purchase will be of a parcel of land (your lot) on which sits a structure (your house).

ADVANTAGES	DISADVANTAGES
To a large degree, "your space" is your own. You can modify or improve it as you wish.	All maintenance and repair costs - interior, exterior and everything in between - are yours
Re-sale value is generally the highest on single family detached homes.	Lack of amenities (for example, pools, playgrounds, etc.) that you may find in other types of housing.
If you need more room, you can usually add on to the existing house.	You are responsible for landscaping and lawn upkeep costs.
Generally there are no property management fees as there are in condominiums and many townhouses.	In most areas, single family homes are more expensive than townhouses or condominiums.

- You like your "space". The idea of apartment living gives you the willies.
- The prospect of cutting the lawn, trimming the bushes and shoveling snow excite you (or at least don't send you headed for the nearest bridge).
- You like the idea of modifying your home – changing the color, the appearance, the size. Having someone tell you that you couldn't do that would bother you.
- If you like, you are able to build a single family home (building a townhouse or condominium community gets a little expensive!).

Group B townhouses

Townhouses often can make an excellent "middle ground" between a detached single family home and a full fledged condominium because, to some degree, they offer attributes of both.

For purposes of definition, we will describe a townhouse as a home that is attached to one or more other houses, but which sits directly on a parcel of land that you also own (if you don't own the land, it is a condominium). For this discussion, townhouses can range from duplexes and triplexes all the way through huge townhouse communities consisting of hundreds of similar homes.

There is a good degree of variance in the way townhouse communities are structured. It may be a simple agreement (as is often the case of duplexes and triplexes) that each parcel of land and the home that sits on it is separately owned. In the case of larger townhouse communities, you will generally have an additional shared ownership in the common areas of the complex as well as any amenities such as swimming pools, park areas, etc. This ownership you will share jointly with all other townhouse owners in the complex.

ADVANTAGES	DISADVANTAGES
May have less exterior maintenance and repairs to be responsible for.	You give up privacy when compared to single family homes.
Having a neighbor's home attached to yours may bring a higher level of security.	Your options for changing the exterior look of your house will be limited.
There may be amenities in the community (for example, pools, tennis courts, playgrounds and the like).	

- You like the idea of your "space" but not having to deal with most exterior maintenance has even more appeal.
- A small backyard "retreat" or deck is just about all the yard you need.
- The idea of having neighbors close doesn't really bother you - you just don't want them above and below as well as next to you!

Group C condominiums

The easiest way to understand the concept of condominium ownership is to see it as an apartment you own (in fact, many condominiums are apartments that have been converted over the years). Your ownership extends inward from your interior walls, floors and ceilings. In addition, you are a partner, with all of the other owners in the complex, of the exterior structure (the foundation, exterior walls and roof) as well as any common areas and amenities (for example, swimming pools, clubhouses, tennis courts, play areas, etc.).

One of the requirements of condominium ownership is the payment of a monthly condo fee, which covers general repairs and maintenance to the common areas of the complex as well as (hopefully) build up a cash reserve for future needs. In general, all exterior maintenance and repairs are the responsibility of the condominium association, although you will be charged for them, either through your association dues or a special assessment (a one time charge assessed to all owners for, as an example, a new roof). The normal day-to-day maintenance of the grounds (some examples are cutting the grass, shoveling snow and maintaining the pool) are also the responsibility of the association. Interior maintenance and repairs (for example, replacing a dishwasher) are the responsibility of the individual owner.

In some areas, a condominium may be the only consideration that fits within your budget. The reason for this is simple. In general, the same square footage will cost less in a condo setting than it will in a single family home or townhouse, due mainly to land cost--you can build many more condos than you can single family homes on the same amount of land.

ADVANTAGES	DISADVANTAGES
You will be responsible for little or no exterior maintenance or repairs.	You will be responsible for payment of Condominium Association fees.
Many condominium communities offer amenities (pools, play areas, tennis courts, etc.) you may otherwise not be able to afford.	You give up more privacy when compared to single family homes as well as townhouses.
Condominiums are often located in locations convenient to centers of employment and shopping.	You only own from your interior walls inward. The rest of the structure and all of the land is owned in common with the other condominium owners.
Condominiums are often more reasonably priced than other forms of housing.	When it is time to sell, it can often take longer to sell a condominium.

- You want absolutely nothing to do with exterior maintenance and repairs.
- You like the idea of amenities (swimming pools, tennis courts and the like) but you don't like the idea of having to pay for them on your own.
- You like the safety of numerous and nearby neighbors.

Source: http://www.ourfamilyplace.com

Now listen to the interviews presented by the other groups and complete the following table:

type of house	characteristics	advantages	disadvantages	ideal house for…
Single family home (detached house)				
Townhouse (terraced house)				
Condominium				

Which type of residential property is more popular in your home town? Do you find different properties in different areas? If so, how would explain this phenomenon?

Talking about Safety

Have a look at the following advice that should help to prevent burglary.
Which ones would you pass on to your tenants?
Do you as landlords take any steps against burglary?

- A Consider fitting a burglar alarm as a deterrent
- B Don´t leave a window open where access would be easy from a flat roof
- C Install a time switch to certain lights in the house so that they will come on automatically even when you are out
- D Consider fitting external security lighting
- E Don´t leave ladders lying around
- F Take stock of your fences and hedges – fences and walls should be secure and high, hedges thick
- G Sheds should be of the lock-up variety
- H Make sure that the conservatory is properly secured
- I Check up on garage locks
- J Keep the side gate closed to prevent easy access to the back of the house
- K Don´t leave anything valuable in the car, remove the stereo system and use a crock lock
- L Demand to see an identity card from all callers unknown to you. Have external meter cupboards installed if you are out all day.
- M Fit a metal grille over vulnerable windows
- N Paint drain-pipes with slippery anti-burglar paint
- O The panes of some double-glazed windows can easily be removed unless they are properly secured
- P Bikes, motorbikes and other vehicles are easy to steal if left lying around the front of the house
- Q Don´t keep computers or other valuable equipment in view
- R Fit windows locks
- S Cancel milk and newspapers when you go away
- T Never keep a spare key under the door mat or a flowerpot
- U Clear panels in the front door are less secure than solid ones
- V Fit a door viewer in a solid front door so that you can see who is at the door before opening it
- W Fit suitable door locks and a door chain/limiter

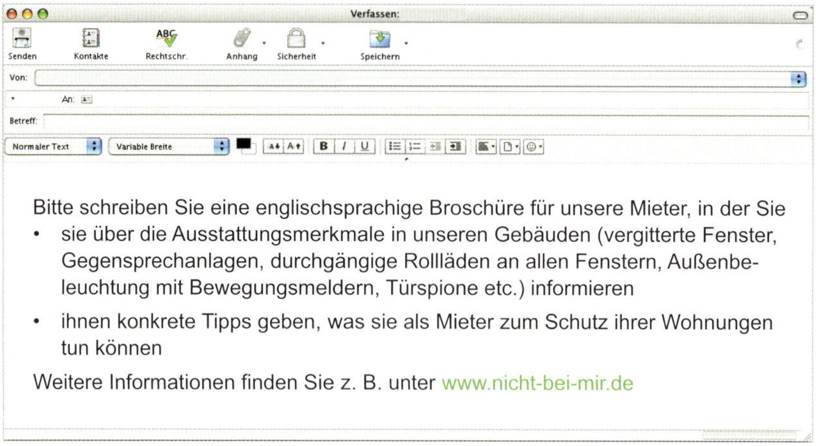

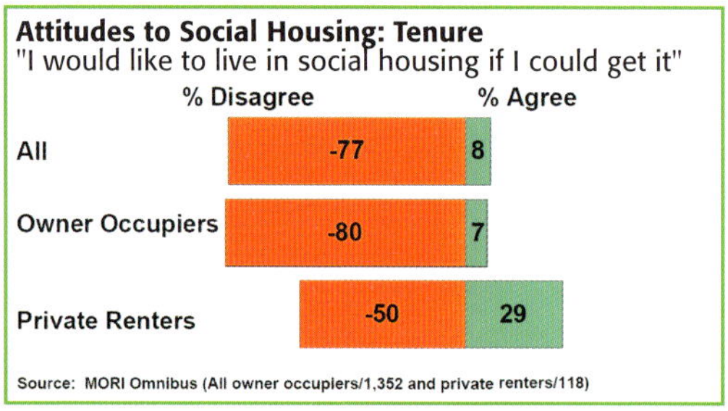

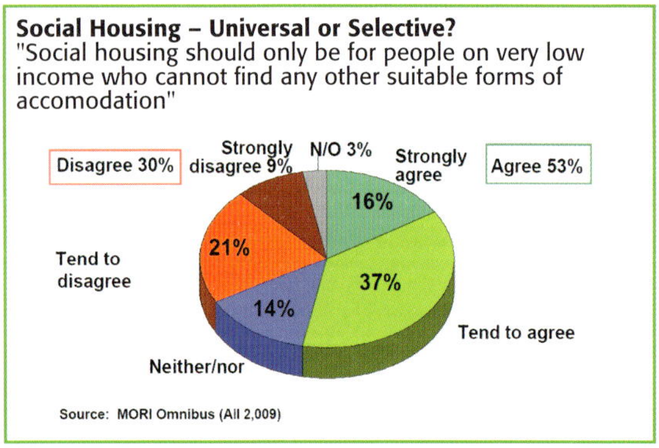

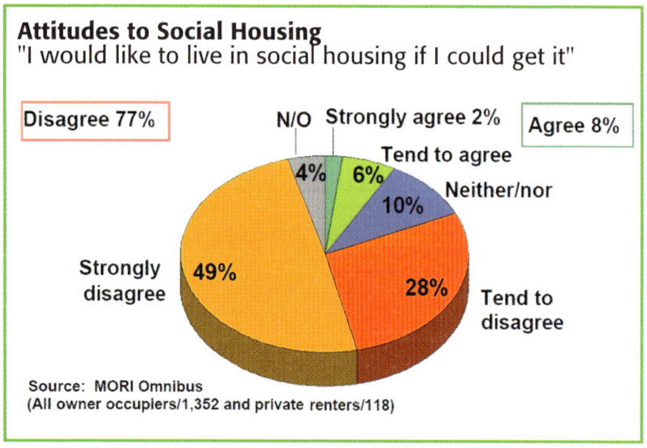

Pre-reading activity:

When you hear the term "social housing", which are your first associations? Are these more positive or negative?
Can you explain why?

One of the main ideas of the following text is "We need a radical shift in thinking to remove the stigma of social housing". Before you read the text, briefly exchange ideas on which steps might be necessary for that.

Now read the text and list the suggestions Zeena Atkins makes in her article.

Assignments:

What – according to the text – are the advantages of homeownership?
What does the author mean by "the housing stigma"?
Which solutions does Zenna Atkins offer or suggest in her article?

The stigma enigma

We need a radical shift in thinking to remove the stigma of social housing, says Zenna Atkins

the guardian

Wednesday January 5, 2005

I like being a homeowner - or at least the luxury of kidding myself that I am; the Royal Bank of Scotland actually owns most of my home and I pay it handsomely each month to say it's mine. You are taken seriously as a grown-up member of society. You feel in control. If I want a new kitchen, I can get one. If I hate my neighbours, I can sell up and move. If I want to paint it pink, no one stops me - although a few neighbours were a little taken aback by my unusually bright Christmas lights.

Whether we agree or not, home ownership has become - or is perceived to be - an almost universal aspiration. There is increasing demand for affordable homes, which ought to make us think about how we provide them. Yet still we assume that people on low incomes or no incomes will be happy renting. We hold to the notion of traditional social housing, where people are marked out by their tenure, not by what kind of neighbours they make.

How might we do things differently? For a start, we might move more quickly away from the accepted norm that people who need social housing should be corralled together, isolated from homeowners, often on estates of the „sink“ variety that have inadequate infrastructure, poor schooling and a lack of local recreation and amenities. The section 106 planning rule goes some way towards this. It requires all new residential schemes to include an affordable home element.

Yet it is not uncommon to see all the social housing tucked away, apartheid fashion, in the least desirable corner of the development. Enlightened registered social landlords (RSLs) - and I count my own housing association, Places for People, among these - are trying to ensure a more diverse „pepper pot“ approach to new housing projects.

But the way the finance stacks up means that almost inevitably the properties with the best views and design are designated for buyers, not social housing clients.

The consequence of this is that RSLs have become, along with local authority housing, the inadvertent agents of stigma. To live in social housing is to be seen to have failed. There is the underlying assumption that if you are "in housing need" at some point in your life, you will always be in housing need.

You are given a social housing tenure for life - and a social stigma to boot. Despite this, we pursue traditional ideas about building up stocks of social housing. Perhaps instead we should create places people want to live in, encourage mixed economic communities, and create more ways for people to step on to (and off) the homeownership ladder. We need to be flexible in how people are able to access and fund these homes.

Admittedly, this requires a radical shift in thinking. We would need to no longer build social housing places, but build affordable homes for people who could choose how they paid for them. The property should not brand you. How you pay for your home should not be public knowledge.

I went to look at a new housing development with a friend recently. A young couple were in the show home before us, and asked where the social stock was going. Could they, they asked politely, reserve a property at the furthest point from "those people"?

Later, I asked the sales staff if this is a commonplace request. All too commonplace, they assured me. Sales were so much easier on sites with no "section 106" properties. From the couple's point of view, they clearly felt they worked hard, saved hard, so why should they live next door to someone who must have "failed" and got their home from "the state"?

With all the best intentions, RSLs are becoming Registered Stigma Landlords. We need to make a distinction between housing as a product, and the set of financial vehicles, tools or options that are available to allow people to access their housing.

That means new ways of delivering the housing agenda: creative ways of facilitating home ownership, such as flexible tenures on properties, so people can switch between renting and owning as their life changes.

Irrespective of status, earnings or opportunity, a decent home in a safe place should be available to all. We must accept that mixed economy communities are far more successful than exclusively poor communities. We must build communities, not estates, and ensure that these are communities of active choice for all, providing good schools, health, retail, leisure and recreational facilities.

The question is how to deliver this. Should the state support home ownership? Should state financial help belong to the housing provider, or should it follow the individual?

Getting private housebuilders to provide social housing is fine, if it brings a greater mix of tenures and incomes. The risk is that they will be able to achieve profit only by segregating the „social" elements.

So perhaps the better option is RSLs. Let us develop commercial housing building arms, new ways to finance the houses we build, and better ways of providing real communities of choice, accessible to all.

Zenna Atkins is chair of Places for People, a housing association. She is an occasional columnist for Society Guardian.

Social Housing – More Government Spending
"If the government wants to increase spending on housing, they should improve social housing"

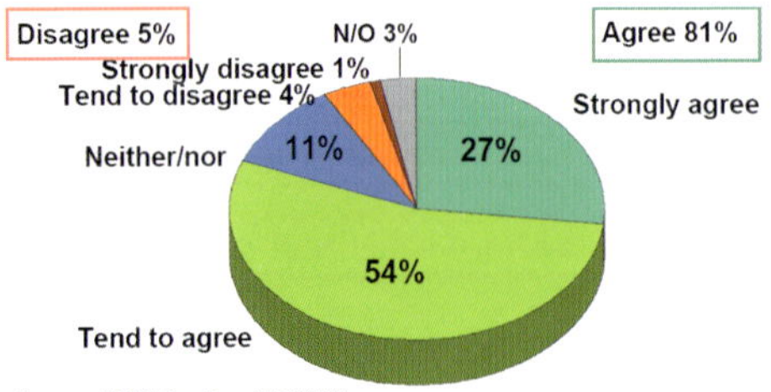

Source: MORI Omnibus (All 2,009)

Social Housing – More Demand for Better Quality Accomodation?
"More people would want to live in social housing if better quality accomodation were available"

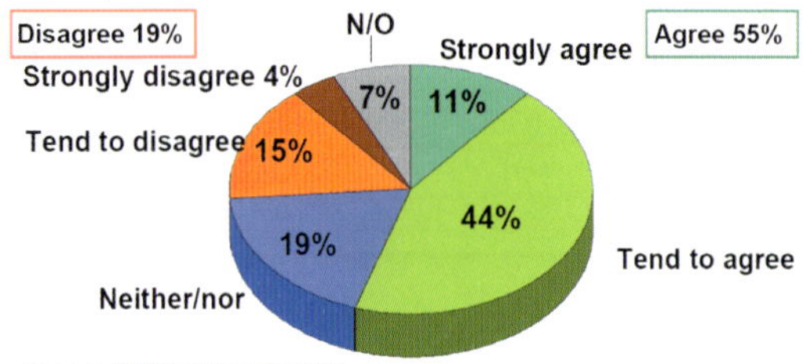

Source: MORI Omnibus (All 2,009)

The ideal flat?

Have a look at the picture. Does this estate meet the demands of modern housing?

Pre-listening activity

Work in pairs. Think of a typical flat which is part of your company's housing stock. Briefly tell your partner about this flat. Then brainstorm

- aspects a family of four would like about these flats
- aspects a family of four would not like about these flats.

While listening activity

Now listen to the following conversation in which some journalists discuss what could and should be done to make flats more attractive for families.

Which requirements are mentioned in the discussion which a modern flat should meet? Complete the table.

THE FLAT ITSELF	THE BUILDING	THE NEIGHBOUR-HOOD/LOCATION

Now design an ideal flat for a family of four (two adults, 2 children, aged 7 and 11.) Present your flat and all your ideas on a poster.

Here are some aspects you should consider:

- the location, the neighbourhood
- the building itself
- amenities and equipment in the building
- the flat itself
- the floor plan

Prepare to present your flat to the rest of the class and discuss your ideas. Which flat do you like best? Why?

Crack your brain…

With the help of the information provided below, complete the floor plan and the table below. Who works in which department and in which office?

The two toilets are next to each other.
The room with the photocopier has got two doors.
The tea kitchen has got no window.
Frau Kleiner's office is next to the tea kitchen.
There's an outside staircase which leads from the car park to the first floor.
The room with the tenant files can be reached by two rooms.
Frau Schulz shares an office with two colleagues.
Herr Lieske works in New Constructions.
Frau Schmitz' office is next to Repairs and Maintenance.
Herr Fahle often complains that the way to the tea kitchen is very long.
Ten people need to leave the building first before they can get to the toilets unless they want to walk through somebody else's office.
Herr Wegner works in Refurbishment.
There are two people working in Refurbishment.
Frau Schmitz works next door to Herr Elbing.
Herr Huber shares an office with two female colleagues and one male colleague.
Frau Reveling works in Major Repairs and Maintenance.
When you enter the building, the ladies' toilet is the first door on the left.
Major Repairs and Maintenance is next to the main entrance.
Frau Gobar's office is next to the tenant files.
Herr Wegner's office is next to one of the toilets.
Herr Fahle's office is next to Frau Kleiner's office.
From his desk, Herr Braun can see the car park.
Frau Gerdes' office has got four windows.
Herr Elbing shares his office with two female colleagues.
Herr Braun's office is next to Refurbishment.
Nobody else has got a desk in the room with the photocopier.
Frau Kleiner works in the Personnel Department.
The tea kitchen is slightly larger than the room with the photocopier.
Herr Lagowski's office is opposite the photocopier.
Frau Reveling shares an office with Frau Tuch and two other colleagues.
Herr Huber works in Major Repairs and Maintenance.
From the tenant files there is a connecting door to Accounting and Controlling.
Four people work in Major Repairs and Maintenance.
Frau Schulz works next door to Herr Lagowski.
There is a total of 15 employees working on this floor of the building.
The room with the tenant files is smaller than the room with the photocopier.

DEPARTMENT 1:	DEPARTMENT 2:	DEPARTMENT 3:	DEPARTMENT 4:	DEPARTMENT 5:
staff:	staff:	staff:	staff:	staff:

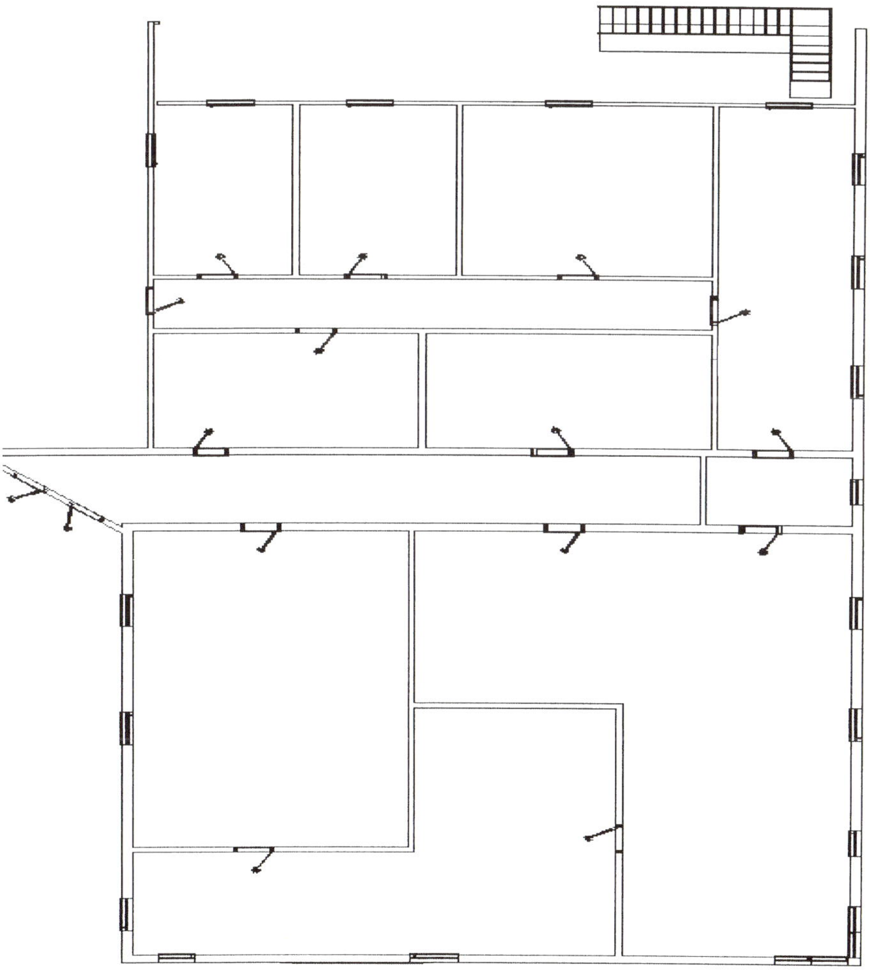

WEB UNIT: Buying property in the country

WWW.

In this WEB UNIT you will come across many words you have not heard of before. It is not always necessary that you learn them, but you should have a dictionary at hand so that you can look up what they mean. If, however, you prefer to use an online-dictionary, go to www.quickdic.org or www.leo.org.

Pre-net activities

What do you already know about buying property in the country? While doing all these web-based activities, please carry on developing this topic web!

WEB UNIT: Buying property in the country

Imagine you had unlimited financial possibilities. What would your ultimate dream house in the English countryside look like? Please write a short text in which you list all its features.

____

____

____

____

____

____

____

____

____

Net-use activities

The wealthy French customer Henri Marceau is considering buying or building a large house in the South of England.

Write down at least five questions about the house in general which you would like to ask Mr Marceau before taking further decisions!

Here are two questions to start you off:

- Rooms - what kind of rooms do you need and how big do they need to be?
- Do you ever work from home?
- ____
- ____
- ____
- ____
- ____
- ____
- ____
- ____

Now write down at least five questions about the floor plan. Here are two questions to start you off:

- Do you favour one, two or three storey designs?
- Do you prefer formal or informal room layouts?
- ____?
- ____?
- ____?

WEB UNIT:
Buying property in the country

Henri Marceau has got some ideas about the location of his new home:

He wants to live

- close to the sea,
- near a larger town,
- close to an airport
- south of London

and also wants to live in the countryside.

Click on:
www.uktouristinfo.com/search/map.php

Name those counties/areas he might take into consideration.

______________________	______________________
______________________	______________________
______________________	______________________
______________________	______________________

Click on:
www.surreyhouses.

Go to "Surrey" to open the fact file ("facts").
Now list the most important information about this region and its infrastructure.

______________________	______________________
______________________	______________________
______________________	______________________
______________________	______________________

Name some advantages and disadvantages of moving to Surrey:

Advantages:

______________________	______________________
______________________	______________________

Disadvantages:

______________________	______________________
______________________	______________________

Click on:
www.propertyfinder.co.uk/

Scroll down to the bottom of the screen and click on "regional property search" on the left.

Then go to the South-West and click on Cornwall.

Name five of the cities which are mentioned on this site:

______________________	______________________
______________________	______________________
______________________	______________________
______________________	______________________

How many properties are currently offered in Penzance?

WEB UNIT:
Buying property in the country

Choose one of the more exclusive properties and make a list of the rooms/ facilities:

Choose any five properties for sale and make a list of terms/adjectives that describe the building/its architecture!

Make a list of the information you get about the building material used.

Click on:
www.homebuilding.co.uk/

and go to "Hidden Charms: Readers' homes"

Now write a short German text in which you present this house to your boss.

WEB UNIT: Buying property in the country

As your French customer is also considering building himself, there are many things to be taken into account before investing any money at all.

Click on: fish4.co.uk/, **go to "homes", then "new homes" and then "self-build".**

Make a list of aspects to consider before buying a building-plot.

No matter if you are planning to buy or build, you will surely need the services of companies in the building trade. Name at least five services/professions any future homeowner is likely to contact!

Click on: www.homebuilding.co.uk/directory/CompanyCat.asp

Complete the following table:

THE BUILDING/CONSTRUCTION ITSELF	INTERIOR DESIGN	OUTSIDE THE BUILDING
Heating	*bathroom accessories*	*fences*
timber frame	*wall coverings*	*driveways*

Post-net activities

Now make some notes to prepare a phone call in which you want to inform Henri Marceau about the research you have done. Also think of any future steps you should suggest to him.

UNIT 2

Describing properties

VOKABELN

A	acre	Fläche von 4.047 m²
	add on	Erweiterung, Zusatz, Zugabe
	advance payment for service charges	Nebenkostenvorauszahlung
	air conditioning	Klimaanlage
	airfield	Flugfeld, Flugplatz
	airport	Flughafen
	all-time high / low	Allzeithoch / -tief
	amenities	Ausstattungsmerkmale
	appointment	Verabredung
	attach (verb)	anbauen, anbringen, anfügen
	attached	angebaut, angefügt
	attic	Attika, Dachgeschoss
	average	Durchschnitt
B	back porch	Anbau, Windfang, Terrasse hinter dem Haus
	bakery	Bäckerei
	balcony	Balkon
	bar chart	Balkendiagramm
	basement	Keller
	bathroom	Badezimmer
	bedroom	Schlafzimmer
	bicycle stand,	Fahrradständer
	biometric access control	biometrische Zugangskontrolle
	block of flats	Blockbebauung
	broadband internet	Breitband-Internet
	budget	Haushalt, Budget
	building block for urbanism	Blockbebauung
	building permission	Baugenehmigung
	built-in cupboard	Einbauschrank
	building permit	Baugenehmigung
	bungalow	Bungalow
	burglar	Einbrecher
	burglar alarm	Alarmanlage
	burglary	Einbruchdiebstahl
	business park, commercial area	Gewerbegebiet
	butchery, butcher's	Fleischerei, Metzger
C	cable TV	Kabelfernsehen
	campsite	Campingplatz, Stellplatz für ein Zelt
	car parking space, car port	Einstellplatz
	cargo	Fracht
	carpet flooring	Teppichbodenbelag
	carpet, carpeted floor	Teppichboden
	cash reserve	Liquiditätsreserve
	cathedral ceiling	Gewölbedecke
	ceiling	Zimmerdecke
	cellar	Keller
	central gas heating	Gaszentralheizung
	central heating	Zentralheizung
	chart	Chart, Diagramm
	children's room	Kinderzimmer
	chimney sweeper	Schornsteinfeger
	climax	Höhepunkt
	climb (verb)	ansteigen
	clubhouse	Clubhaus
	column	Säule, Kolonne, Rubrik
	commercial	gewerblich
	commercial rent	Gewerbemiete
	common areas	Gemeinschaftsflächen
	condensing heating technology	Brennwerttechnologie
	condo fee	Hausgeld (für Eigentumswohnungen)
	condominium	Eigentumswohnung
	conference centre	Konferenzzentrum
	conservatory	Wintergarten, Gewächshaus
	conversion	Umwidmung, Umwandlung
	corner shop	Laden an der Ecke, Tante-Emma-Laden
	crawl space	Souterrain
	cubic	Kubik-
	cul-de-sac	Sackgasse
D	decade	Dekade, Dezennium, Jahrzehnt
	deck	Dachterrasse
	decrease (verb)	abnehmen
	department store	Kaufhaus, Warenhaus
	deposit	Kaution, Anzahlung
	destination, place of excursions	Ausflugsziele
	detached house	freistehendes Haus
	deterrent	abwehrend, abschreckend
	dining room	Esszimmer
	dishwasher	Geschirrspülmaschine
	door chain	Türkette
	door mat	Fußmatte
	door viewer	Türspion
	double glazed windows	Doppelverglasung
	drain pipes	Entwässerungsrohre
	dramatic	dramatisch
	drastic	drastisch
	drop (verb)	(ab-)fallen
	dry cleaning	Reinigung
	due diligence	Kauf- / Prospektprüfung
	dues	Abgaben, Gebühren, Rechte
	duplex	Zweifamilienhaus
E	eat-in kitchen	Wohnküche
	end unit	Endreihenhaus
	enquiry	Anfrage
	erect (verb)	errichten
	estate, housing estate	Wohngebiet
	estate agent	Immobilienmakler
	eviction	Zwangsräumung
	exactly (adv.)	genau, präzise
	explode (verb)	explodieren
	exterior	Außen-
	exterior walls	Außenwände
F	fall (verb)	(ab-)fallen
	fan	Ventilator
	fashion boutique	Modeboutique
	fenced	eingezäunt
	fitted	eingebaut
	fitted kitchen	Einbauküche
	fixed	befestigt
	floating city	schwimmende Stadt
	floor	Fußboden
	floor covering, flooring	Bodenbelag
	floor plan, layout	Grundriss

	flow chart	Ablaufdiagramm
	footage	Länge, Gesamtlänge
	foundation	Fundament
	fraction	Bruchteil
	front window	Vorderfenster
	furnished	möbliert
	furnishing house	Einrichtungshaus
G	garage	Garage
	garage	Werkstatt
	gas heating	Gasheizung
	gate	Tor
	grille	Gitter, Fenstergitter, Gittertür
	ground floor	Erdgeschoss
	grow (verb)	anwachsen
	growth	Wachstum
	guest toilet	Gäste-WC
H	half	halb
	hallway light	Hauslicht
	halve (verb)	halbieren
	hangar	Hangar
	heating	Heizung
	heating costs	Heizkosten
	heating technology	Heiztechnologie
	high	Spitze, höchster Punkt
	holiday park	Ferienpark
	hook-up	Zusammenschaltung, Anschluss
	housing benefit	Wohngeld
	housing market	Wohnungsmarkt
I	incorporation	Eingemeindung, Gesellschaft (Unternehmensform)
	increase (verb)	(an-)steigen
	inner courtyard, patio	Innenhof
	insulation	Isolierung
	insurance	Versicherung
	intercom system, interphone	Gegensprechanlage
	investment opportunity	Investitionsmöglichkeit
J	jumbled	durcheinander, ungeordnet
	jurisdiction	Rechtsprechung
K	kitchen	Küche
L	landlord	Vermieter
	laundry room	Waschküche, Wäschezimmer
	lawn	Rasen
	lease (verb)	verpachten
	leisure	Freizeit
	letting agent	Immobilienmakler (Vermietung)
	lift	Fahrstuhl
	lighting system	Beleuchtungssystem
	line graph	Liniendiagramm
	living room	Wohnzimmer
	location	Lage, Ort
	lock	Schloss
	loft	Loft, Wohnung über zwei Etagen
	lot	Bauplatz, Baustelle
	lottery license shop	Lottoannahmestelle
	low	Tiefpunkt
	low rent	niedrige Miete

M	maintenance and repair	Wartung und Instandsetzung
	mall	Einkaufszentrum, Promenade
	manor house	Herrenhaus, Schloss
	mansion	herrschaftliches Wohnhaus
	marble	Marmor
	mercantile	kaufmännisch
	metal-grilled window	vergittertes Fenster
	microwave	Mikrowelle
	migrate (verb)	wandern, abwandern, ziehen, migrieren
	migration	Migration
	motion detector	Bewegungsmelder
	move-in	Einzug
	multi-family house	Mehrfamilienhaus
	multi-storey	mehrgeschossig
	multi-storey car park	Parkhaus
N	neighbourhood	Nachbarschaft, Wohnviertel
O	open-plan living area	Wohnfläche
	option-to-buy	Vorkaufsrecht
	ordinance	Anordnung, Verfügung
	outbuilding	Außengebäude, Nebengebäude
	outside lighting	Außenbeleuchtung
	outside staircase	außen liegendes Treppenhaus
P	pane	Glasscheibe
	partition wall	Trennwand
	patio	Patio, Innenhof
	peak	Höchstwert, Höchststand
	percentage	Prozentsatz
	perpetual, for an unlimited period	unbefristet
	photo shop	Fotogeschäft
	pie chart	Kuchendiagramm
	playground	Kinderspielplatz
	plummet (verb)	(ab-)stürzen
	pool	Swimmingpool
	porch	Portal, Veranda, Vorbau, Wintergarten
	potential	Potenzial
	privacy	Privatsphäre
	property	Eigentum
	pull-down stairs	ausziehbare Dachstuhltreppe
	purchase (verb)	kaufen, erwerben
R	real estate property	Immobilieneigentum
	real estate tax, tax on land and buildings	Grundsteuer
	recreation park	Erholungsanlage
	rectangular	rechtwinklig
	refrigerator, fridge	Kühlschank
	refurbish (verb)	sanieren
	regulation	Regelung, Rechtsvorschrift
	remain (verb)	bleiben, verbleiben
	rent	Miete
	rent excluding service charges	Kaltmiete
	repair jobs	Reparaturarbeiten
	re-sale value	Wiederverkaufswert
	residential	wohn-
	residential area	Wohngebiet
	retail shop	Einzelhandelsgeschäft
	rise (verb)	(an-)steigen
	rolling grill	durchgängige Rollläden

UNIT 2

Describing properties

	roof	Dach
	roughly	ungefähr, zirka
	RSL = Registered Social Landlord	Sozialwohnungsunternehmen in Großbritannien
	RV	Wohnwagen, Campingmobil
S	safety	Sicherheit
	sales floor, sales area	Verkaufsfläche
	self-contained central heating	Etagenheizung
	semi-detached	einseitig angebaut
	service charges	Nebenkosten
	service enterprise	Dienstleistungsbetrieb
	shed	Schuppen, Lagerhaus
	shop	Ladenlokal
	shopping park	Einkaufspark
	shower	Dusche
	single family home	Einfamilienhaus
	sink (verb)	absenken, absacken
	site	Baustelle
	skylights	Dachluke, Dachfenster, Oberlicht
	skyscraper	Wolkenkratzer
	small business enterprise	Kleingewerbe
	social housing	sozialer Wohnungsbau
	social housing, council housing, RSL housing	Sozialwohnung
	solid	solide
	spare key	Ersatzschlüssel
	sprawling	sich der Länge nach hinstrecken / ausdehnen
	stagnate (verb)	stagnieren, stillstehen
	stagnation	Stagnation, Stillstand
	stationery	Briefpapier
	steady	gleichmäßig, beständig, dauerhaft
	stop	Stopp
	storage facilities	Lagerräume
	storey	Geschoss
	subdivision	Unterabteilung
	suburb	Vorort
	subway	U-Bahn
	sudden	plötzlich
	sun blinds	Sonnenblenden
	surgery	Arztpraxis, Behandlungsraum
T	table	Tabelle
	takeaway bar	Lokal mit Speisen zum Mitnehmen
	tea kitchen	Teeküche
	tenancy agreement	Miet-, Pachtvertrag
	tenant	Mieter
	tenant files	Mieterakten
	tennis court	Tennisplatz
	tenure	Miet- / Pachtverhältnis
	terrace	Häuserreihe, Terrasse
	terraced house	Reihenhaus
	thorough	sorgfältig
	tiled	gefliest
	tiled floor	Fliesenboden
	time switch	Zeitschaltung
	tobacco products	Tabakwaren
	townhouse	Stadthaus
	trade chain	Handelskette
	traffic connections	Verkehrsverbindungen
	triplex	Dreifamilienhaus
	turning-point	Wende, Wendepunkt
	two-persons household	Zweipersonenhaushalt
	two-room apartment	Zweizimmerwohnung
U	underground parking	unterirdisches Parkhaus
	unexpected	unerwartet
	unfurnished	unmöbliert
	urban development, urban extension	Stadterweiterung
	utility costs	Versorgungskosten für Strom, Wasser, Gas usw.
V	vacancy	Leerstand
	vessel	Schiff
	villa	freistehendes Einfamilienhaus, Villa
	vineyard	Weingut
W	walk-in (adj.)	begehbar
	warehouse	Lagerhaus
	waste container	Abfallbehälter
	wealthy people	wohlhabende Menschen
X	x-axis	X-Achse
Y	y-axis	Y-Achse

SELF-ASSESSMENT GRID AFTER UNIT 2

Gehen Sie die einzelnen Abschnitte des gerade abgeschlossenen Kapitels noch einmal durch und überprüfen Sie sich selbstkritisch. Was haben Sie gelernt? Was sollten Sie wiederholen bzw. vertiefen? Was bereitet Ihnen Schwierigkeiten? Schreiben Sie kurze Kommentare in die Kästchen, die Ihren Lernzuwachs für Sie selbst erläutern. Arbeiten Sie nach eigenen Prioritäten Unterpunkte nach, wenn Sie mehrheitlich Ihre Kommentare in der rechten Spalte gesetzt haben.

Was ich in diesem Kapitel gelernt habe…	**Wie ich meinen Fortschritt einschätze**		
	Ich fühle mich beim Sprechen/Schreiben und beim Hören bzw. Lesen zu diesem Aspekt insgesamt sicher und verstehe einen Großteil der Informationen bzw. kann einen Großteil der Informationen wie beabsichtigt weitergeben; auch wenn ich Fehler mache, habe ich insgesamt Vertrauen in meine Sprachbeherrschung.	Ich kann vieles von dem, was für diesen Aspekt wichtig ist, mündlich und schriftlich ausdrücken bzw. beim Hören und Lesen verstehen; allerdings fehlen mir einige Fachvokabeln und auch die grundsätzliche Sicherheit, mich frei über diesen Aspekt auszutauschen.	Ich habe zu diesem Aspekt einige Fachbegriffe und Redewendungen gelernt und verstehe auch Informationen; jedoch erschließen sich mir noch nicht alle Zusammenhänge; sowohl die Textrezeption (Hören und Lesen) als auch das Sprechen und Schreiben bereiten mir noch Probleme; ich weiß, dass ich einige Aspekte nacharbeiten sollte.
den Fachwortschatz zur Beschreibung von gewerblichen und Wohnimmobilien in ihrer Funktion und gemäß ihren Eigenschaften anzuwenden.			
wie man ein kurzes englischsprachiges Exposé schreibt.			
Grundaspekte zur Sicherheit und zur Vorbeugung von Einbrüchen zu berücksichtigen.			
Anforderungen an moderne Mietwohnungen zu reflektieren und darzustellen.			
Grundlagen des Telefonierens in der englischen Sprache anzuwenden.			
wie man eine Diagrammbeschreibung anfertigt.			
wie man zu schreibende Texte im Vorfeld strukturieren kann.			

UNIT 3

Dealing with customers

In dieser Unit lernen Sie:

- den Fachwortschatz zur Beschreibung der Geschäftspartner und Mieter eines Wohnungsunternehmens / Vermieters
- die unterschiedlichen Arten und Medien der Bürokommunikation sowie deren angemessene Verwendung in diversen Situationen des Tagesgeschäfts eines Wohnungsunternehmens
- die Grundlagen und die englischen Fachtermini für den mündlichen und schriftlichen Umgang mit Mietern / Wohneigentümern
- die Grundlagen und den englischen Fachwortschatz zu mündlichen und schriftlichen Vereinbarungen
- kulturübergreifende Aspekte der Mieterkommunikation
- Lernstrategien der Wörterbucharbeit

Dealing with people in your business

Work in pairs. Have a look at these pictures and with the help of the vocabulary list at the end of the book, briefly quantify your business relationship with these people.

Have a look at the pictures and find the suitable English word.

How often do you contact these people or companies? Copy and fill in the table.

VERY OFTEN	SOMETIMES	JUST OCCASIONALLY
tenant		
...		

Means of communication

Copy and complete the following mind map with terms you already know. Then work through the text and complete your mind map.

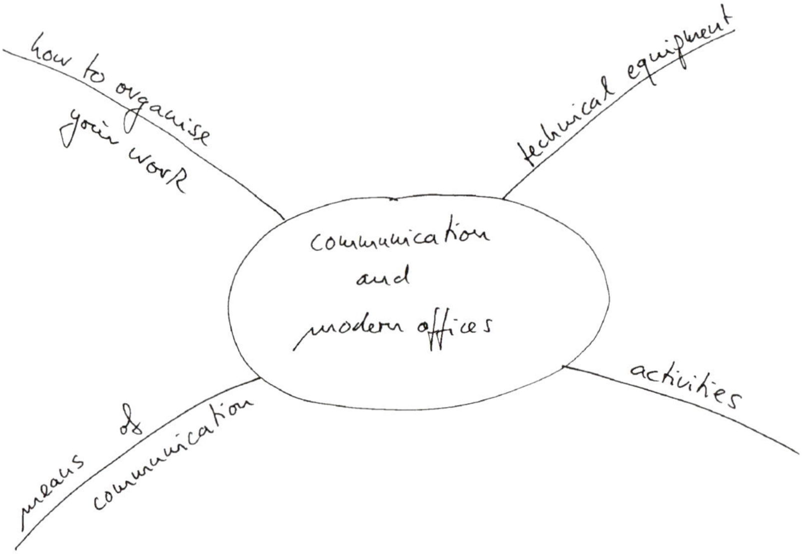

Communication in a modern office

In order to communicate efficiently, a modern office has to be full of technology and modern equipment. One of the most important means of communication today surely is the telephone. You can easily speak to anyone in any part of the world if this person has got a phone himself and is available. A fax machine makes use of phone lines as well, but it is used to send written documents e.g. as a confirmation of what has been discussed over the phone. In a modern office a lot of writing and typing has to be done. Nowadays, very often computers are used for that. A computer is a machine that is used to run a lot of different and often complicated programmes. Spreadsheet calculations, specialist software and database applications or word-processing are now done by computers. They can be found in almost every office because these modern computers are fast and very reliable and make the exchange of data simple. The information they produce is stored on hard-drives, disks or CD-ROMS for further use. The information or the data the different computer programmes need or give are shown on the screen. In order to save space, in many of today's offices you find flat-screen monitors.

With the help of e.g. a mouse, modern computers using the most common operating system are told what you want them to do. You only click on an icon, for example "print", and the command will be followed which means that a text or a diagram will be printed.
More and more business people now take their computers with them when they leave the office. These small portable computers are called note-books or laptops. They are no bigger than a small brief-case in which some files may be kept.
Internet access is a very important feature in today's office world, too. You can obtain unlimited information and also present your company on the world wide web, thus providing information about your business.
When your data should be passed on to somebody else who also uses a computer, you either give them data carriers (disks, USB-sticks, CD-ROMS, DVDs etc.) or you use existing networks (internet, intranet, local area networks (LAN)) and wireless local area networks (WLAN). One of the most comfortable ways of transmitting data is the use of email. If two office machines are connected in any sort of computer network, you can easily send huge amounts of data within seconds to any part of the world. Once your information should be presented to somebody on paper (e.g. in a letter), it must be printed out. This can easily be done with the help of printers. These machines are used to print the texts, diagrams or any data which you see on the monitor. Modern laser printers are very fast and produce high-quality documents. They are also available as "all-in-one-solutions", i. e. can print, copy, scan and send faxes.
Sometimes you have got a document on paper which you would like to store electronically for future reference. Then you use a scanner which reads the text for you and automatically sends it to the computer and its programmes. Most scanners found in modern offices today are flat-bed scanners.
But as you all know, some of the writing (especially if you have to fill in forms) is still done by electric typewriters. One disadvantage of these office machines is that the data or the texts you have produced cannot be stored. Thus, you always have to make a photocopy of your text. This is what you use the photocopier for. It is a machine which helps if texts must be duplicated.
The papers that you want to keep are collected in files. Each file has got a name or a number on it so that you always know what is in the file.
All the files are kept in a filing cabinet. It is very important that you keep this in order because otherwise you will never find any of your papers or contracts when you need them!

When you only make notes you normally do not use computers for this but do this with a pen. A normal pencil can be wiped out again when you use a rubber or, as the Americans say, an eraser. This is not possible with a fountain-pen. A fountain-pen uses ink; you normally use fountain pens for signatures. They are more expensive than pencils.
You see that some of the daily office work is still done as it was done a long time ago. Even your grandparents collected all the daily incoming mail in so-called in-trays; every incoming letter must be read and filed. First, it must be stamped so that you know when you received this letter. A stamp is used for this. There are various stamps which help you when you have to write the same text (for example the date) again and again.
If you want to photocopy valuable information, you sometimes have to prepare the copy. This means that you may need scissors for cutting out pictures, passages of an article etc.
Some clerks in offices write important messages on so called post-its which can be fixed on your desk or at the phone. When you make notes while speaking on the phone, you may write down important information on a pad. When you have finished your day at the office and have written a lot of letters, all the letters which must be sent to other companies or other departments are collected in the out-tray.

Look at your mind map and the text once again and make a list of activities that describe your daily office work. Here are some examples to get you started...

- to file documents
- to photocopy tenancy agreements
- to phone tenants
- to answer the phone

...

Which are the tasks that are part of your office routine? Categorise these activities by saying how often you do them.

On average, I have to

activity	several times a day	once or twice a day	several times a week, but not every day	just occasionally
answer the phone	X			
...	...	...	...	...

Oral or written communication?

Brainstorm advantages and disadvantages of both oral and written communication. When do you talk? When do you write?

Now listen to the recording and make notes on oral vs written communication.

	ADVANTAGES	DISADVANTAGES	USED WHEN?
oral communication			
written communication			

Now have a look at these means of communication. Which is your favourite? Which one do you dislike? Why?

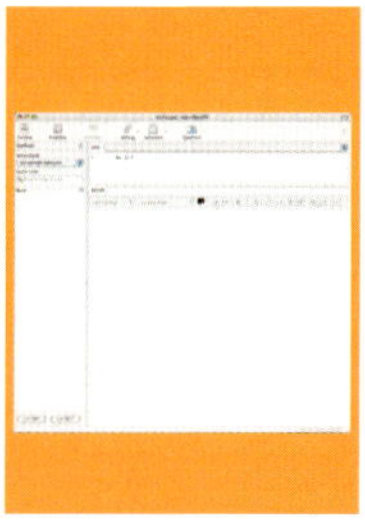

Work in small groups. Please work out characteristics of these means of communication. What are their advantages and disadvantages? When do you use them?

	ADVANTAGES	DIS-ADVANTAGES	USED IN WHICH BUSINESS SITUATION
fax			
business letter			
email			
phone call			
face-to-face meeting			

Have a look at the following situation and then decide if you would send a fax, an email, a business letter, phone them or meet face-to-face. Give reasons for your answer.

- You send an enquiry for a new heating system in one of your buildings.
- You want to know the exact date when one of your tenants moves out.
- A tenant asks for permission to remove walls in his flat. You reply to his request.
- You inform your tenants about a rent increase.
- You need to change the time of a meeting with business partners.
- One of your tenants thinks of buying his flat and needs further information.
- A tenant asks you to explain the utility costs in detail.
- A tenant again has not paid the rent. You send him a second reminder.
- You confirm the time of arrival at an airport to be picked up for a business conference.
- You are not satisfied with the repair works an electrician carried out.
- You inform a colleague in another part of the building about the time a meeting starts.
- You inform the tenants about a change in ownership.
- You inform the tenants that repair works on the water pipes will be carried out. For a short time in the morning there will be no water.
- You report a gas leak in one of your buildings.
- You ask your boss for an extra day off.
- You inform your tenants about an increase in the advance payment of utility costs.
- One of your long-term commercial tenants asks you for a reduction in rent.

Carry out a brief survey in class: What is the most common means of communication in your company? When do you use which means?

Email Overload

How many business emails do you get a day? How many do you consider important?

What are your associations when you hear the term email overload?

Which steps are taken in your company to prevent too many and dangerous emails?

Now listen to the recording and make notes on the following aspects:
- definitions of email overload
- consequences of email overload
- steps suggested against email overload

AFX

ONPEH

SERNAW NOPHE

PEONVLEE

POCTEURM

BEMLOI

LACL

TEGSIRNAU

POPCOIHETRO

LEERTT

ALMEI

MUTSERCO

FEIL

KEDS

CESNARN

RALPEST

SIRSCOSS

REWSAN

OSMUE

NIRREPT

LAFT-NERECS

DAP

NI-RAYT

DAPTSSREEHE

DWRO-SINESCPGOR

SABAEDAT

WONRETK

Unscramble each of the clue words.

Lernstrategien Wörterbucharbeit

Wenn Sie Texte lesen, in denen Ihnen unbekanntes Vokabular vorkommt, sollten Sie auch hier Lern- und Vorgehenstechniken befolgen und nicht kopflos agieren:

- Bleiben Sie nicht sofort am ersten Ihnen unbekannten Wort hängen und schlagen es nicht sofort im Wörterbuch nach. Dies stoppt Ihren Leseprozess. Arbeiten Sie sich stattdessen durch den gesamten Text und markieren Sie Ihnen unbekannte Wörter.
- Lesen Sie den Text ein zweites Mal. Einiges wird sich Ihnen nun erschließen.
- Versuchen Sie jetzt, die Ihnen unbekannten Wörter erst aus dem Kontext zu erschließen. Kennen Sie das Wort in dieser oder sehr ähnlicher Form in einer anderen Sprache?
- Erst jetzt sollten Sie ein Wörterbuch oder ein Glossar zu Hilfe nehmen.
- Ein zweisprachiges Wörterbuch scheint schneller Klärung zu bringen, jedoch bietet ein einsprachiges Wörterbuch im Sinne der Wortschatzarbeit mehr. Das Beispiel „tenant" verdeutlicht dies: Im zweisprachigen Wörterbuch finden Sie „Mieter/Mieterin". Ein englischsprachiges Wörterbuch hingegen bietet neben der Definition noch kontextrelevante weitere Wörter: „someone who pays rent to use land or a building that is owned by someone else; „the landlord can evict a tenant who doesn't pay the rent".
- Einsprachige Wörterbücher bieten neben der Worterklärung auch Synonym-Wörter an. Für „tenant" lernen Sie das gleichbedeutende Wort „renter".
- Wenn Sie häufig Fachtexte lesen, wird Ihnen ein allgemeinsprachiges Wörterbuch nicht immer helfen. Investieren Sie in ein gutes Fachwörterbuch oder legen Sie eine eigene Vokabelliste an, die Sie z. B. mit Hilfe des Computers ständig erweitern und sortieren können.
- Wenn Sie nicht sicher sind, welcher von zwei oder mehreren Begriffen in dem von Ihnen verwandten Zusammenhang richtig ist, können Sie dies mittels einer Konkordanzsuche schnell überprüfen: Geben Sie „Ihre" Begriffe im Zusammenhang auf einer Suchmaschinenseite im Internet ein. Wie hoch ist jeweils die Trefferquote? Woher stammen die Seiten, die diese Verwendung anzeigen?
- Misstrauen Sie Internetseiten, die Ihnen auf Knopfdruck ganze Textpassagen übersetzen. Die Fehlerzahl bei falschen Wortbedeutungen oder Grammatikverstößen ist sehr hoch.

Dealing with tenants

In your opinion, what are the most important aspects that contribute to a successful landlord-tenant relationship?

Start in pairs and agree on your top five. Then get together with another pair and again agree on your top 5. When you have finally agreed on your top five in a group of eight, discuss your results in class.

Here's a list to choose from. Of course you can add other criteria as well.

good manners
wealth
knowledge of legal matters
cleanliness
good looks
mutual trust
personal liking
common interests
good reputation
a secure income on both sides
an extremely detailed tenancy agreement
reliability
friendliness
politeness
both parties fulfilling their rights and obligations

Are there different criteria for tenants than for landlords? If so, why?

Landlording

Now listen to the recording and make notes on Hermann's relationship to his tenants. What is his philosophy?

Letting as a Service Business

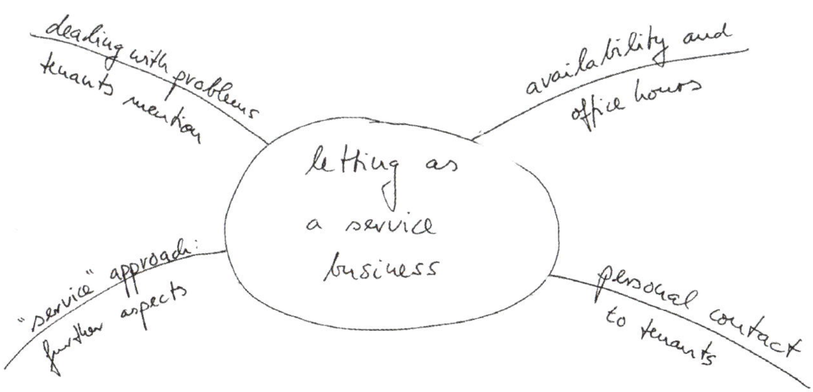

Copy and complete the mind map brainstorming ideas that make letting a service for your tenants.

Service Business

Fill in the gaps.

be reminded	emergency service line	operation	agreeable	prompt
provide	follow-ups	firm	staffed	promptly
perception	denied	estimate	breakdown	deserves
interruption	recorded	be informed	timely	
out of service	service desks	recorded	housing company	communication policy
response	effective			

Tenant Relations: A Service Business

A good relationship between the housing company as the landlord and its tenants is paramount to the successful ____________________ of the housing business.

This consequently means that the ____________________'s personnel should constantly ____________________ that this is a service business - in this case, the service they ____________________ is the maintenance and administration of usable space and ____________________ communications and ____________________. All personnel should accept and apply this service approach.

The importance of service personnel being ____________________, courteous, and yet ____________________ cannot be overemphasized. The teams dealing with the tenants must know their tenants, receive comments courteously, and act on them promptly - an extremely important point. A tenant's ____________________ that a legitimate complaint will receive ____________________ and courteous attention is communicated quickly throughout the building. Even when an answer is negative, the tenant ____________________ a courteous explanation of why his request was ____________________.

Good communication between management and tenants is essential in establishing and maintaining positive tenant/management relations. When a major ____________________ occurs, the tenants should promptly ____________________ and given an ____________________ of how long the equipment will be ____________________. Furthermore, the tenants should also promptly be informed of any upcoming holidays, anticipated ____________________ in service, programmed preventive maintenance, or other problems concerning the property.

With regard to telephone and service request responses, it should be the ____________________ that all service calls from tenants receive a prompt response from the service team and that any required ____________________ be ____________________. In order to promote better communication and control of maintenance requests, ____________________ should be available and ____________________ during normal business hours. An emergency service line must be available to tenants 24 hours a day.

If a tenant calls for a work request, this matter should be properly____________ and passed on to the individual in charge. These reports are recorded and reviewed by the person responsible for the building and his engineering or technical staff. Follow-up calls are made to the tenants on a periodic basis to ensure timely completion of work requests.

Which of the aspects mentioned in the text do you consider most important? Which of these does your company provide?

Dealing with difficult tenants

What is your definition of a difficult tenant? How do you deal with tenants who behave in an anti-social way?

Do these methods always work?

Brainstorm and collect approaches you use in your companies.

At GW BO, you find the following task waiting for you...

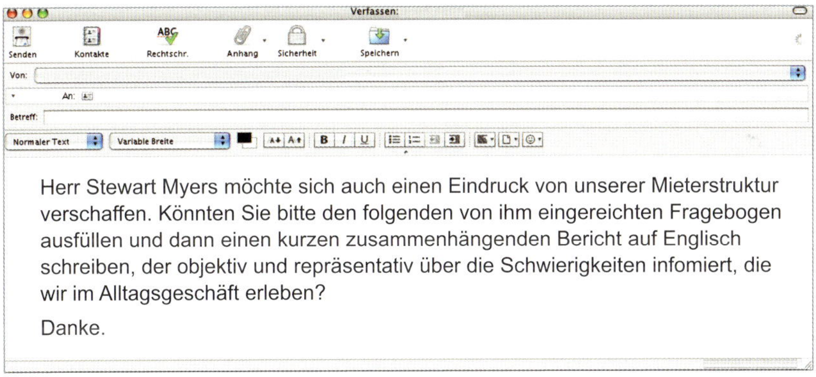

Herr Stewart Myers möchte sich auch einen Eindruck von unserer Mieterstruktur verschaffen. Könnten Sie bitte den folgenden von ihm eingereichten Fragebogen ausfüllen und dann einen kurzen zusammenhängenden Bericht auf Englisch schreiben, der objektiv und repräsentativ über die Schwierigkeiten infomiert, die wir im Alltagsgeschäft erleben?

Danke.

Which forms of difficult tenant behaviour are you frequently confronted with? Please tick the boxes.

- ❑ abusive, verbal behaviour
- ❑ assault
- ❑ begging
- ❑ noisy car stereos
- ❑ criminal behaviour
- ❑ damage to property
- ❑ domestic violence
- ❑ drug and alcohol misuse/abuse
- ❑ neighbour intimidation
- ❑ noise pollution
- ❑ disturbance caused by animals
- ❑ overgrown, unkempt gardens
- ❑ parking illegally & abandoned vehicles
- ❑ racist behaviour / racial harassment
- ❑ rubbish and dumping of litter
- ❑ running a business from home
- ❑ stalking
- ❑ threatening behavior
- ❑ use of inappropriate places for sport/activities
- ❑ vandalism, graffiti
- ❑ youths and young people who cause problems

Now have a look at the following text dealing with two approaches from the UK.

TextTextText
TextTextText
TextTextText
ARBEIT
TextTextText
TextTextText

Posters set to shame Asbo louts

People given anti-social behaviour orders (Asbo) in Nottingham face being named and shamed on leaflets.

The city council is set to publicise the identity of offenders on posters and leaflets delivered to neighbours.

They hope it will help people inform them if they spot offenders breaching conditions of orders.

New Home Office guidance earlier this year urged police and local authorities to do more to publicise the names of adults and children as young as 10. Council leader Cllr Jon Collins said: "Our aim is to discourage those on Asbos from breaching their orders, deter others from anti-social behaviour and let people know that we take this very seriously."

"The posters will also help people to notify the authorities if anyone who has been given an asbo breaches it."

Council officers will have to carry out risk assessments on whether the proposed publicity for people is reasonable.

The posters will carry photographs of offenders and details of why courts have imposed anti-social behaviour orders.

The city council's executive board is set to approve the move when it meets next week.

Last year a judge ruled in favour of a north London council which sent out thousands of leaflets naming a gang given anti-social behaviour orders.

The gang and their parents mounted the unsuccessful High Court challenge against Brent Council claiming their right to privacy had been infringed.

Civil rights group Liberty has previously claimed the posters could lead to vigilante action.

Source: BBC Television Centre

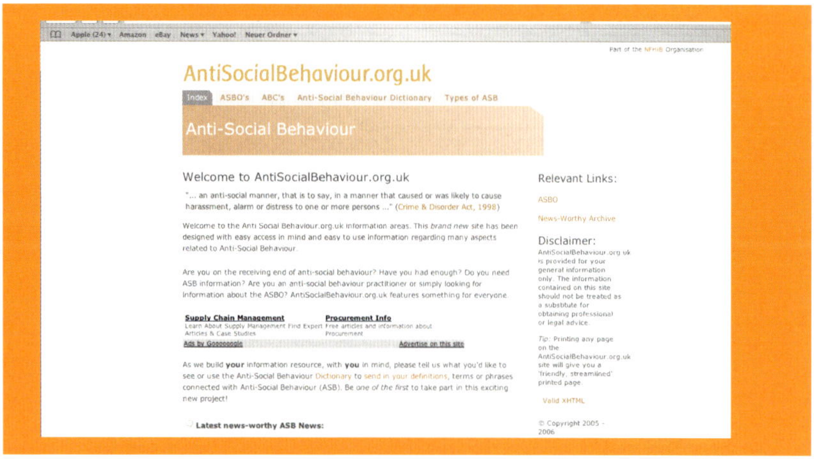

Rights group criticises "Asbo TV"

Civil rights campaigners have voiced concern about a new channel allowing households in east London to monitor local CCTV cameras, dubbed "Asbo TV".

The project will enable Shoreditch residents to compare suspicious characters with an on-screen "rogue's gallery" from their living-room. Viewers can then alert police to anyone in breach of an anti-social behaviour order (Asbo) or committing a crime.

Asbo Concern said the scheme was a "gimmick" and would be open to abuse.

The CCTV channel is part of a £12m online community network project being set up in the area under a 10-year government-funded regeneration programme in one of the country's most deprived areas. About 1,000 residents in the Haberdasher and Charles Square estates will pilot the scheme from March before it is rolled out to more than 20,000 households across Shoreditch, giving viewers access to some 400 cameras.

They will be asked to pay about £3.50 a week for the full service, which includes cheap local calls, a free set-top box providing digital TV, public service channels and high-speed internet access.

Atul Hatwal, strategy director of the Shoreditch Digital Bridge, said while crime in the area has fallen, the community safety channel will address the fear of crime.

"The scheme aims to empower members of the local community to support police in tackling crime and supporting each other in making Shoreditch a safer place," he said.

But Matt Foot, co-ordinator for Asbo Concern, which campaigns against the misuse of the Asbo, said the channel was "a complete waste of money".

"While the rest of the project sounds quite positive, the community safety channel is a gimmick," he said. "There are professionals trained to monitor CCTV and it should be left to them."

"Here, you will have a situation of people spying on each other, which raises concerns about vigilantism and vulnerable people such as children being bullied on CCTV."

Source: BBC Television Centre

Should we have ASBOs and CCTV cameras in German neighbourhoods as well? Are there any other steps which could be taken?

Discuss.

Oral communication

Look at the various elements of oral communication and explain what they stand for.

What is your definition of a successful communicator in business? Exchange your definitions in class.

facial expression
gesture
body language
touch
space
time

words
terminology

volume
rate
pitch

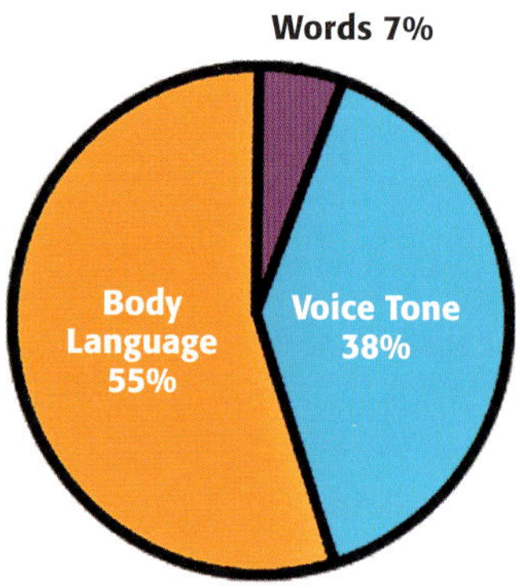

Referring to your definitions of a good communicator, comment on this landlord and the way he communicated. Suggest alternatives how to deal with this situation. Role play an ideal way to communicate with these tenants.

Hugh met the prospective tenant dressed in his jump suit. He had been on his way to the fitness studio and their call interrupted him. Hugh told them that he was inconvenienced.

He took them through the property and made sure they understood that he wouldn't tolerate any funny business.

"I expect this place to be clean all the time. If you have a problem, I expect you to take care of it. It had better be a big emergency and you had better not caused it before you call me. I don't want any parties and no more than one guest at a time. I live only three doors away so I'll know."

"The rent is due on the first and you're out of here if it's not paid by the third. You pay for all the utilities including the water and the garbage, and you take care of the garden in front. I've been taken by tenants before and I know all the tricks and I'm not about to be taken again, got it?"

Work in pairs. Have a look at the following role play cards. One of you should take the role of the person called using the information provided. The other one is the caller and should make up the missing parts of the conversation so that a logical phone call will be the result. Present your phone calls to the class.

Situation 1 *You work for a commercial letting agent in the centre of Essen. One of your customers just built a shopping centre and is advertising for 15 retail shops to be let. You receive a phone call from a representative of the British company Fashion&More which is planning to enter the German market.*

Person called: Thank caller for call and for interest in retail shops

Caller: ______________________________

Person called: 10 shops are still available, ground floor and first floor; sizes from 85m^2 to 1500 m^2

Caller: ______________________________

Person called: flooring material can be chosen by tenant

Caller: ______________________________

Person called: yes, electrical fixtures and appliances suitable for fashion store

Caller: ______________________________

Person called: yes, free car park for customers available; also very good infrastructure and excellent shopping facilities nearby

Caller: ______________________________

Person called: say you will send a more detailed property description within the next two days

Situation 2 *You work for a large national letting agent with branches in Dortmund, Stuttgart, Düsseldorf, Hamburg and Munich. You receive a call from a potential customer in London. This company is planning to send four senior executives to Germany for half a year.*

Person called: answer the phone and ask for caller's requirements

Caller: ______________________________

Person called: yes, you also offer short-term lets for 6 months; which size of flats? Where?

Caller: ______________________________

Person called: smaller flats (1 bedroom) available in Stuttgart and Hamburg; location? furnished?

Caller: ______________________________

Person called: Prices in city centre generally higher than in surrounding area; price range for small furnished flats from €7 to €18/m^2

Caller: ______________________________

Person called: No, rent does not include any utility costs (give examples)

Caller: ______________________________

Person called: Sure, promise to send further description of flats and some photos as soon as possible

Caller: ______________________________

The phone rings. On the other end of the line one of your English speaking tenants lets you know the following… What do you say? Remember to take the caller seriously and remain polite.

The bulb in my kitchen light doesn't work anymore.	I have changed my mind about the colour of the carpets. Can I have blue instead?

Can we have a barbecue in the summer for all residents?	My brother who lives in Canada will be coming over, he needs to stay here for six months. I think I have got enough space.

Will we all be taken over by the Americans now?	My tap in the bathroom drips.

Can I have a little monkey?	The key-card to the underground parking does not work anymore.

We need more storage space.	Because of some financial problems, we won't be able to pay the full rent.

I don't like the caretaker.

My neighbours always cook garlic. I can't stand the smell.

My new neighbour has got a cat. I'm allergic to cats!

The tumble-driers in the laundry room don't work again.

When I came into the cellar this morning, there was the smell of gas.

The people downstairs never clean their windows.

I would like to have a new toilet seat.

When I come home in the evening, I have nowhere to park my car.

How often do I have to open all windows to air the rooms?

I cannot understand the people through the intercom.

I think the lift is very old.

Can we all vote on the design of the new facade?

I would like to have parquet flooring.

I am going to move out next week.

Never ever did we use that much water! The utility costs are far too high.

Copy and complete the table.

DEFINITION	TERM USED FOR THIS SERVICE	WHEN WE NEED THIS SERVICE
to fight fires	fire brigade	in cases of emergency
to clean soot from chimneys	chimney-sweeper	periodically, according to government regulations
to control the affairs of a community, to maintain order, enforce the law, and prevent and detect crime		
to carry out the installation, maintenance, repair, or operation of electric equipment and circuitry	electrician	needed for repairs, new installations, maintenance and controls;
to install and repair pipes and plumbing		
to paint walls and other parts of buildings		
to look after or take charge of properties		
determining and drawing up plans for the future physical arrangement and condition of a community		
to give legal advice and assistance to clients and represent them in court or in other legal matters		
to run a business establishment in which money is kept for saving or commercial purposes or is invested, supplied for loans, or exchanged		
to make something, such as a service available		
to hear and submit a decision on cases at law.		
the exchange of thoughts, messages, or information by signals		
one that makes or repairs locks		
the warming of a room or building by a furnace or another source of energy		
one that builds, especially a person who contracts for and supervises the construction of a building		
coverage by a contract binding a party to indemnify another against specified loss in return for premiums paid		
one who lays tiles		

DEFINITION	TERM USED FOR THIS SERVICE	WHEN WE NEED THIS SERVICE
the business of supplying an essential commodity, such as water or electricity, or a service, such as communications or transportation, to the public		
one who lays or repairs roofs		
a skilled worker who makes, finishes, and repairs wooden objects and structures		
a person, an enterprise, or an entity that manufactures something		
someone whose business is to supply a particular service or commodity		
to bring in (goods or materials) from a foreign country for trade or sale		

Work in pairs. Have a look at the following role play cards. One of you should take the role of the person called using the information provided. The other one is the caller and should make up the missing parts of the conversation so that a logical phone call will be the result. Present your phone calls to the class.

Situation 1 *You work for a housing company in Germany which also runs some student hostels in German university towns.*

You receive a call from a university in Taiwan which is looking for accommodation for their students.

Person called: Thank caller for getting in touch; ask for requirements

Caller: ____

Person called: yes, small flats available (1 bedroom; $20m^2$) close to university; suitable for student accommodation

Caller: ____

Person called: all-inclusive rent can be arranged; length of tenancy agreement? How many apartments?

Caller: ____

Person called: Furnished apartments possible: kitchenette, bathroom unit, 2 built-in cupboards, bed and desk

Caller: ____

Person called: weekly cleaning service can be arranged according to tenant's specifications

Caller: ____

Person called: send detailed offer in writing next week

Situation 2 *You are the representative of a cleaning contractor and are called by a prospective customer asking for a detailed presentation of your service.*

Person called: Thank customer for calling and ask for requirements

Caller: ______________________________

Person called: You offer your services around the clock (extra charge for unusual hours)

Caller: ______________________________

Person called: You clean both manufacturing facilities and offices

Caller: ______________________________

Person called: For an offer you need precise requirements

Caller: ______________________________

Person called: No problem cleaning his office buildings (one storey, 1,000 m^2) and five-storey headquarters (120 windows of 2.5 m^2 each) regularly/daily

Caller: ______________________________

Person called: Yes, you only use environmentally friendly agents

Caller: ______________________________

Person called: Detailed offer within the next five days

Caller: ______________________________

Situation 3 *You are employed with a British producer of carpets and flooring material. You receive a phone call from a large housing company in Germany.*

Person called: Thank caller for calling and ask for requirements

Caller: ______________________________

Person called: Yes, of course you also sell flooring material products to Germany. Quantity? Product group?

Caller: ______________________________

Person called: You also supply British student hostels; market leader; products range from simple flooring material to exclusive carpets and wooden floors; requirements?

Caller: ______________________________

Person called: No problem; standard products are in use all over the UK; useful life in normal use between 5 and 7 years

Caller: ______________________________

Person called: colours and materials can be chosen; suggest to have a look at your homepage www.carpetworld.co.uk; you will send catalogue and price lists as well

Caller: ______________________________

Person called: Possible for order of that size; you will certainly offer substantial discount

Written communication

Useful connectives

ADDING	SEQUENCING	EMPHASISING
and also as well as moreover too furthermore	first of all next then first, second, finally meanwhile after	above all in particular especially significantly indeed notably
COMPARING	**CAUSE AND EFFECT**	**QUALIFYING**
equally in the same way similarly likewise as with like	because so therefore thus consequently	however although unless except if as long as apart from yet
ILLUSTRATING	**CONTRASTING**	
for example such as for instance as revealed by in the case of	whereas instead of alternatively otherwise unlike on the other hand	

Matching exercise: an offer for heated towel rails

Complete the following sentences by matching the first part on the left with the suitable one on the right.

Firstly, we are glad to offer you…	1	A	…without busting your budget.
They also come with a 5 year guarantee…	2	B	…and have been tested to comply with all EU and UK laws.
In turning to us, you have chosen one of…	3	C	…against faulty manufacturing and materials.
Please find enclosed our brochures and price lists…	4	D	…will meet your requirements and satisfy your tenants' needs.
We are sure that our range of goods…	5	E	…the designer towel rails are exceptionally well made, beautifully designed and, best of all, have distinctly unpretentious prices.
These radiators are of the highest quality …	6	F	…our series of traditional heated towel rails.
Thank you for your enquiry for heated towel rails…	7	G	…that will keep your towels comfy and warm without the need for the rail to be plumbed into the central heating system.
Providing heating solutions in quirky and innovative style…	8	H	…all our heated towel rails offer a quality product at exceptional value for money.
Whatever product group you choose,…	9	I	…the leading suppliers of bathroom equipment in the UK and Europe.
Manufactured in a factory which also supplies major brand names,…	10	J	…which will give you a first impression of our products.
We would be pleased to welcome you in our showroom in Oxford…	11	K	…which we received today.
The heated towel rails we offer basically…	12	L	…they are built to a high standard.
Our range of electrical towel warmers incorporates sleek modern design with instant heating…	13	M	…come in three categories.
This great range will bring warmth and style to your bathroom…	14	N	…to give you more specific information and discuss your needs in more detail.
Should you have any further questions…	15	O	…we would grant on an order that size.
Of course on that occasion we can as well talk about possible discounts…	16	P	…please do not hesitate to contact us by phone, fax or email.

1	2	3	4	5	6	7	8	9	10	11	12	13	14	15	16

Now arrange the sentences in a logical order and copy the entire letter into your exercise books.

All about bathrooms

(Begriffe aus zwei Wörtern mit Bindestrich eintragen)

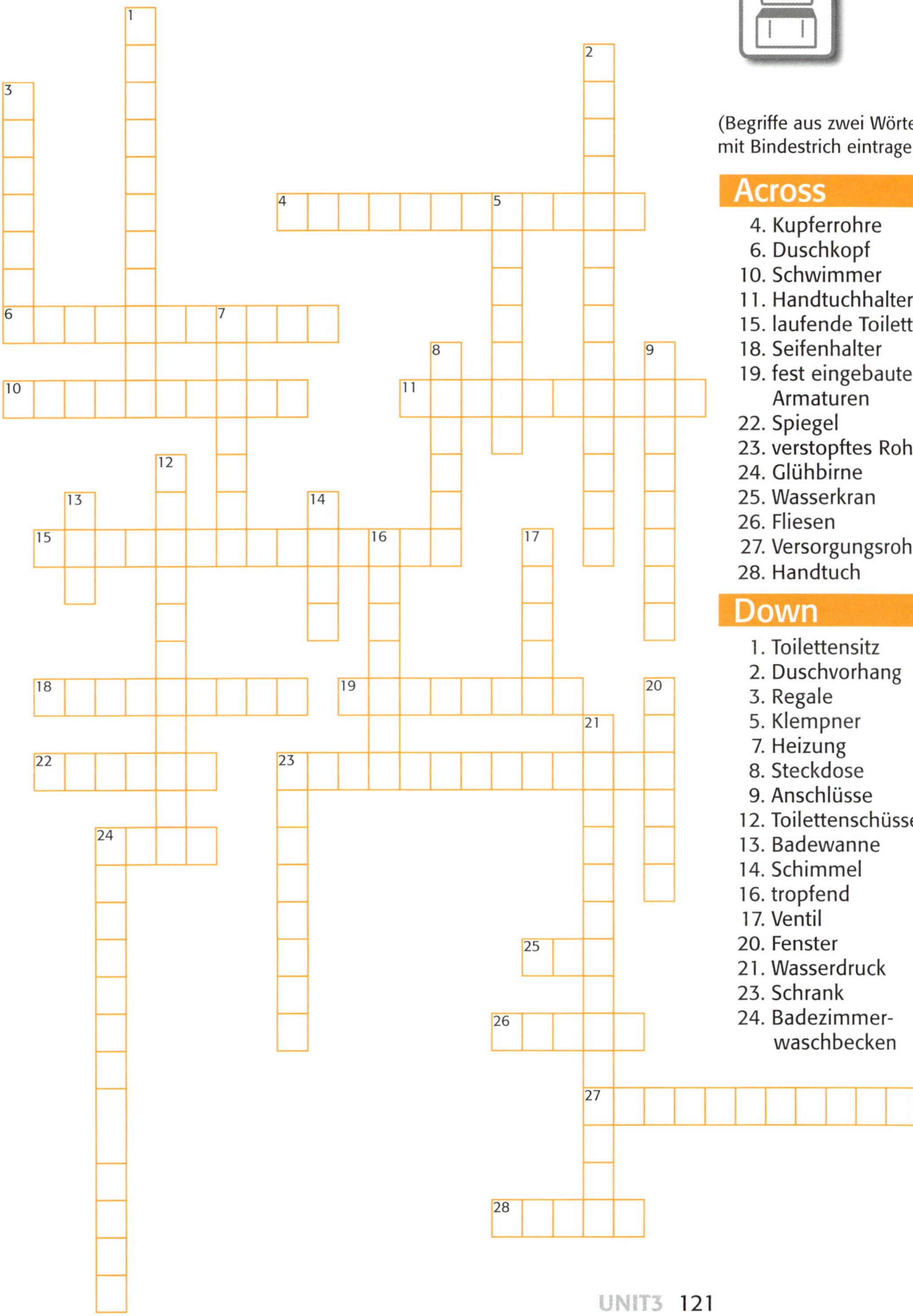

Across

4. Kupferrohre
6. Duschkopf
10. Schwimmer
11. Handtuchhalter
15. laufende Toilette
18. Seifenhalter
19. fest eingebaute Armaturen
22. Spiegel
23. verstopftes Rohr
24. Glühbirne
25. Wasserkran
26. Fliesen
27. Versorgungsrohr
28. Handtuch

Down

1. Toilettensitz
2. Duschvorhang
3. Regale
5. Klempner
7. Heizung
8. Steckdose
9. Anschlüsse
12. Toilettenschüssel
13. Badewanne
14. Schimmel
16. tropfend
17. Ventil
20. Fenster
21. Wasserdruck
23. Schrank
24. Badezimmer-waschbecken

Verfassen:

Senden Kontakte Rechtschr. Anhang Sicherheit Speichern

Von:

An:

Betreff:

Für die Sanierung unserer Wohnanlagen in Harpen benötigen wir unterschiedliche Angebote auch aus dem englischsprachigen Ausland.
Unter www.europages.com finden Sie Lieferanten- bzw. Herstelleradressen. Bitte schreiben Sie einige Unternehmen mit der Bitte um ein aussagekräftiges Angebot an. Hier sind die deutschsprachigen Vorgaben zu diesem Brief:

Situation: komplette Badsanierung in unseren Mehrfamilienhäusern, insgesamt benötigt 250 Waschtischbatterien, die die folgenden Kriterien erfüllen müssen:

- attraktives, zeitloses Design
- energiesparend und extrem belastbar
- Wasser sparend durch Durchlaufkontrolle
- tropffrei
- optionale Temperaturbeschränkung
- hohe Lebensdauer
- Nachweis eines Belastungstests
- oberflächenbeständig

Auf Grund des hohen Auftragsvolumens kommen nur knapp kalkulierte Preise in Betracht.

Wir erwarten eine 3-Jahres-Garantie auf alle Komponenten.

Für den Fall eines vorteilhaften Angebots können Folgeaufträge in Aussicht gestellt werden.

Ansprechpartnerin im Einkauf ist Frau Berger. Bei Rückfragen unter Zusatzinformationen Kontaktaufnahme per Mail unter berger@gwbo.de oder unter der Durchwahl -459.

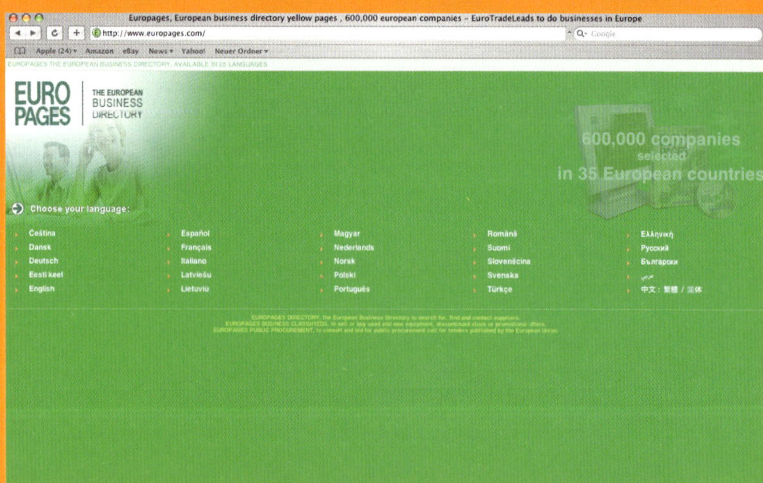

Source: EUREDIT SA

Writing an enquiry: sample phrases

OPENING LINES

Your name has been given to us by the Chamber of Commerce in ...

We saw your products in ... earlier this year.

Your advertisement in this month's issue of ... states that you can offer ...

We have seen your advertisement in ...

You were recommended to us by ...

We learn from your sales literature that you are selling ...

We found your name and address on the internet and were impressed by the range of products you have on display.

I am replying to your advertisement in ... and would like to know more about the ... you offer.

ASKING FOR DETAILS

Could you please quote your best price for ...

We would be glad to receive specifications of your ..., together with you current export price list and details of trade discount.

Could you please send us your catalogue and pricelist?

Please let us have your price list for the above product and state your terms of payment.

We would very much appreciate your sending us further information about your range of products and your terms of business.

Please let us have your price list and further details about the terms of payment.

We shall be pleased to receive your answer soon.

We should appreciate an early reply.

When replying, could you please enclose a sample of ...

We intend to place a substantial order and would therefore like to know what discounts you allow.

Can you guarantee delivery within three weeks after receiving orders?

INTRODUCING YOUR COMPANY/EXPLAINING THE SITUATION

Our company is a regional housing company in Germany. At present, we are considering to ... the ... in ... of our properties. Therefore, we are looking for a supplier of ...

We are a leading housing cooperative in northern Germany. As we are planning to privatise a majority of our housing stock, we are currently refurbishing 350 of our flats. Thus, we are looking for a supplier of ...

CLOSING LINES

We look forward to hearing from you.

If your prices are competitive, you can be sure of a large order.

Should your prices and products meet our expectations, we might consider future business.

UNIT 3

Dealing with customers

Commercial Correspondence

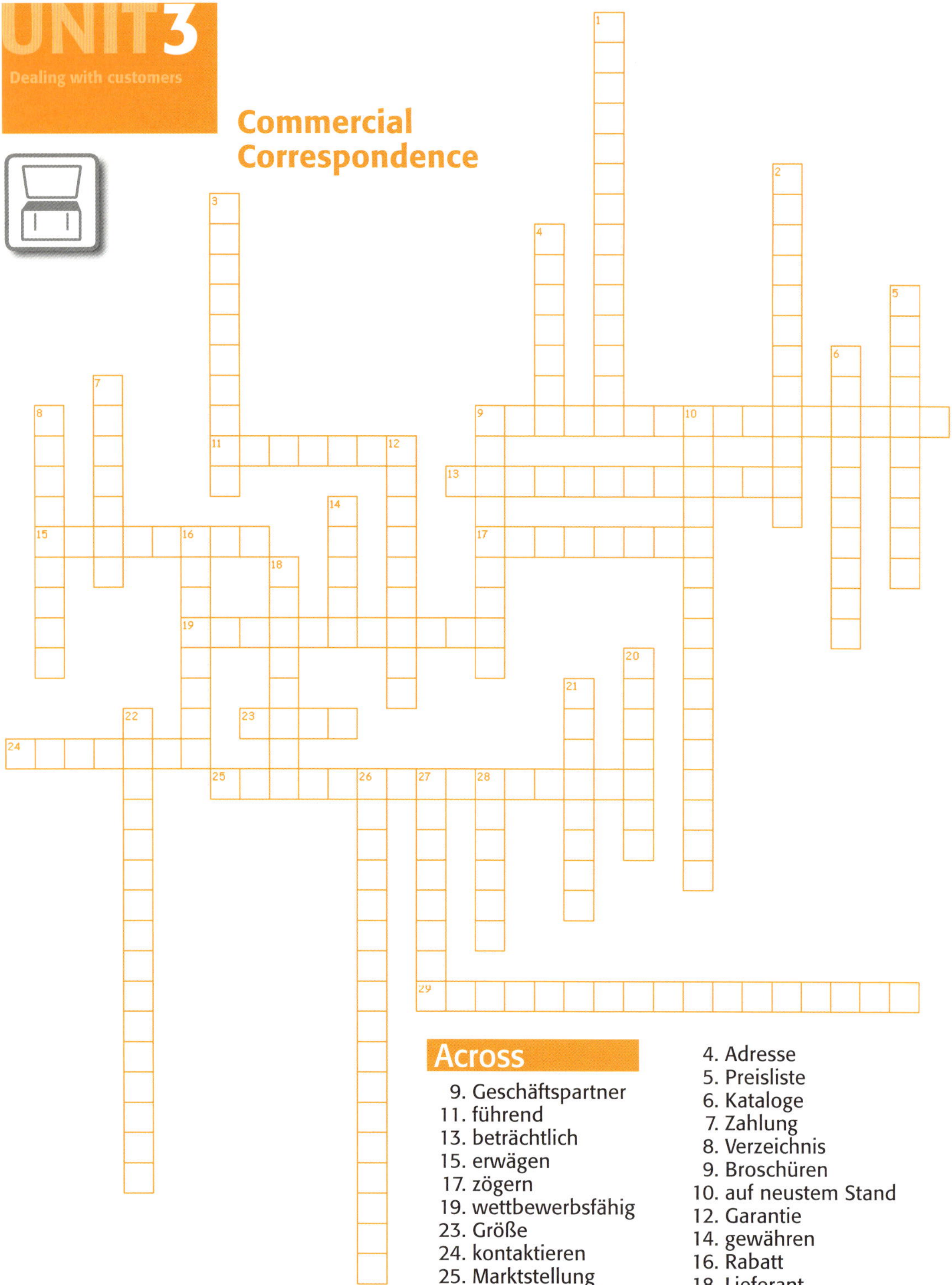

(Begriffe aus zwei Wörtern mit Bindestrich eintragen)

Across

9. Geschäftspartner
11. führend
13. beträchtlich
15. erwägen
17. zögern
19. wettbewerbsfähig
23. Größe
24. kontaktieren
25. Marktstellung
29. Produktsortiment

Down

1. Empfehlung
2. gelbe Seiten
3. vorteilhaft
4. Adresse
5. Preisliste
6. Kataloge
7. Zahlung
8. Verzeichnis
9. Broschüren
10. auf neustem Stand
12. Garantie
14. gewähren
16. Rabatt
18. Lieferant
20. Bedürfnisse
21. Lieferung
22. Verkaufsunterlagen
26. Geschäftsbedingungen
27. Hersteller
28. Muster

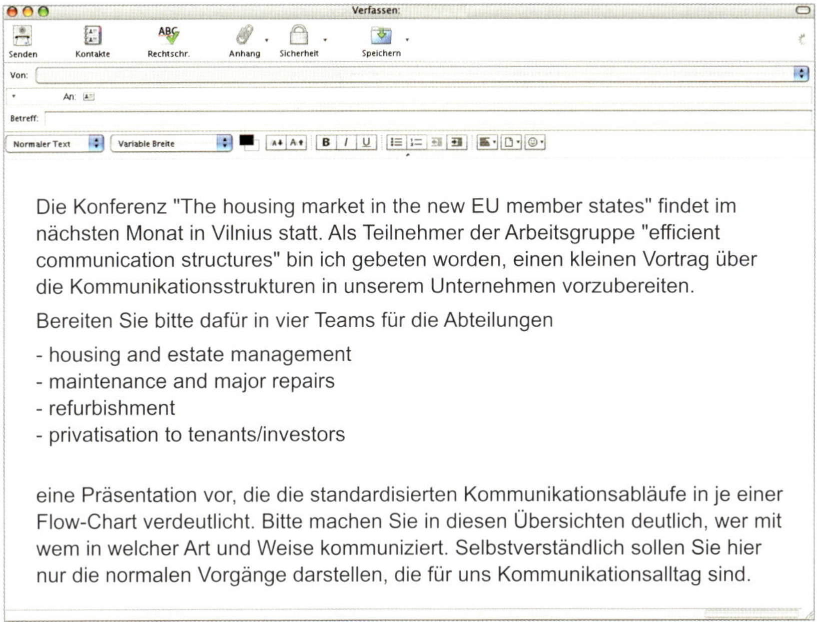

Die Konferenz "The housing market in the new EU member states" findet im nächsten Monat in Vilnius statt. Als Teilnehmer der Arbeitsgruppe "efficient communication structures" bin ich gebeten worden, einen kleinen Vortrag über die Kommunikationsstrukturen in unserem Unternehmen vorzubereiten.

Bereiten Sie bitte dafür in vier Teams für die Abteilungen

- housing and estate management
- maintenance and major repairs
- refurbishment
- privatisation to tenants/investors

eine Präsentation vor, die die standardisierten Kommunikationsabläufe in je einer Flow-Chart verdeutlicht. Bitte machen Sie in diesen Übersichten deutlich, wer mit wem in welcher Art und Weise kommuniziert. Selbstverständlich sollen Sie hier nur die normalen Vorgänge darstellen, die für uns Kommunikationsalltag sind.

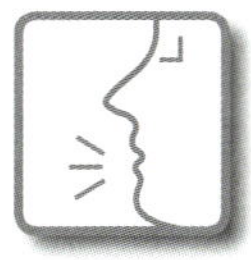

Talking about legal documents

"Dealing with business partners" – this is the title of Unit 3. But what does "dealing" actually mean?

Well, the English phrase "to deal with somebody" can comprise numerous and manifold forms of interaction.

In its extensive sense, it means any kind of communication. In its distinctively intensive sense, it refers to any kind of oral and / or written agreements.

A "deal" is the result of a contracting activity.

Most of the time, "dealing" is a process in which you

- identify your own feasible interests, wishes, desires, claims, etc.;
- assess whether or not you can legitimately ask other persons to fulfil, to honour, to deliver, etc. your interests, wishes, desires, claims, etc;
- select and get in touch with your potential partner(s) in order to communicate your goals;
- negotiate with your selected partner(s) so as to obtain what you wish;
- conclude an oral or written agreement with your partner(s) that determines precisely the type of goods to be delivered, of services to be provided, etc. and the conditions under which this business transaction will have to be handled.

YOU MAY NEVER EVER MAKE ILLEGAL DEALS !

You will now listen to a text which will give you a lot of details on how to conclude agreements, how to "make a deal".

Pre-listening activity

- think about situations in life, when you actually deal with people (when buying rolls for breakfast, when buying some pieces of furniture or even when getting your child baptised in church, etc.) and write them down;
- describe the typical set of negotiations and deals (where, when, with whom, what is it all about?);
- make a list of your personal "deals" and the corresponding oral and written agreements you've concluded in your life and you've kept on file at home;
- work in pairs and role-play a simple deal of your choice.

While-listening activity

Now listen to the audio document and take notes while listening.

Please pay special attention to the following points:

- What are the advantages and inconveniences of oral vs. written agreements?
- Who can draft a contract?
- Do you need a lawyer to conclude an agreement?
- Do contracts require a special form?
- Where can you find contract forms?
- What are the indispensable core elements every contract needs to contain (the "W"-questions)?
- What do you keep on file in connection with a contract?
- Whose signature is required to make a contract legally binding?
- Which issues should never be dealt with in a contract?
- What is meant by "anticipate problems"?
- What is required to make a contract legally binding?

Post-listening activity

1. Discuss in class:

- which kind of issues you can handle with oral agreements and for which businesses you absolutely need written ones;
- identify the advantages and inconveniences of oral and written agreements;
- typical issues that require agreements with a limited / unlimited duration in time;
- situations when the inherent purpose of a contract ceases to apply.

Please write down the results of your debate.

2. Please make a list of all agreements which are relevant for your everyday business.

Cross-cultural communication

How others see us…

Have a look at this list of common statements about Germans. Do you agree with them? Tick the appropriate box and discuss your results in class.

STATEMENT	I AGREE	I DO NOT AGREE	IT DEPENDS
Business dress in Germany is very conservative.			
Businessmen wear dark suits, solid, conservative ties, and white shirts.			
Women also dress conservatively, in dark suits and white blouses.			
Chewing gum while talking to someone is considered rude.			
Germans are strongly individualistic.			
The German thought process is extremely thorough, with each aspect of a project being examined in great detail. This process is often times very time-intensive. However, once the planning is over, a project will move very quickly and deadlines are expected to be honored.			
Germans do not like surprises. Sudden changes in business transactions, even if they may improve the outcome, are unwelcome.			
German citizens do not need or expect to be complimented. In Germany, it is assumed that everything is satisfactory unless the person hears otherwise.			
Punctuality is a necessity in Germany. Arrive on time for every appointment, whether for business or social. Being late, even if it is only by a few minutes, is very insulting to a German executive.			
In business situations, shake hands at both the beginning and the end of a meeting. Additionally, a handshake may be accompanied with a slight bow. Be sure to look directly into the person's eyes while shaking hands.			
When being introduced to a woman, wait to see if she extends her hand.			
Business is viewed as being very serious, and Germans do not appreciate humor in a business context.			
In business meetings, age takes precedence over youth. If you are in a group setting, the eldest person enters first.			
Germans keep a larger personal space around them, approximately 6 inches more space than North Americans do.			
People that have worked together for years still shake hands each morning as if it were the first time they met.			
German men frequently great each other with **Herr** ‚last name', even when they know each other very well.			

Source: Stephen Taylor & Matt Priest – www.InternationalBusinessCenter.org

Culture is like an iceberg. The tip of the iceberg is easy to see. This includes the visible aspects and do's and taboos of working in other cultures.

The remaining huge chunk of the iceberg hidden below the surface includes the invisible aspects of a culture such as the values, traditions, experiences and behaviors that define each culture.

Discuss the significance of this statement for your business. Exchange your experience and also how you managed to overcome any intercultural problems that arose.

What – in your opinion – are tips for successful cross-cultural communication?

Did you know...

In some forms of communication, silence is to be expected before a response, as a sign of thoughtfulness and deference to the original speaker, yet at other times, silence may be experienced as a sign of hostility. In the West, twenty seconds of silence during a meeting is an extraordinarily long time, and people will feel uncomfortable with that. Someone invariably will break in to end the uncomfortable silence. But the same customs around silence are not universal.

In the West, we often try to build immediate rapport through humor, but of course, this is not universally seen to be appropriate in all contexts. The use of laughter can be experienced as a sign of disrespect by some, and so it is important to understand that this is another area where misunderstandings can be very likely to occur.

The same issues arise over the issue of interrupting. In some cultures, interruption, vocal, emotional expression, etc. are considered to be the default conversational style, particularly among those considered to be equals, or among men. Many people of Northern European or American extract might mistake this kind of conversation for argument and hostility, but that would not be the case.

Different cultures may have different customs around who addresses whom when and how, and who has the right, or even the duty, to speak first, and what is the proper way to conclude a conversation. Think about it: no matter where you are, some ways of commencing a conversation or concluding one will be considered as rude, even disrespectful. These are artificial customs, to a certain degree, and there is probably no universally right or wrong way to go about these things, short of behaviors that all cultures would likely consider to be vulgar or abusive. This topic includes modes of address, salutations, levels of deference to age or social position, acceptable ways to conclude gracefully and so on. Obviously, and to the dismay of many of us in the West, this will also cover gender differences.

In some places, it is considered vulgar to speak openly about money, for example, let alone about the kinds of intimate family issues that commonly form the basis of afternoon television "talk" shows in the West. Travelers or business people should learn the customs that surround the making of deals, the transaction of commerce, and the degree to which details are specified in advance and enumerated in writing across cultures (not all places are as prone to hire lawyers and create detailed contracts as we are in the West).

In some cultures, it is more appropriate to take turns in an interactive way, and in others, it is more important to listen thoroughly and without comment, without immediate response, lest a response be taken as a challenge or a humiliation, particularly depending on the context of the conversation, the audience, and the levels of personal knowledge/relationship between the two people interacting. For example, a Western couple or pair of executives may feel perfectly comfortable interacting in a give and take way in a public market, but if that public market is in a part of the world where such a public display of give and take is considered to be in bad taste, then they may be giving offense without ever realizing it.

In some places, less is definitely more, whereas in other places, it is more valued to wrap a rather small point up in a longer preamble, followed by an extended wrap-up. For Westerners, this can be maddening, as we tend to value speaking directly and to the point. Then again, there are clearly circumstances where Westerners say too much and lose their ability to communicate well, depending on the context. Of course, patterns around presumed areas of deference based on age and social standing can influence how much is appropriate to say, depending on the culture.

Dr. A. J. Schuler is an expert in leadership and organizational change. To find out more about his programs and services, visit *www.SchulerSolutions.com* or call (703) 370-6545.

Either in business or in your private life, have you ever come across situations like the ones described above? How did you react? What sort of advice would you give others?

Tenant satisfaction survey

Verfassen:

Senden | Kontakte | Rechtschr. | Anhang | Sicherheit | Speichern

Von:

An:

Betreff:

Bitte bereiten Sie als Projekt einen Fragebogen an unsere englischsprachigen Mieter vor (tenant satisfaction survey). Ich habe Ihnen als Information einige zentrale Ergebnisse aus der Auswertung eines Fragebogens kopiert, die ich als Vorbereitung der Konferenz in Vilnius von einem Kollegen aus Swindon, England, erhalten habe. Der Gesamtbogen kann auch im Internet abgerufen werden:

http://www.swindon.gov.uk/tenant_participation_survey_2003-04.pdf

Diese Ergebnisse können nur eine Orientierung sein, der tatsächliche Fragebogen sollte natürlich auf unsere Bedürfnisse zugeschnitten werden. Bitte beachten Sie, dass die einzelnen Fragen klar verständlich formuliert werden und dass die Antwortmöglichkeiten eine unkomplizierte Auswertung zulassen sollen.

Chart 1:

Overall Satisfaction with Housing Service Provided by Swindon Borough Council

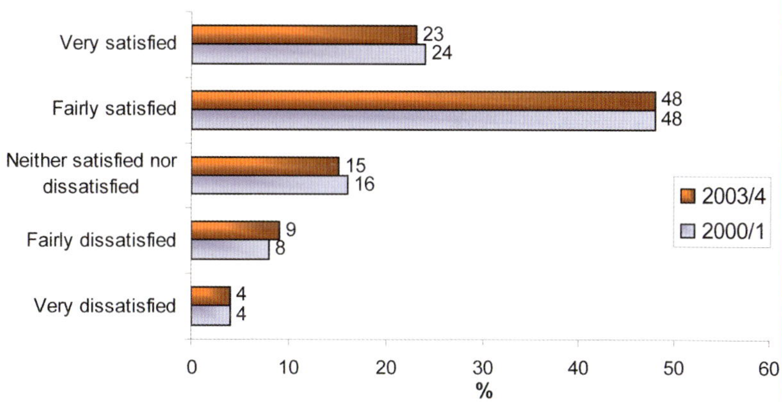

Base: All answering
(2003/2004: 946, 2000/1:921)

Chart 2:

Overall Satisfaction with Accomodation

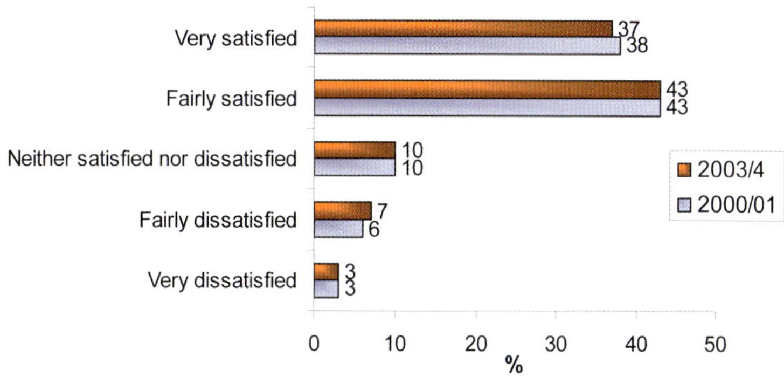

Base: All answering
(2003/2004: 953, 2000/1:924)

Chart 3:

Opinion of Number of Rooms in Home, by Household Composition

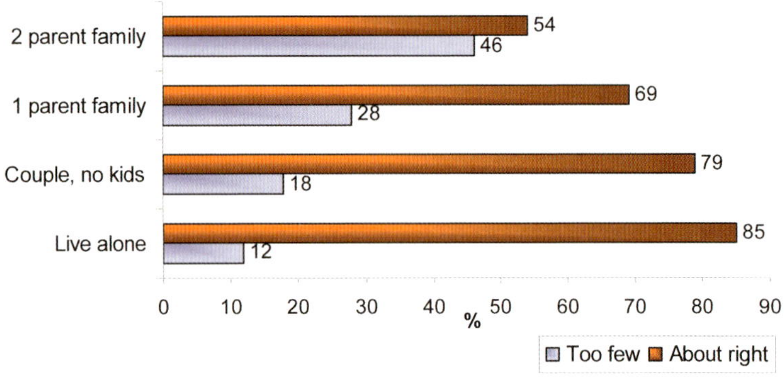

Base: All answering (953)

Chart 4:

Satisfaction with General Condition of Property, by Age

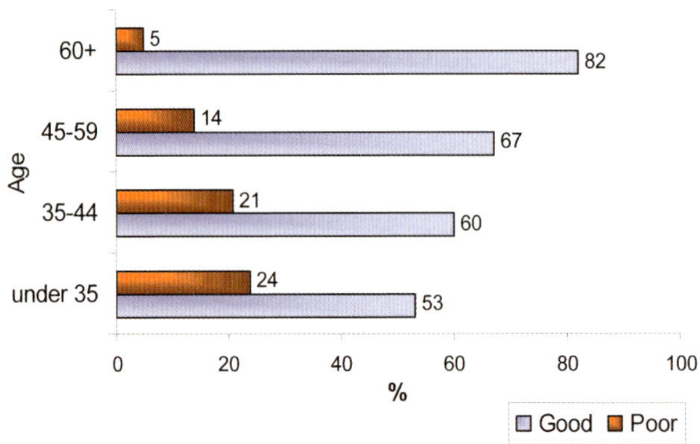

Base: All answering (955)

Chart 5:

Problems in the Area

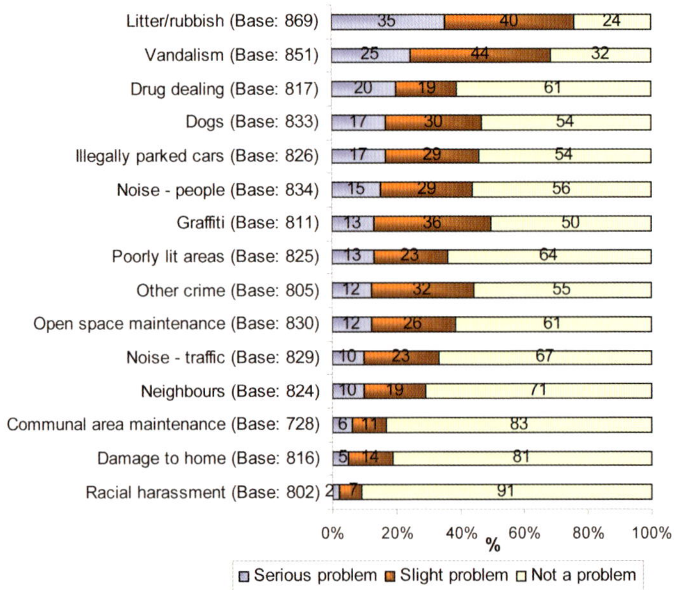

Base: All answering
(see individual problem)

Chart 6:

Preference for improving services

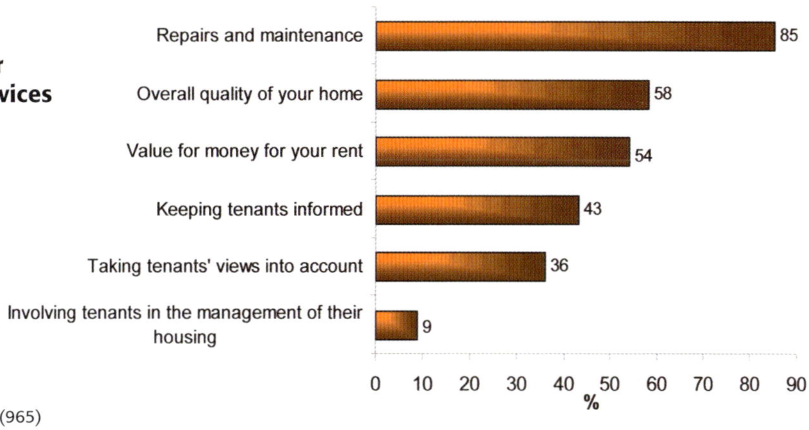

Base: All answering (965)

Chart 7:

Ratings of Last Completed Repair

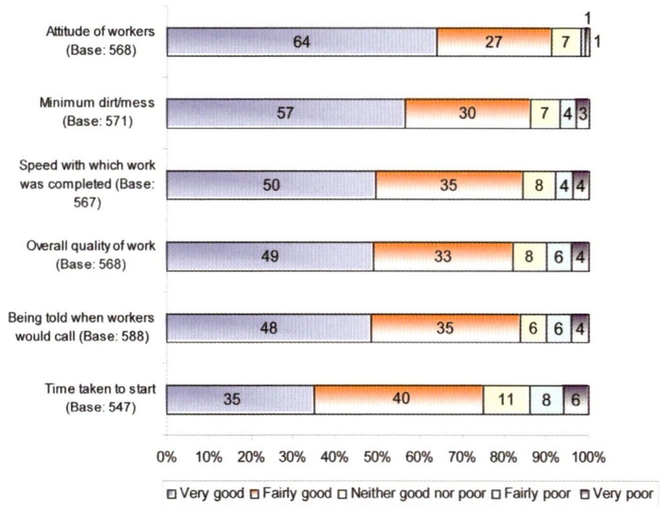

Base: All answering
(see individual repair)

Chart 2:

Length of Tenure/ Residence in Current Home

	Current Home	Swindon tenant
Base:	*(954)*	*(949)*
	%	%
Under 1 year	6	3
1-2 years	11	6
3-5 years	17	11
6-10 years	21	15
11-20 years	22	22
21+ years	23	43
Mean (years)	12.08	18.06

Base: All answering

Source: RBAresearch Ltd

Vokabeln

A	abusive	missbräuchlich, beleidigend
	accommodation	Unterbringung
	acknowledgement	Anerkennung, Bestätigung
	advertise (verb)	werben, Anzeigen schalten
	advertisement	Werbung
	agent	Makler
	air (verb)	lüften
	alert	alarmieren
	answer phone	Anrufbeantworter
	Asbo	einstweilige Anordnung wegen antisozialen Verhaltens
	assault	Angriff, tätlicher Übergriff
	assume (verb)	annehmen, übernehmen, vermuten, unterstellen
B	bank	Bank
	barbecue	Grill
	bathroom sink	Badezimmerwaschbecken
	begging	Bettelei
	bow	Bogen
	branch	Niederlassung
	breach (verb)	brechen, verletzen, zuwiderhandeln
	breakdown	Betriebsstörung
	briefcase	Aktenkoffer
	bulb	Glühbirne
	bust (verb)	sprengen
C	caretaker	Hausmeister, Hauswart
	cell phone	Handy
	challenge	Herausforderung
	chamber of commerce and industry	Industrie- und Handelskammer
	chimney	Kamin, Schornstein
	circuitry	Kreislauf, Schaltkreis, Schaltschema
	city council	Stadtrat
	civil rights campaigner	Bürgerrechtler
	cleaning service	Reinigungsdienst
	cleanliness	Sauberkeit
	commence (verb)	beginnen
	commodity	Verbrauchsgut
	competitive	wettbewerbsfähig
	comply (verb)	übereinstimmen mit
	confirmation	Bestätigung
	considerable	beachtlich
	copper pipe	Kupferrohr
	court	Gericht
	court order	Gerichtsentscheidung, gerichtliche Mahnung
	courteous	höflich, zuvorkommend
	craftsman	Handwerker
	craftspeople	Handwerkerschaft
D	damage	Schaden, Beschädigung
	data carrier	Datenträger
	database	Datenbank
	deadline	Termin
	default	schlecht, fehlerhaft
	delivery	Lieferung
	deny (verb)	verneinen, verleugnen, bestreiten, dementieren
	deprived area	Stadtteil mit besonderem Entwicklungsbedarf, sozialer Brennpunkt, benachteiligtes Quartier
	deter (verb)	abschrecken, abhalten von
	diagram	Diagramm
	discount	Rabatt
	display	Display
	disturbance caused by animals	Störung durch (Haus-)Tiere
	domestic violence	häusliche Gewalt
	drip (verb)	tropfen
	dripping	tropfend
	due	fällig
	duplicate (verb)	verdoppeln
E	electrician	Elektriker
	emergency	Notfall
	energy provider	Energieversorger
	enquiry	Anfrage
	entity	Entität, Einheit
	envelope	Umschlag
	environmentally friendly	umweltfreundlich
	estimate	Kostenvoranschlag
	examine (verb)	untersuchen
	executive	Führungskraft
F	face-to-face	gegenüber
	facial expression	Gesichtsausdruck
	favourable	günstig
	fight fire (verb)	Brand bekämpfen
	file	Akte, Datei
	file (verb)	nachverfolgen, ablegen
	fire brigade	Feuerwehr
	fittings	Anschlüsse
	fixture	fest eingebaute Armatur
	flat-bed scanner	Flachbettscanner
	flat-screen monitor	Flachbildschirm
	float-ball	Schwimmer
	flooring material	Bodenbelag
	follow-up	nachverfolgen
	furnace	Ofen
G	garbage	Müll
	gardener	Gärtner
	garlic	Knoblauch
	gas leak	Leck in der Gasleitung
	gas provider	Gasversorger
	German Tenants' Protection Association	Deutscher Mieterschutzbund
	gesture	Geste, Gebärde
	government-funded	staatlich gefördert
	grant (verb)	einräumen, gewähren
	guarantee	garantieren, gewährleisten
H	handicapped-equipped bathroom equipment	behindertengerechte Badezimmerausstattung
	harassment	Belästigung
	headquarter	Hauptsitz
	heating system	Heizung
	hesitate	zögern
	hostility	Feindlichkeit
I	icon	Symbol
	improve (verb)	verbessern
	in charge	verantwortlich, zuständig
	inconvenience	Belästigung, Unbill
	indemnify (verb)	entschädigen
	indispensable	unerlässlich
	infringe (verb)	verletzen
	insurance company	Versicherungsunternehmen
	intimidation	Einschüchterung
	in-tray	Posteingangskorb
J	jump suit	Overall, Trainingsanzug
K	kitchenette	Kochnische
L	land registry	Kataster
	law	Gesetz

	lawyer	Rechtsanwalt
	leading	führend
	leaking toilet	laufende Toilette
	legal advice	Rechtsberatung
	legal matter	Rechtsangelegenheit
	legally binding	rechtsverbindlich
	length	Länge
	liability insurance	Haftpflichtversicherung
M	manufacturer	Hersteller
	market leader	Marktführer
	market position	Marktstellung
	mirror	Spiegel
	misuse	Missbrauch
	mobile, mobile phone	mobil, Mobiltelefon
	mortgage bank	Hypothekenbank
	mould, mold (AE)	Schimmel
	mutual	gegenseitig
N	network	Netzwerk
	noise pollution	Lärmbelästigung
	noisy	laut, lärmend
O	occur (verb)	auftreten, passieren, geschehen
	offender	Angreifer, Straftäter
	offer	Angebot
	operating system	Betriebssystem
	oral communication	mündliche Kommunikation
	order	Auftrag
	outlet	Steckdose
	out-tray	Postausgangskorb
	overemphasize	überbewerten
	overload	Überlastung
P	painter	Maler
	paramount	höchst, überragend, vorrangig, Haupt-
	parquet flooring	Parkettfußboden
	permission	Genehmigung
	personnel	Personal
	pest-control	Kammerjäger
	pilot scheme	Pilotvorhaben
	pitch	Steigung
	plumber	Klempner
	plumbing	Installateurarbeit
	police	Polizei
	preamble	Präambel
	price list	Preisliste
	property description	Immobilienexposé
	public utility company	Stadtwerke
	punctuality	Pünktlichkeit
	purpose	Ziel, Zweck
Q	quirky	schnörkelig, schrullig, schrill, sonderbar
R	racist	rassistisch
	range of products	Produktportfolio
	rapport	Verbindung, Verhältnis
	recommend (verb)	empfehlen
	reduction	Verringerung, Reduktion
	reminder	Mahnung
	rent increase	Mieterhöhung
	representative	Vertreter
	reputation	Leumund, Ruf, Reputation
	request	Anfrage, Anforderung
	requirement	Anforderung, Erfordernis
	rights and obligations	Rechte und Pflichten
	risk assessment	Risikobeurteilung
	rogue	Schlingel, Spitzbub
	rude	grob
S	sales literature	Verkaufsprospekt
	sample	Muster
	satisfied	zufrieden
	shelf, shelves	Regal(e)
	short-term lets	befristeter Mietvertrag
	shower curtain	Duschvorhang
	shower head	Duschkopf
	showroom	Ausstellungsraum
	sign (verb)	unterzeichnen
	sleek	geschmeidig, glatt
	smell of gas	Gasgeruch
	social services department	Sozialamt
	soot	Ruß
	spreadsheet	Kalkulationsblatt, Tabellenkalkulation
	spy (verb)	spionieren
	stalking	Stalking
	stamp	Briefmarke
	stapler	Hefter
	state-of-the-art	auf dem neusten Stand
	storage space	Lagerraum
	store (verb)	speichern
	student hostel	Studentenwohnheim
	suit	passen, taugen, übereinstimmen
	supply pipe	Versorgungsrohr
	survey	Erhebung, Gutachten, Studie
	suspicious	verdächtig, suspekt
T	tap	Wasserkran
	telephone company	Telefongesellschaft
	television company	Fernsehgesellschaft
	tenants' association	Mieterbund
	tie	Krawatte
	tile	Fliese
	toilet bowl	Toilettenschüssel
	toilet seat	Klobrille
	towel	Handtuch
	towel rail	Handtuchhalter
	trust	Vertrauen
	tumble-drier	Wäschetrockner
U	unsatisfied, dissatisfied	unzufrieden
	urban planner	Stadtplaner
	urban regeneration programme	Stadterneuerungsprogramm
	urge (verb)	drängen, dringend bitten
	useful life	Nutzungsdauer
V	vandalism	Vandalismus
	vigilant action / vigilant justice	Selbstjustiz
	vulgar	abgeschmackt, geschmacklos, vulgär
W	warranty	Garantie
	WASCs – water and sewerage companies	Wasserversorgungsunternehmen
	washbasin	Waschbecken
	water pipe	Wasserrohr
	water pressure	Wasserdruck
	wealth	Wohlstand
	wheelchair	Rollstuhl
	window	Fenster
	wooden floor	Holzfußboden
	word-processing	Textverarbeitung
	written communication	schriftliche Kommunikation
Y	yellow pages	Gelbe Seiten

SELF-ASSESSMENT GRID AFTER UNIT 3

Gehen Sie die einzelnen Abschnitte des gerade abgeschlossenen Kapitels noch einmal durch und überprüfen Sie sich selbstkritisch. Was haben Sie gelernt? Was sollten Sie wiederholen bzw. vertiefen? Was bereitet Ihnen Schwierigkeiten? Schreiben Sie kurze Kommentare in die Kästchen, die Ihren Lernzuwachs für Sie selbst erläutern. Arbeiten Sie nach eigenen Prioritäten Unterpunkte nach, wenn Sie mehrheitlich Ihre Kommentare in der rechten Spalte gesetzt haben.

Was ich in diesem Kapitel gelernt habe…	**Wie ich meinen Fortschritt einschätze**		
	Ich fühle mich beim Sprechen/Schreiben und beim Hören bzw. Lesen zu diesem Aspekt insgesamt sicher und verstehe einen Großteil der Informationen bzw. kann einen Großteil der Informationen wie beabsichtigt weitergeben; auch wenn ich Fehler mache, habe ich insgesamt Vertrauen in meine Sprachbeherrschung.	Ich kann vieles von dem, was für diesen Aspekt wichtig ist, mündlich und schriftlich ausdrücken bzw. beim Hören und Lesen verstehen; allerdings fehlen mir einige Fachvokabeln und auch die grundsätzliche Sicherheit, mich frei über diesen Aspekt auszutauschen.	Ich habe zu diesem Aspekt einige Fachbegriffe und Redewendungen gelernt und verstehe auch Informationen; jedoch erschließen sich mir noch nicht alle Zusammenhänge; sowohl die Textrezeption (Hören und Lesen) als auch das Sprechen und Schreiben bereiten mir noch Probleme; ich weiß, dass ich einige Aspekte nacharbeiten sollte.
den Fachwortschatz zur Beschreibung der Geschäftspartner und Mieter eines Wohnungsunternehmens / Vermieters anzuwenden.			
die Arten und Medien der Bürokommunikation zu unterscheiden sowie diese in diversen Situationen des Tagesgeschäfts eines Wohnungsunternehmens angemessen zu verwenden.			
die Grundlagen und die englischen Fachtermini für den mündlichen und schriftlichen Umgang mit Mietern / Wohneigentümern anzuwenden.			
die Grundlagen und den englischen Fachwortschatz zu mündlichen und schriftlichen Vereinbarungen anzuwenden.			
kulturübergreifende Aspekte der Mieterkommunikation zu berücksichtigen.			
Lernstrategien der Wörterbucharbeit anzuwenden.			

UNIT 4 Aspects of Letting

In dieser Unit lernen Sie:

- den Fachwortschatz zur Beschreibung von Rechten und Pflichten von Mietern und Vermietern anzuwenden
- die wesentlichen Bestandteile eines Mietvertrags und der Miete darzustellen und zu erläutern
- grundlegende Aspekte der Betriebskosten zu erläutern
- die Fachtermini zur Beschreibung einer Wohnung in einem Wohnungsübergabeprotokoll anzuwenden
- die Grundzüge einer Hausordnung darzustellen
- den Fachwortschatz, um Informationen und Tipps zum Energiesparen und zur Müllentsorgung zu geben
- wesentliche Bestandteile der Beendigung eines Mietverhältnisses in der erforderlichen Korrespondenz darzustellen
- Leerstand und mögliche Ursachen zu beschreiben
- den Fachwortschatz zu relevanten Versicherungen anzuwenden
- Anbahnung und Abschluss eines Pachtvertrages für eine Gewerbeimmobilie darzustellen
- die Anwendung und Erarbeitung des Fachwortschatzes „Mülltrennung“ in einer Web-Unit zu Abfallmanagement
- Lernstrategien: richtig lesen auf dem Weg zu einem detaillierten Textverständnis

UNIT 4

Aspects of letting

Landlords and tenants – rights and obligations

Have a look at these pictures and briefly explain what you see. What have they got to do with rental properties and aspects of letting? Copy and complete the following table.

THE LANDLORD…			THE TENANT…		
…has the right to…	…has the obligation to…	… is not allowed to…	…has the right to…	…has the obligation to…	… is not allowed to…

UNIT 4
Aspects of letting

Now have a look at the following text and complete your table with those aspects you have not mentioned yet.

The responsibilities of the landlord are:

- to provide the premises in a reasonable state of cleanliness
- to provide and maintain the premises in a reasonable state of repair with regard to age and character of the premises
- to comply with all legal requirements to do with buildings, health and safety
- to compensate the tenant for any reasonable expenses that the tenant has incurred in making repairs, if the problem was serious and urgent and the tenant made a reasonable attempt to notify the landlord of the problem
- to take all reasonable steps to ensure that any other tenants do not interfere with the reasonable peace, comfort or privacy of the tenant in using the premises
- to not interfere with the supply of electricity, water, phone, gas or any other services, except where this is necessary to avoid danger to any person or to enable maintenance or repairs to be carried out

As a tenant you are required to:

- pay rent as and where it is due under the tenancy agreement
- ensure that the premises are used principally for residential purposes
- keep the premises reasonably clean and tidy
- notify the landlord as soon as possible of any damage or of the need for any repairs
- ensure that any maximum number of residents specified in the agreement is complied with
- not intentionally or carelessly damage the premises, or permit anyone else to do this
- not use the premises, or permit them to be used, for any unlawful purpose
- not interfere with the reasonable peace, comfort, or privacy of your neighbours or of any of the landlord's other tenants

When the tenancy comes to an end, the tenant must:

- vacate the premises
- remove his or her property from the premises
- leave the premises in a reasonably clean and tidy condition, and remove all rubbish
- return all keys (and security cards or other devices) to the landlord
- leave all the chattels (such as furniture) that the landlord provided for the tenant's use

Landlords are entitled to enter the premises to inspect them or to do necessary repairs and maintenance, provided they have given prior notice.

A tenant can sub-let the premises only if this is not explicitly forbidden under the tenancy agreement.

One of you is the landlord, the other one takes the role of the tenant.

The tenant: Look at the extracts from a tenancy agreement and choose five aspects you would like to have explained in detail. Ask the landlord detailed questions, e.g. what does this obligation mean for you? Why does the landlord need this aspect in the agreement etc.

The landlord: Choose five aspects from your tenancy agreement which you consider very important. Explain these aspects in detail and make sure that the tenant fully understands what they mean.

not to alter or change or install any locks on any doors or windows in or about the property or have any additional keys made for any locks without the prior written consent

to use the property as a single private dwelling and not to use it or any part of it for any other purpose nor to allow anyone else to do so

not to do or permit in or on the property any act or thing which may be a nuisance, damage or annoyance to the landlord or to the occupiers of the neighbouring premises

to keep the premises including all driveways, pathways, lawns, hedges and rockeries, neat, tidy and properly tended and to keep any garage in good order

to pay the deposit as security for the performance of the obligations and to pay and compensate for any breach of those obligations

not to use the property for any illegal or immoral purpose

not to damage or injure the property and contents or make any alteration or addition to it without the prior written consent

to replace all broken glass in doors and windows damaged

may at reasonable times on giving 24 hours' notice (unless in the case of an emergency) enter the property for the purpose of viewing, inspecting its condition and state of repair or for the purpose of repair and maintenance

to pay promptly to whom they are due expenses (including water and sewerage charges, gas, electric, light and telephone relating to the property)

to pay the rent on the days and in the manner specified to the landlord

to keep the drains free from obstruction and to keep the chimney swept as often as necessary

to immediately pay the value of replacement of any losses or damages and not to remove or permit to be removed any equipment belonging to the property

not to receive paying guests or carry on or permit to be carried on any business, trade or possession on or from the property

not to assign, or sublet, part with possession of the property, or to let any other person live at the property

to reinstate the property to the same order that it was provided at the commencement of the tenancy

to take all reasonable precautions to prevent damage by frost

to notify promptly in writing of any disrepair, damage or defect in the property or of any event which causes damage to the property

provided the rent has been paid, permit and make sure that the tenant can have quiet enjoyment of the property without interruption

to keep the interior of the property and contents in good clean condition and complete repair (damage by accidental fire and reasonable wear and tear excepted) and to keep the property at all times well and sufficiently aired and warmed during the tenancy

not to keep any animals or birds or other living creature on the property without the landlord's written consent

to permit the landlord or any person authorised by the landlord at reasonable hours in daytime to enter and view the property with prospective tenants or purchasers

Managing your rental property

Have a look at these activities associated with rental properties. Arrange them (i.e. the letter representing this activity) in a logical order using the time line provided. You may want to use some aspects more than once.

A clean up your rental property for further letting
B inspect the property with the tenant, using a move-in check-list
C go through the aspects of the tenancy agreement making sure the tenant understands all details
D advertise for a new tenant during period of notice
E allocate the respective utility costs
F confirm the notice given by your tenant
G hand out keys for the flat
H inspect the property with the tenant
I collect the deposit
J carry out necessary repair works
K inspect the property with the tenant, using the move-out check-list
L refund the deposit and the interest payment
M solve any problems associated with rent arrears
N settle disputes among tenants
O collect keys for the flat and confirm the receipt
P carry out necessary maintenance works
Q organise the tenant's move-out
R organise the tenant's move-in
S start a tenant file and collect all necessary information about your tenant
T inform tenant about repair and maintenance works
U if necessary, provide advice on debt management
V provide information on saving energy and reducing utility costs
W provide information on housing benefit etc.
X use possible vacancies for major refurbishments etc.
Y answer possible queries on billings of utility costs
Z collect all written correspondence in the tenant file

beginning
of tenancy

→

end
of tenancy

→

Add any further steps which you consider important. Present your results to the class.

Tenancy agreements

tenancy agreement	how	rights	covers	tenant
standing order	landlord	contract	letting	responsibilities
charges	furniture	property	due	responsibilities
provided	house rules	rights	end	pets
conditions	external	structural	property	utility costs
heat	terms	refunded	deposit	written
rented accommo-dation	services	respond	internal decorations	safe
tenant	complaints	well-maintained	renting	bills
clean	property	on time	law	rental agree-ment
avoid	rent	care	electricity	address
in full	amenities	tenant	utilities	owner
responsibilities	refrain	danger	apartment	damage
conditions				

A ______________________ is the ______________________ between ______________________ and ______________________. It sets out the ______________________ and ______________________ tenants and landlords have while renting/______________________ the ______________________.

When moving into ______________________, the tenant should be given a ______________________ tenancy agreement. However, both parties do not need a written tenancy agreement to have ______________________.

A tenancy agreement should list the ______________________ and ______________________ both parties need to stick to. It should contain information about:

- the name and ______________________ of your landlord
- the address of the ______________________ the tenant is ______________________
- how much ______________________ he has to pay

- how long the ______________________ can live in the property

A tenancy agreement could include the following:

- when the rent is ______________________ and ______________________ it should be paid (for example, by cheque, by ______________________, etc.)
- what the rent ______________________. Does it include ______________________, e.g. ______________________? Are there any extra ______________________, for example for cleaning or gardening?
- whether the tenant has to pay a ______________________, and if so, what it covers and under which circumstances the tenant might not be ______________________
- how the tenancy can be brought to an ______________________,
- what ______________________, if any, will be ______________________
- what ______________________ tenants have for ______________________ (the landlord will be responsible for ______________________ and ______________________ repairs)
- any other relevant information or ______________________, for example about ______________________, guests or smoking.

The owner's responsibilities toward the tenant are to provide ______________________, ______________________, and other ______________________ which are paid for by the tenant; to ______________________ in a timely manner to the tenant's ______________________; to keep the building and surrounding property in a ______________________, ______________________, and ______________________ condition; and to follow all other provisions provided by ______________________ and by the agreement with the tenant.

Providing quality services to the tenants should be top priority. If the tenants believe that the landlord does not ______________________ about them, then they will not be likely to care about the ______________________ or about paying their rent ______________________.

What, then, are the responsibilities of the ______________________? In general, the tenant's are to pay the ______________________, ______________________ and other services ______________________ and on time; to keep the ________________ in good condition; and to ________________ causing ________________ to the property. The tenant should also ________________ from activities that would cause ________________ or annoyance to other tenants and should adhere to the ________________ provided by the law and by the ________________ with the ________________.

Periods of letting

Pre-listening activity

What are the advantages / disadvantages of fixed-term and periodic tenancy agreements? Complete the mind map.

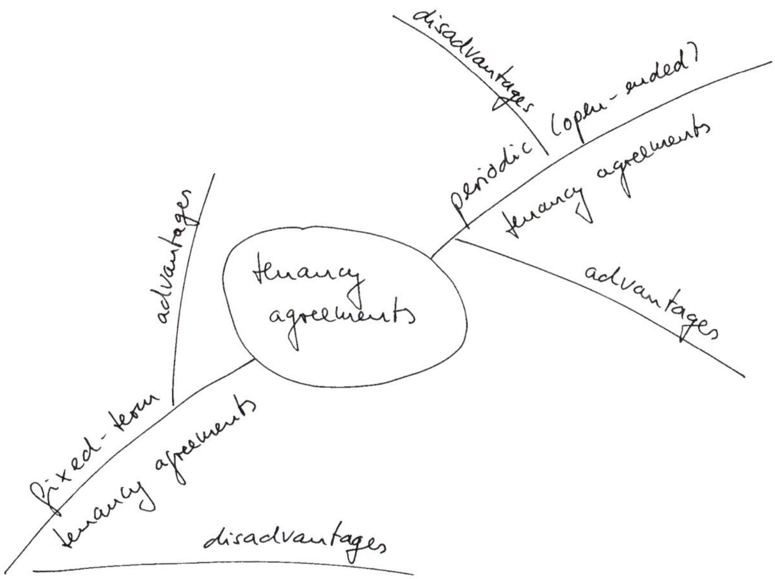

Now listen to the recording and add information on these types of tenancy agreements

Post-listening activity

Which type of tenancy agreement is more common in your company? Why?

How to be an effective landlord

Work in teams. Each team should have a look at one of the key tasks an effective landlord has to do quite regularly.

Have a look at the tips listed below in a jumbled order and copy those which have to do with your task.

Do you agree with these tips? Give reasons. Add more tips which you consider important. Please prepare to explain to the others what these tips mean in detail.

Please also produce a list of technical terms that have to do with your task.

Give a short talk to the class in which you explain what your task means for being an effective landlord.

CHOOSING TENANTS	COLLECTING AND RETURNING DEPOSITS	THE RENT
INSPECTION AND ENTRY	NON-PAYMENT AND EVICTION	REPAIRS AND MAINTENANCE
MANAGING THE PROPERTY	AGREEMENTS BETWEEN LANDLORD AND TENANT	

Tips on how to be a good landlord

- Select your tenants carefully.
- When writing a newspaper ad to let your unit, make sure to give accurate descriptions.
- The owner's responsibilities toward the tenant are to provide heat, electricity, and other services paid for by the tenant; to respond in a timely manner to the tenant's complaints; to keep the building and surrounding property in a safe, clean, and well-maintained condition; and to follow all other provisions provided by law and by the agreement with the tenant.
- It's unlawful to discriminate against an applicant because of race, national origin, religion, marital status, sex or physical disabilities.
- The landlord should keep tenant records that will allow him to see which tenants will have leases expiring and which tenants will be moving out in the next few months.
- Before the apartment is turned over to a new tenant, the landlord must check that the apartment is ready for occupancy and that all equipment (appliances, lights, toilets, taps) is in good working order.
- If a tenant has in any way damaged your property beyond what would be considered normal wear and tear, you have the right to keep funds considered as security deposits and/or cleaning deposits.

- Normal use will age any property to some extent.
- Include a statement in your rental agreement that requires an immediate inspection at the time the tenant gives notice of his leaving.
- A security deposit is an up-front payment that is held as collateral against any financial default or damage to the unit or other property.
- It's usually best to find a family or a person that can be recommended by a current tenant of yours.
- In a rental property, vacant units are unoccupied apartments or commercial units that do not generate income for the property. The income lost from these units is referred to as a "vacancy loss" and occurs if there is any period of time when the full rent is not collected for the unit. It is in the interest of the owner and the property's cash flow to minimize vacancy loss.
- Never let to the first person through the door.
- Use move-in and move-out check lists to clearly monitor the status of your flat.
- Include a final inspection the last day the tenant occupies your property.
- Only enter your property for repairs and maintenance works after approval from the tenant.
- Perform a thorough check of each applicant.
- If the tenant fails to live up to the terms of the agreement, this deposit will help you to defray some of the costs of evicting the tenant.
- The tenant has a right to occupy the apartment provided that he meets the other terms of the agreement, such as paying rent on time.
- Your main consideration for determining the rental amount is based on rents of comparable rental units in the area.
- Make sure your tenants know exactly when the rent is due.
- Make it clear that you expect prompt payment.
- This deposit might be applied to any damage that occurs while the tenant is occupying the unit.
- Even though you carefully selected your tenant from all the other applicants, things can go wrong. Job loss, illness, divorce, all kinds of things can hinder someone's ability to make timely rental payments. You may want to go easy on a tenant with a good payment record.
- You may offer your current tenants an incentive for recommending strong prospects.
- An open-ended lease contains no fixed term and allows the tenant to continue renting the apartment until she decides to leave.
- The more people who live in a unit, the more wear and tear, noise, damage, etc. One way to keep the crowds down is to limit the number of tenants per unit. Have this stipulated in your rental agreement.
- If booze and drug parties, loud noise or music, or property destruction occurs, you may have grounds for eviction.
- If the unit has been damaged beyond normal wear-and-tear, or if there are outstanding financial obligations from the tenant (such as unpaid rent), the landlord should deduct such expenses from the security deposit and refund the balance, if any, to the tenant.
- The move-out inspection should use the same form that was completed for the move-in inspection so that any conditions noted at that time are taken into account.

- If the tenant intends to move out, the landlord should review the move-out procedures with the tenant and schedule a move-out inspection and a move-out date.
- Do not interfere in your tenants lives.
- Once the inspection is completed, the tenant must sign the move-out inspection form.
- Send a letter advising the tenant of move-out procedures and the requirements for the return of his security deposit. This letter should state the tenant's obligation to return all unit and common area keys; thoroughly clean the unit (including appliances); remove all furniture, belongings, and trash; and provide a forwarding address.
- Each tenant file should contain the following documents: copy of tenant lease; tenant correspondence; apartment inspection forms; legal paperwork accounting forms; rent or service charge increases; status of security deposit.
- After the inspection, the landlord must determine whether any damages or cleaning charges should be deducted from the security deposit.
- Possible services that may be obtained from contractors include cleaning of stairwells, corridors and other interior common areas; trash pick-up on the surrounding grounds; pest control; snow removal; grounds or landscape maintenance; elevator maintenance; non-routine services such as concrete repairs, major painting projects, or major roof repairs or replacement; an annual outside audit of the property's financial records; or legal services.
- If the tenants believe that the landlord does not care about them, then they will not be likely to care about the property or about paying their rent on time. If the tenants feel that they are being treated fairly and that there is a sense of partnership with the owner and the housing manager, then they may be more willing to do their part to keep the property in good condition.
- Preventive maintenance is the process of scheduling and performing routine care and component replacement to reduce unscheduled interruptions of service.
- Routine maintenance is the process of inspecting equipment and facilities and responding appropriately if conditions deviate from their normal condition, and of responding to requests for repairs from tenants.
- Emergencies are defined as events that interrupt essential services in the building or otherwise endanger tenants, such as no heat in winter, no water, odour of gas, major water leak damage (or risk of damage) to units or the common areas, frozen pipes, or a power outage.
- Any drug related criminal action in the building or the locality may also result in tenant eviction.
- Be particularly careful where a tenant has left the property unoccupied for extended periods.
- Encourage tenants to report defects promptly and to allow you access by always dealing with problems as quickly as you can.
- If things go wrong, never try to use force or other means to gain entry or try to evict a tenant - you must apply for a court possession order giving specific grounds.
- If the tenant always refuses to comply with the requirements of the lease, even after he has been warned, or go against the central, state or local law

and other tasks of the tenant as cited in the rental contract, the landlord can evict him.

- Tenant eviction can also be caused by unlawful deeds or if the actions of the tenants threat the security of people residing in the building or in the surrounding area

Have a look at the building below and match the building components and correct terms.

basins, baths, wcs, pipework, water heaters	window frames and glass	gutters and down-pipes	roof tiles	garden walls
drains	chimney	water supply	gas supply	other gas and electrical appli-ances supplied by landlord
internal doors	ceilings	gas and electric space heaters	floors	walls
cold water and tank boiler	electric wiring	stairs	insulation	gas/electric meter box

Source: University of Birmingham

UNIT 4
Aspects of letting

Work through the following material (1-5) and prepare an English text in which you explain the concept of "Warm-" and "Kaltmiete".

Explaining the rent

1. THE RENT

fixed monthly amount as written down in the tenancy agreement; to be paid to the landlord in advance

+

variable costs for any utilities associated with the flat; costs for

- heating,
- water,
- sewage,
- waste removal,
- chimney sweeping,
- garden upkeep,
- services provided by the caretaker,
- street cleaning
- insurances
- property taxes
- lifts and communal areas
- laundry facilities

Often, these costs have to be paid to the landlord (who is charged by the utility providers) in advance; should the tenant's payment be higher than the actual consumption, the tenant will be refunded at the end of the billing period; in case the consumption exceeds the payment, the tenant will be asked to pay the difference.

GERMAN	definition	symbol	GERMAN	definition	symbol	GERMAN	definition	symbol
Grund-steuer			Wasserver-sorgung			Entwässe-rung		
Heizungs-kosten			Warm-wasser-kosten			Aufzug		
Straßen-reinigung			Müllab-fuhr			Hausreini-gung		
Garten-pflege			Schorn-steinreini-gung			Allgemein-beleuch-tung		
Sach- und Haftpflicht-versiche-rungen			Hauswart			Gemein-schaftsan-tenne		
Wasch-einrich-tungen								

A		**1:** a capital tax on property imposed by municipalities; based on the estimated value of the property	I	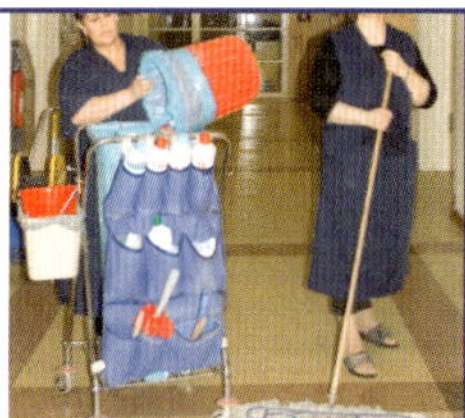	**2:** costs associated with a lift in the building
B	**LIABILITY INSURANCE.**	**3:** costs for waste matter carried away in sewers or drains	J		**4:** costs for any utility to warm a building
C		**5:** costs for any facility that provides a source of water and for the water itself	K		**6:** costs for waste removal
D		**7:** costs for the cleaning of public roads and sidewalks	L		**8:** costs associated with the supply of hot water

E		**9:** costs for cleaning of the chimney	**M**		**10:** costs for the cleaning of stairways and other common areas
F		**11:** costs for garden upkeep	**N**		**12:** costs for any electricity used in common rooms (such as lighting the staircase etc.)
G		**13:** costs for any insurance needed to run the building	**O**		**14:** costs associated with any communal areal installation
H		**15:** costs for any laundry facilities provided for the tenants	**P**		**16:** any costs associated with the services offered by a caretaker

3. Die zweite Miete: Nebenkosten

Jedes Jahr flattern den Mietern die Nebenkostenabrechnungen ins Haus, längst als zweite Miete bezeichnet. Nicht nur die Kosten für Strom und Heizenergie wie Gas und Öl haben mittlerweile einen Höchststand erreicht, auch Wasser, Abwasser und Steuern haben kräftig an der Preisschraube gedreht.

Der Deutsche Mieterbund befürchtet, dass diese enormen Preissteigerungen auch im nächsten Winter weitergehen werden. Die Eigentümerverbände wie z. B. *Haus und Grund* schließen sich dieser Auffassung an. Mieter sollten schon jetzt für die kommende Heizkostensaison Rücklagen bilden. Empfohlen wird eine Summe von 20 bis 30 € monatlich. Darüber hinaus ist konsequentes Energiesparen angesagt.

38 % der Gesamtmiete gehen mittlerweile für die Nebenkosten drauf, bei weitem der höchste Wert seit 1945. Alleine im letzten Jahr betrug die Steigerung dieses Anteils 4 %. In einigen Regionen kann diese Belastung sogar noch höher ausfallen.

Hauptverursacher für den Preisauftrieb sind also vor allem die Energiekosten. Ein Drei-Personen-Haushalt in einer 70-Quadratmeter-Wohnung muss in diesem Jahr gut 300 Euro mehr für Licht, Heizung und Warmwasser zahlen, etwa 30 Prozent mehr als noch vor fünf Jahren, so der DMB. Für Gaskunden beispielsweise sind das ca. 135 Euro mehr als noch 2000, für Heizölverbraucher schätzungsweise 160 Euro. Für Strom muss die Familie Mehrbelastungen von 170 Euro schultern.

Doch nicht nur die Mieter sind von dieser wachsenden Belastung betroffen. Auch die Vermieter leiden unter dem enormen Kostendruck. Für Modernisierungen und Investitionen bleiben immer weniger Finanzmittel übrig.

4. Betriebskosten

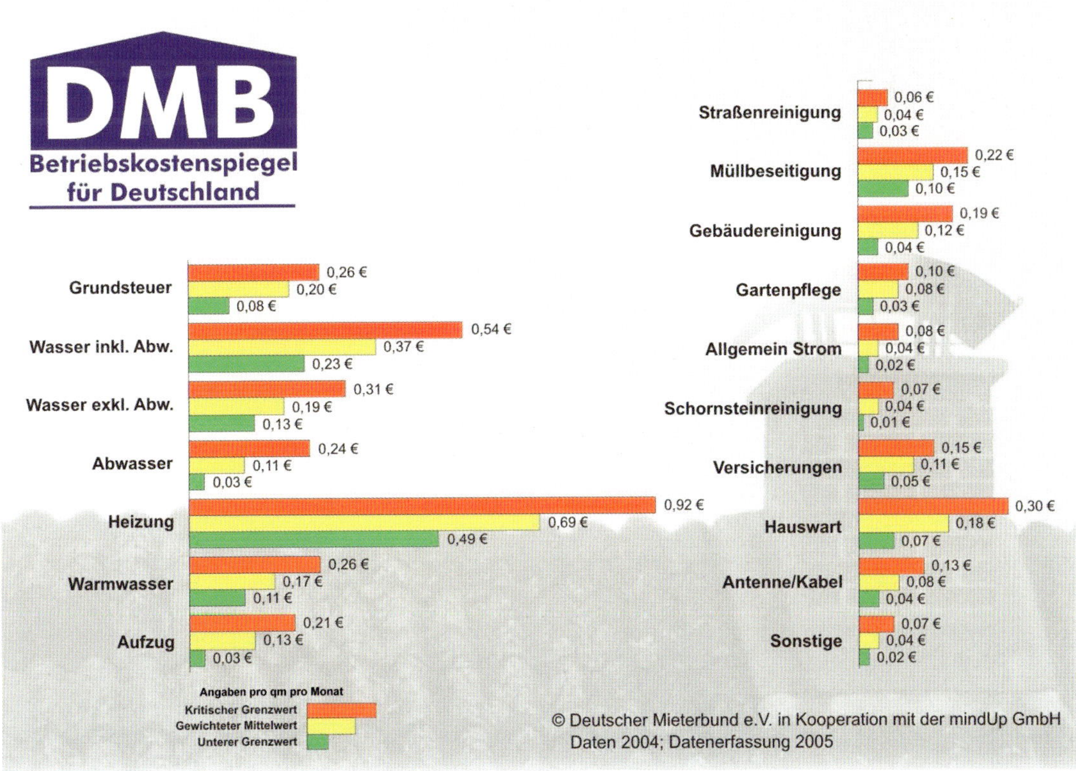

5.

Most tenants have to pay additional charges to cover the cost of maintaining the building they live in. These costs cover the share of the cost of maintaining the building they live in. These charges, also called service charges, usually cover things like repairs, cleaning, and shared amenities such as porters and communal gardens. All tenants normally have to pay a share of everything even if they don't use some of the services. For example, even if you live on the ground floor and never use the lift, you will probably still have to pay something towards its maintenance. If you are not sure what your service charges cover, check your lease. It should say clearly:

- what services you have to pay for and when
- how your landlord can collect the charges
- how service charges are calculated
- how they are divided between you and any other tenants

The amount you pay can vary from one year to the next (variable service charges). If your lease doesn't give enough information about service charges or what it says isn't fair (for example if it means your landlord makes a profit), get advice. You are entitled to a written breakdown of your service charges to check whether the costs are reasonable. You have the right to inspect and take copies of accounts, receipts and any other relevant documents.

Richtig lesen auf dem Weg zu einem detaillierten Textverständnis

Richtiges und aktives Lesen ist der Schlüssel zu einem detaillierten Textverständnis. Wenn Sie einen Ihnen unbekannten Text mit dem Ziel eines genauen Textverständnisses lesen, haben sich die folgenden Schritte und Vorgehensweisen bewährt:

Schritt 1

Verschaffen Sie sich anhand des Titels, möglicher Bilder und Grafiken, des Erscheinungskontextes und der Abschnittüberschriften einen ersten Überblick über den Text. Was ist das Thema? Worum geht es vermutlich im Einzelnen?

Schritt 2

Stellen Sie vor dem eigentlichen Leseprozess Fragen an den Text und werden somit beim Lesen zu jemandem, der aktiv nach Informationen sucht. Dieser Schritt verändert Ihre Rolle von einem passiv Aufnehmenden zu einem Leser, der Vorwissen zu dem Thema des Textes aktiviert und schneller Bedeutungszusammenhänge versteht und konstruiert.

Schritt 3

Lesen Sie den Text. Markieren Sie Wichtiges und streichen die Wörter an, die sich Ihnen nicht durch einen Rückgriff auf bisher Bekanntes erschließen. Klären Sie unbekannte Vokabeln. Wenn Ihr Ziel ein Detailverständnis des Textes ist, bedeutet dieser Schritt eine aufmerksame, intensive Arbeit am Text. Wenn Sie zwischendurch den Faden verloren haben, müssen Sie erneut beginnen, bis sich Ihnen der gedankliche Aufbau des Textes in seinen Einzelheiten erschließt.

Schritt 4

Nach Abschluss der Lektüre sollten Sie den Text für sich rekapitulieren. Habe ich Antworten auf meine im Vorfeld gestellten Fragen erhalten? Welche Detailinformationen habe ich gerade aufgenommen? Haben sich meine Vorannahmen bestätigt? Sollte Ihnen dieses nicht möglich sein, müssen Sie den Text erneut lesen. Zur Sicherung des Textverständnisses hat es sich bewährt, dass Sie sich Notizen machen. Diese können Sie abschnittsweise sortieren oder auch in Form eines textrestrukturierenden Mindmaps wiedergeben, in dem Sie die zentralen Themen des Textes an die einzelnen Hauptzweige schreiben und dieses dann vervollständigen.

Schritt 5

Der abschließende Schritt bedeutet ein Rekapitulieren des gerade Erfassten. Überfliegen Sie den Text mit seinen Abschnittsüberschriften und fragen sich: Ist mir klar, worum es hier genau geht? Wenn Sie die vorherigen Schritte sorgfältig ausgeführt haben, ist dieser Schritt schnell ausgeführt und verschafft Ihnen die Gewissheit: Ich habe diesen Text in all seinen Details verstanden!

The Salt Lake Tribune

Devices help save on utility costs in apartment complexes
Utah entrepreneur: Tenant use is measured and billed individually; conservation can result
By Rosemary Winters

Dave Jenkins coupled his concern for the environment with recognition of a market niche when he launched Conservice five years ago in North Logan. The entrepreneur saw the utility billing service as a way to reduce water consumption and energy use among apartment dwellers - and make a buck.

Because most apartment buildings have one master meter for each utility, Conservice installs sub-meters on apartments so tenants can be directly responsible for the amount they consume.

"What we find is that when you pay for what you use, you use less," Jenkins says.

It also means property managers don't have to include utilities in rent prices, which can cause rent to rise rapidly with the cost of energy. And tenants are more likely to report leaky faucets and toilets immediately, Jenkins says. Many will stop wasteful practices such as leaving unused lights on or letting the shower run several minutes to warm up.

"It absolutely makes it easier to evaluate rent," says Janae Jarvis, regional manager for Logan-based Wasatch Property Management, a Conservice client. "The program is very easy to administer."

The industry is relatively new to the United States, but has grown rapidly in the past 10 years. More than 1.2 million apartments receive utility bills from businesses such as Conservice, according to the National Multi Housing Council.

Jenkins, chief executive of Conservice, started the company in 2001 after working for a property management company and finding its utility billing service subpar. Conservice developed a wireless technology that allows it to read meters remotely and capture the data for analysis and billing.

A $3 to $4 service charge is added to each tenant's bill, and property managers are not charged.

The company has grown from annual revenue of $400,000 in 2002 to close to $5 million in 2005. Conservice has 72 employees and bills close to 200,000 apartments in more than 35 states. It's become one of the largest utility billing service companies in the nation.

In addition to submetering, Conservice also provides Ratio Utility Billing Systems, or RUBS, which estimate an apartment unit's usage based on factors such as apartment size, number of fixtures and number of occupants. RUBS is used by clients that cannot or do not want to install submeters.

RUBS has generated some controversy in recent years. A study released in 2004 by the U.S. Environmental Protection Agency found no evidence that RUBS lowered water use from traditional in-rent billing. In contrast, submetering cut consumption by 15.3 percent. Savings ranged from 11 percent to 26 percent, or 15 percent to 48 gallons per apartment per day.

Conservice has seen consumption drop in apartment complexes billed through RUBS, although less than in submetered properties, Jenkins says. Tenants' bills are still impacted by the amount they use, and they tend to police other residents to keep those bills low, he says. Jenkins points to a 1999 study prepared for the housing council and the National Apartment Association that reported drops in water use of 6 percent to 27 percent in RUBS properties and 18 percent to 39 percent in submetered apartments.

"Common sense would dictate when people start paying for water, regardless of the form of measurement, they will use less," says Marc Treitler general counsel for Conservice.

Jenkins hopes the company's services will help reduce the need for new water development in the arid West and keep water prices low.

Conservice also supplies water-saving devices, such as sink aerators and low-flow toilet flappers, and it attaches conservation tips to its bills.

"There's a limited supply of resources," Jenkins says. "Let's work together to use those resources wisely."

Source: The Salt Lake Tribune

ASSIGNMENTS

1. **Write a brief company profile of Conservice, the utility billing service company.**
2. **What is meant by Ratio Utility Billing Systems (RUBS)?**
3. **What, according to the text, are the main advantages of submetering the individual tenant's consumption?**
4. **Which methods do you use in your companies to allocate the costs of water, gas and electricity?**

Letting and presenting a flat

At GW BO one of your colleagues sends you a short note and the following letter:

Verfassen:

Senden Kontakte Rechtschr. Anhang Sicherheit Speichern

Von:

An:

Betreff:

Ein von mir betreuter Mieter will gegen die Nebenkostenabrechnung angehen, die er von uns bekommen hat. Obwohl ich sie ihm am Telefon versucht habe zu erklären – mein Englisch reicht dafür nicht ganz aus –, hat er nun den Mieterschutzbund eingeschaltet. In einem Brief hat er mir dieses mitgeteilt und auch die Kopie des Schreibens an den Mieterschutzbund beigefügt. Können Sie mir dieses bitte kurz zusammenfassen, damit ich eine entsprechende Stellungnahme vorbereiten kann?

Danke!

Clive Bullock
Essener Landwehr 55
44787 Bochum

Mieterschutzbund Bochum
Sprockhöveler Str. 63
44801 Bochum

March 27, 200...

Dear Sir or Madam,

billing of utility costs

First of all I would like to point out that I'm glad that it is possible for me to write this letter in English as my German isn't good enough to discuss legal problems.

I'm renting a flat from GW BO here in Bochum and was now sent the bill for my utility costs. Now I've got several questions which I hope you can answer:

Although I pay a lump sum of 91.00 EUR per month for my utility costs, I should now pay another 356 EUR. How can this amount be explained and what does it consist of? On which basis was the lump sum calculated at the beginning of the billing period?

How is the actual consumption of water and energy metered for every tenant? What is the difference between transferable and non-transferable costs?

Is it right that all insurance costs are passed on directly to the tenants?

If all this is not acceptable, what can I do against this bill of utility costs?

You see that there are many questions I cannot answer myself. Therefore, I would be glad if one of your English-speaking staff could find the time to explain to me all the details in a personal meeting.

I would be pleased to hear from you soon by letter or by email (bullseye@surfeu.com).

Thank you very much for your assistance.

Yours faithfully
Clive Bullock

Explaining the rent

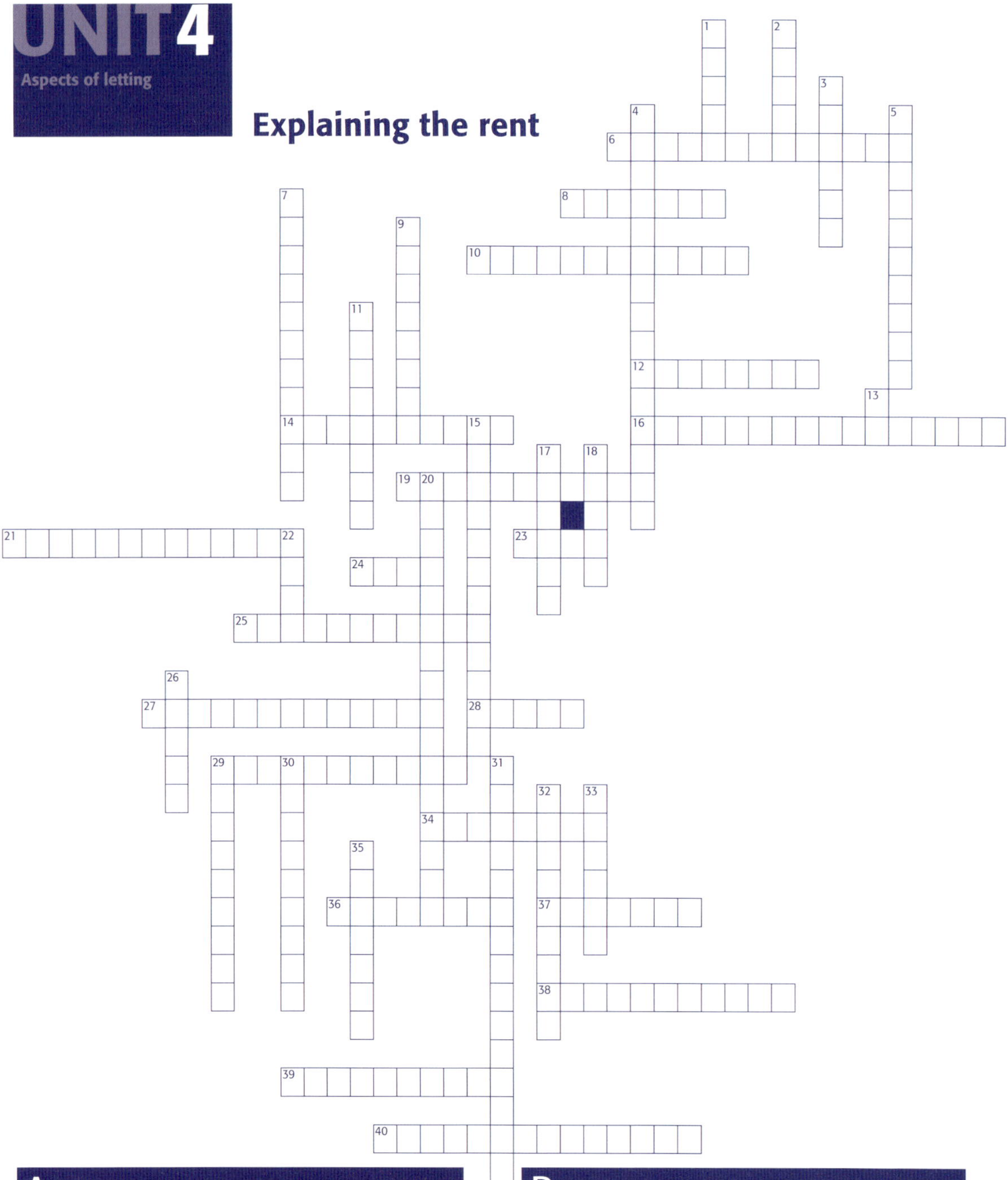

Across

6. Modernisierung
8. Heizung
10. Waschküche
12. Schätzung
14. im Voraus
16. Stromrechnung
19. Einzelablesung
21. Müllabfuhr
23. einsparen
24. Abrechnung
25. Wasseruhr
27. Gartenpflege
28. messen
29. Verbrauch
34. Steigerung
36. Vertrag
37. monatlich
38. Strom
39. Verbrauchszuweisung; Umlage
40. Abrechnungszeitraum

Down

1. Wasser
2. Steuern
3. tatsächlich
4. Energiekosten
5. Versicherungen
7. Berechnung
9. Kabelfernsehen
11. veränderlich
13. bis
15. Gemeinschaftsräume
17. Abwasser
18. festgelegt
20. Versorgungsunternehmen
22. Aufzug
26. verschwenden
29. Hausmeister
30. Treppenhaus
31. Straßenreinigung
32. Gasuhr
33. Erstattung
35. zur Verfügung stellen

Back at GW BO

DAY 1 Tuesday, 10 a.m. the phone rings...

Landlord:
Sie arbeiten für GW BO in Bochum. Sie haben eine 95 m² große 3-Zimmer-Wohnung (Küche, Diele, Bad) in der Nähe der Stadtmitte Bochums inseriert. Die Kaltmiete beläuft sich auf 490 €, an Nebenkosten entstehen weitere 110 € monatlich.
Erklären Sie dem Interessenten, wie sich diese Nebenkosten zusammensetzen.
Die Wohnung ist zentral gelegen, in der Nähe gibt es eine Straßenbahnhaltestelle und ausreichende Einkaufsmöglichkeiten. Die Stadtmitte ist in 10 Minuten zu Fuß zu erreichen. Die Wohnung befindet sich im 2. OG eines Mehrfamilienhauses und hat einen kleinen Balkon.
Die Wohnung wird in vier Wochen nach Abschluss einiger Reparaturarbeiten (neue Fliesen in Küche und Badezimmer) bezugsfertig.
Beantworten Sie die Fragen eines englischsprachigen Anrufers, der zum ersten Mal in Deutschland eine Wohnung anmieten möchte.

Holen Sie des Weiteren alle für Sie für eine Vermietung relevanten Informationen ein.

Potential tenant:
Sie sind Michael (Fiona) Bishop und haben in der Zeitung eine Anzeige für eine Wohnung gesehen, die Sie interessiert. Gerne möchten Sie mit Ihrer Verlobten (Ihrem Verlobten) dort einziehen. Sie haben in Deutschland einen 2-Jahres-Vertrag bei einer Speditionsfirma (haulage company) als Sachbearbeiter, Ihre Frau arbeitet als Bibliothekarin (librarian).

Sie haben diese Informationen: 95 m² große 3-Zimmer-Wohnung (Küche, Diele, Bad) in der Nähe der Stadtmitte Bochums. Fragen Sie nach der Lage der Wohnung und nach der Umgebung. Lassen Sie sich die Miete erklären (aus England kennen Sie bisher nur „furnished property").

Sie kennen den Preis von 490 €, wissen aber nicht, was „Kaltmiete" und „Warmmiete" bedeutet.

Lassen Sie sich die „Nebenkosten" erklären.

Geben Sie alle relevanten Informationen über sich.

Vereinbaren Sie einen Besichtigungstermin für morgen, 15 Uhr.

DAY 2 Wednesday, 3 pm

You prepare for the meeting in the afternoon and have another look at the floor plan to be able to present the flat properly.

Then, at 3 pm, you meet the Bishops and show them the flat giving them all the necessary information. Your first impression is that they quite like the flat but ask for another day to take a final decision. They promise to get in touch either by phone or in writing.

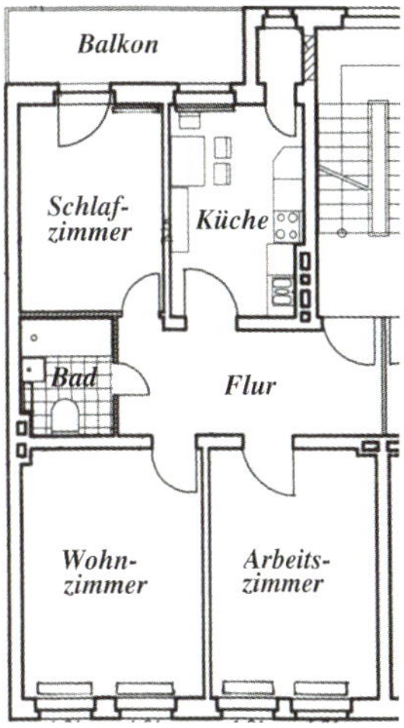

DAY 3 Thursday

Since you are quite sure that the Bishops are seriously interested in the flat, you have a look at your notes again to be prepared to answer possible questions about the tenancy agreement your company asks them to sign. You also talk to the head of repairs and refurbishment and get the answer that the tenants can choose the tiles in the kitchen and in the bathroom as long as they stick to the spending limit. Any additional costs would have to be borne by them.

DAY 4 Friday

You find the following letter in today's mail:

Dear Sir or Madam,

3-bedroom flat 42 Kolkstraße in Bochum

Thank you once again for showing us round the flat in Kolkstraße last Wednesday.

We very much like this flat and have come to the decision that we would like to rent it. There is one question, however, which we did not really understand on Tuesday: Obviously there are some repair works that need to be carried out (tiles in kitchen and bathroom). Who is going to pay for them? If you have to do these works anyway, would there be a chance for us to suggest which tiles we prefer?

Since we are not at all familiar with any legal aspects of renting accommodation in Germany, we would very much like to discuss these matters with you in detail, if at all possible.

We really appreciate that you speak English as our German definitely is not yet good enough to talk about all matters involved. As you asked us to send you any questions we might have in advance to prepare for this meeting, we enclose two documents we would like to refer to when we'll meet: The first one is a hand-written list of questions we would like to ask which have to do with the flat itself. Sure, we had the chance to see the flat and you really gave us enough time on Monday - but we have to admit that we didn't pay enough attention to all the details which have come up in the meantime.

Secondly, we have been told that in Germany the landlord quite often completes a kind of move-in check-list. As we are not familiar with any of these lists in German, we have photocopied an English list we would very much like to take as a basis for this inspection. Maybe we can compare your German list with our document?

Could you please also do us a huge favour and prepare a short summary of a German Mietvertrag and a Hausordnung? We know that these things are important documents but none of our friends seems to be able to tell us in detail what they include.

We suggest that we come to your office on Tuesday at 4 pm on our way home from work. Should this be inconvenient for you, please call us and suggest another date. It is probably best to contact me on my mobile: 0172 7362718293.

Once again, thank you very much for your understanding and the troubles you took for helping us.

Looking forward to seeing you in your office on Tuesday.

Yours faithfully,
Michael Bishop

Our check list

- Who lives around us in the building? What about in adjacent properties and in the neighbourhood generally?
- Is the exterior of the building clean and well maintained?
- Does a caretaker live there or nearby?
- Are there private grounds around the building?
- Does the apartment need to be painted? If so, who will paint it and/or pay for the paint?
- Does the building have a security system?
- Are the hallways well lit? Are there fire extinguishers and smoke detectors?
- Is the street well lit?
- Does the apartment door have an adequate lock? Is there a dead bolt?
- What happens if we lose our keys?
- Who do we call for emergencies or repairs? Is there someone on call at all times for emergencies?
- Are there laundry facilities in the building? If not, are there facilities nearby?
- Is there storage space allocated for us outside the apartment?
- Is there a private secure mailbox?
- Is private parking available? If so, is it free?
- How close are grocery and convenience stores to the apartment? What about other shops, restaurants, entertainment, etc.?
- How, where, and when do we dispose of trash?
- Are there sufficient wall outlets?

- Are there sufficient phone jacks?
- How many windows are there in the flat? Do they open and close? Do they lock? Are screens provided?
- Who pays for utilities? What is the average cost per month?
- How is the apartment heated (gas or electric)? Who pays for and/or controls the heat? When is it turned on?
- Are the appliances gas or electric? When were they last serviced?
- Is there ample water pressure in both the kitchen and bathroom?
- Who pays for water? Do the faucets, traps, or toilets leak?
- Are there any signs of water damage around water fixtures or on the ceiling?
- Are there restrictions on decorating the flat?
- Are draperies, curtain rods, or blinds included?
- Are there any restrictions regarding guests, parties, etc.?
- Is there sufficient privacy?
- Are there limits to the number of occupants permitted in the apartment?
- What are the requirements for a full refund of our security deposit?
- Are pets or children allowed?

TENANT´S MOVE IN AND OUT CONDITION CHECK LIST

(Form first Completed by Landlord, Next, Tenant(s) fill out Comments & Sign at bottom, **Original to Landlord and Copy to Tenant(s)**)

Tenant Name(s)			
Address & Apt. No.	City	State	Zip

Move-in Date	Inspection Date	Time	By
Move-Out Date	Inspection Date	Time	By

Unless otherwise noted, the premises are clean, in good working order and undamaged. Use the key codes provided.

KEY CODES: **NC** - needs cleaning, **NP** - needs painting, **RP** - replace, **NR** - needs repair, **NS** -needs spot cleaning
NSP - needs spot painting, **SC** - scratched ______

BEDROOM 1	Move-In	Move-Out	Est. Cost
FLOOR			
WALLS			
CEILING			
DOORS			
WINDOWS			
SCREENS			
CLOSET			
SHADES/BLINDS			
ELEC FIXTURES			
LIGHT BULBS			

BEDROOM 2			
FLOOR			
WALLS			
CEILING			
DOORS			
WINDOWS			
SCREENS			
CLOSET			
SHADES/BLINDS			
ELEC FIXTURES			
LIGHT BULBS			

BEDROOM 3			
FLOOR			
WALLS			
CEILING			
DOORS			
WINDOWS			
SCREENS			
CLOSET			
SHADES/BLINDS			
ELEC FIXTURES			
LIGHT BULBS			

HALL/STAIRS/ENTRY			
WALLS			
CEILING			
DRAPES/BLINDS			
CLOSET			
DOORS			
FLOOR			
WINDOWS			
SCREENS			
ELEC FIXTURES			
LIGHT BULBS			

LIVING ROOM	Move-In	Move-Out	Est. Cost
FLOOR			
WALLS			
CEILING			
DOORS			
WINDOWS			
SCREENS			
SHADES			
CLOSET			
ELEC FIXTURES			
LIGHT BULBS			

KITCHEN			
FLOORS			
WALLS			
CEILING			
DOORS			
WINDOWS			

BATH			
FLOORS			
WALLS			
CEILING			
DOORS			
CABINETS			
DRAWERS			
SINK/FAUCET			
SHELVES			
MIRROR			
TUB/SHOWER			
CAULKING			
COUNTER TOPS			
FAN			
BOWL/SEAT			
TOWEL RACKS			
WINDOW			
ELEC FIXTURES			
LIGHT BULBS			

NO. OF KEYS			
FRONT DOOR			
LAUNDRY ROOM			
MAIL BOX			

MECHANICAL			
HOT WATER HEATER			
SMOKE DETECTOR			
THERMOSTAT			
FURNACE			
AIR CONDITIONER			
AIR COND. FILTER			

COMMENTS ______

______

______

______

I/We (the tenant(s)) understand that unless otherwise noted, all discrepancies will be tenant's responsibility and will be deducted from the security deposit at time of move out.

______
Tenant (Signature)

______
Tenant (Signature)

______
Landlord / Agent (Signature)

Tenant's Forwarding Address ______

______

______

DAY 5 Monday

In order to be able to explain to the Bishops what they are expected to sign, you have a closer look at your "Übergabeprotokoll" and compare it with the document they photocopied for you.

ÜBERGABEPROTOKOLL

Mieter: ....
Ort: ....
Straße: ....
Lage (Stockwerk): ....

Zustand - Mängel - fehlende Ausstattung

DIELE

Fußboden: ❑ Parkett ❑ Laminat
❑ Teppich ❑ PVC ❑ Estrich ....
Türen: ....
Decken: ....
Wände: ....
Elektroinstallation: ....
Heizkörper: ....

BAD

Fußboden: ❑ PVC ❑ Fliesen ....
Wände: ❑ Fliesen ❑ ....
Badewanne ❑ Dusche ❑ ....
WC: ....
Waschbecken: ....
Armaturen: ....
Sonstiges: ....
Türen: ....
Decken: ....
Elektroinstallation: ....
Heizkörper: ....
Fenster: ....

KÜCHE

Fußboden: ❑ Fliesen ❑ Laminat
❑ PVC ❑ Estrich ....
Türen: ....
Decken: ....
Wände: ....
Elektroinstallation: ....
Heizkörper: ....
Fenster: ....
Sonstige Ausstattung: ....

WOHNZIMMER

Fußboden: ❑ Parkett ❑ Laminat
❑ Teppich ❑ PVC ❑ Estrich ....

Türen:	....
Decken:	....
Wände:	....
Elektroinstallation:	....
Heizkörper:	....
Fenster:	....
Sonstiges:	....

SCHLAFZIMMER

Fußboden: ❑ Parkett ❑ Laminat ❑ Teppich ❑ PVC ❑ Estrich	....
Türen:	....
Decken:	....
Wände:	....
Elektroinstallation:	....
Heizkörper:	....
Fenster:	....
Sonstiges:	....

KINDERZIMMER

Fußboden: ❑ Parkett ❑ Laminat ❑ Teppich ❑ PVC ❑ Estrich	....
Türen:	....
Decken:	....
Wände:	....
Elektroinstallation:	....
Heizkörper:	....
Fenster:	....
Sonstiges:	....

ABSTELLRAUM

....

KELLER

....

Schlüssel	..... Hauseingang ..... W.-Eingang ..... Zimmer
Zählerstände	Gas: .... Wasser: .... Strom: ....

Der/die Mieter bestätigt/en, die Wohnung in o. g. aufgeführtem Zustand übernommen zu haben. Die Wohnung ist – bis auf die nachfolgend genannten Restarbeiten – frei von Mängeln:

....

Der Vermieter verpflichtet sich, folgende Arbeiten bis zum .... durchzuführen:

....

....

Ich/Wir erkennen die Richtigkeit der vorstehenden Wohnungsübergabe an:

Ort/Datum.........................	Ort/Datum.........................	Ort/Datum.........................
Vermieter.........................	Mieter.............................	Zeuge/n...........................

Furthermore, you look at your standard „Hausordnung" and prepare a brief summary of the individual topics in English.

HAUSORDNUNG

Fassung 1979

Das Zusammenleben in einer Hausgemeinschaft erfordert gegenseitige Rücksichtnahme aller Hausbewohner. Um das ungestörte Zusammenleben zu erreichen, ist die nachfolgende Hausordnung als rechtsverbindlicher Bestandteil des Mietvertrages einzuhalten.

I. Schutz vor Lärm

1) Vermeidbarer Lärm belastet unnötig alle Hausbewohner. Deshalb ist Musizieren während der allgemeinen Ruhezeiten von 13 bis 15 Uhr und von 22 bis 7 Uhr untersagt. Fernseh-, Radio- und Tongeräte sind stets auf Zimmerlautstärke einzustellen; die Benutzung im Freien (auf Balkonen, Loggien usw.) darf die übrigen Hausbewohner nicht stören.

2) Sind bei hauswirtschaftlichen und handwerklichen Arbeiten in Haus, Hof oder Garten belästigende Geräusche nicht zu vermeiden (Klopfen von Teppichen und Läufern, Staubsaugen, Rasenmähen, Basteln und dergleichen), so sind diese Verrichtungen werktags in der Zeit von 8 bis 12 Uhr und von 15 bis 18 Uhr vorzunehmen.

3) Baden und Duschen sollte in der Zeit von 22 bis 6 Uhr unterbleiben, so weit auf Grund der Bauart des Gebäudes die Nachtruhe der übrigen Hausbewohner gestört wird.

II. Sicherheit

1) Zum Schutz der Hausbewohner sind die Haustür von 22 bis 6 Uhr und die Kellereingänge und Hoftüren ständig verschlossen zu halten.

2) Haus- und Hofeingänge, Treppen und Flure erfüllen ihren Zweck als Fluchtweg nur, wenn sie freigehalten werden. Sie dürfen daher nicht zugeparkt oder durch Fahr- und Motorräder, Kinderwagen usw. versperrt werden.

3) Das Lagern von feuergefährlichen, leicht entzündbaren sowie Geruch verursachenden Stoffen in Keller- oder Bodenräumen ist untersagt. Auf dem gemeinsamen Trockenboden dürfen keine Gegenstände abgestellt werden.

III. Reinigung

1) Haus und Grundstück sind rein zu halten. Verunreinigungen sind von dem verantwortlichen Hausbewohner unverzüglich zu beseitigen.

2) Die Hausbewohner haben die Kellerflure, Treppen, die Treppenhausfenster, Treppenhausflure und den Boden abwechselnd nach einem bei Bedarf aufzustellenden Reinigungsplan zu reinigen.

3) So weit vertraglich nichts anderes vorgesehen, haben die Hausbewohner abwechselnd nach einem bei Bedarf vom Wohnungsunternehmen aufzustellenden Reinigungsplan:

- die Zugangswege außerhalb des Hauses einschließlich der Außentreppen,
- den Hof,
- den Standplatz der Müllgefäße,
- den Bürgersteig vor dem Haus,
- die Fahrbahn, sofern es das in der Gemeinde geltende Ortsrecht bestimmt,

zu reinigen. Schnee und Eisbeseitigung und das Streuen bei Glätte erfolgt nach einem vom Wohnungsunternehmen aufzustellenden Plan. Maßnahmen gegen Winterglätte müssen zwischen 6 und 21 Uhr wirksam sein, so weit nicht durch behördliche Bestimmungen hierfür andere Zeiten festgelegt worden sind.

Kinderspielplätze

Die Sauberhaltung des Sandkastens nebst Umgebung gehört zu den Obliegenheiten der Eltern, deren Kinder im Sandkasten spielen. Das Spielen fremder Kinder auf dem zum Hause gehörenden Grundstück ist grundsätzlich nur in Gemeinschaft mit Kindern der Hausbewohner gestattet. Die Eltern der spielenden Kinder haben darauf zu achten, dass das benutzte Spielzeug nach Beendigung des Spielens aus dem Sandkasten entfernt wird. Haustiere sind vom Spielplatz fernzuhalten.

DAY 6 Tuesday 4 pm

Meet the Bishops

Work in groups of three. One of you works for GW BO, one of you is Michael, the other one is Fiona Bishop.

Role-play the situation. Try and address as many of the issues that might logically come up considering the correspondence before.

DAY 7 Wednesday

The Bishops have signed the tenancy agreement and have paid a deposit of two months' rent. The move-in date is the first of the following month. As you have also discussed the matter of the kitchen and bathroom tiles, you contact your tiler to arrange for the works to be carried out.

April 30th

You hand over the keys so that the Bishops can move in the following day, May 1st.

Energy costs

Have a look at the enclosed brochure which suggests ways to reduce the high energy consumption in buildings. Referring to your knowledge of energy consumption, insulation and other effective measures in your buildings, prepare a short talk on this subject. Make sure that you give your talk a clear structure and end it by clearly expressing your opinion on this matter.

Energy use in buildings

In the EU 15, buildings account for 40 % of all energy use of which half could be saved through simple and effective measures, such as **better insulation**. This is a poor state of affairs.

The story on the new Member States is even worse. As in the EU 15, the new Member States use over 40 % of their energy in buildings. CO_2 emissions per square meter of floor space are 35 % higher, due in large part to lower levels of thermal insulation. This means more waste but also a greater opportunity to save energy.

80 % is simple

Simple energy efficiency measures including improved wall, roof and cellar insulation, better windows and a more efficient boiler were shown to reduce energy use by 80 % in a Polish terraced house. These measures have a pay back period of only 9 years, yet will continue saving money for the entire lifetime of the house.

A crises waiting to become a success story

What the new ECOSYS study demonstrates is that by ensuring that energy efficiency is central to the renovation process, this process can be changed from an expensive burden to an economical, social and environmental success story:

- **Economical:** An appropriate energy efficiency retrofit would create 1.7 billion EURO a year in energy savings – substantially offsetting the overall annual renovation costs for existing buildings.
- **Social:** Retrofit programmes would not only create between 150,000 and 230,000 new jobs (EURIMA estimate), but would radically improve housing conditions and would protect vulnerable sections of society from future increases in energy prices.
- **Environmental:** Carbon dioxide emissions would be reduced by 14 million tonnes a year and air pollution could be reduced dramatically.

Which measures are most cost effective?

Insulation:

In the new Member States taking action to improve insulation levels almost always delivers costs savings. This is the case whether or not the measure is taken as part of the normal renovation cycle or solely to improve energy efficiency.

Insulation of external walls:

In all the countries under investigation, insulation measures were found to create cost savings when coupled with ongoing renovation.

In all countries except Estonia, Latvia and Lithuania, non-coupled measures were seen to create cost savings.

Insulation of roofs:

The insulation of roofs cannot be done as a coupled measure in the new Member States as the placing of insulation under rafters must be seen as an independent measure of maintenance of the roof. Nonetheless, improving insulation levels always creates costs savings in all the countries under investigation.

Insulation of cellar ceilings:

In all countries except Estonia, Latvia and Lithuania measures to improve insulation of the cellar ceiling are cost-effective. However, as for roofs this measure can only be carried out as an independent measure as the cellar ceiling is not usually subject to maintenance.

Other measures:

Replacing windows and changing the heating system were also investigated.

Windows: Upgrading windows to better levels of energy efficiency during a renovation cycle is always cost-effective in the new Member States.

Heating: Replacement of current heating systems with newer condensing gas boilers is seen to be cost effective in larger buildings if done as part of the replacement cycle of a boiler.

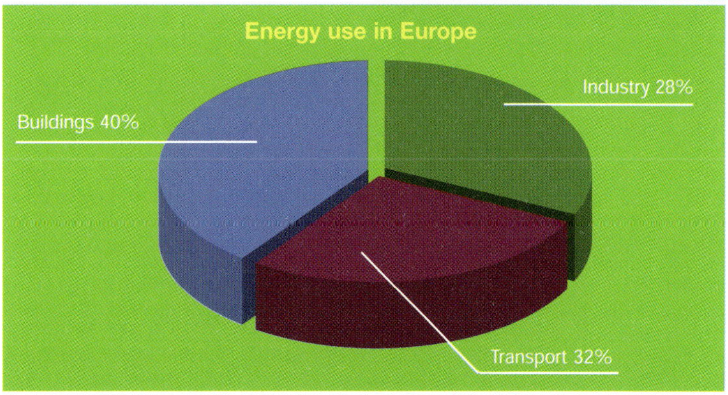

Source: EURIMA (European Insulation Manufacturing Association), http://www.eurima.org

Now explain the following diagram in English.

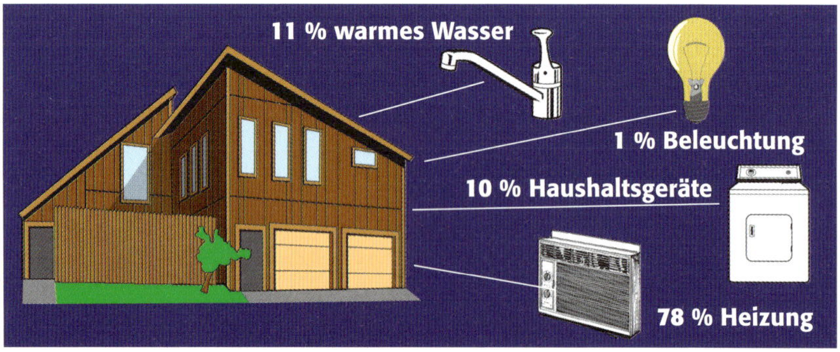

Now get together in four groups (heating, hot water, electrical appliances and lighting). In your groups, come up with ideas how your tenants could reduce their energy costs. Prepare to present your ideas to the rest of the class. Listen to the other presentations and discuss the suggestions made. Agree on those ideas that seem to be most practical and easy to communicate. Then complete the following tables.

Tips on reducing costs for …

HEATING	HOT WATER	ELECTRICAL APPLIANCES	LIGHTING

Listening Comprehension

Now listen to the recording on tips to reduce heating costs. Which other tips are mentioned? Which ones are more important for homeowners than tenants?

Enquiry for digital thermostats

Auf einer Haustechnikmesse in Schweden habe ich an einem Stand im Frühjahr einen neuartigen programmierbaren Heizungsregler gesehen, mit dem jede Gastherme individuell zeitgesteuert noch energiesparender eingestellt werden kann.

Bitte schreiben Sie eine unterschriftsreife Anfrage an den britischen Hersteller (Energy Technology Ltd, 10-16 Squires Walk, Lowestoft; NR32 4LA, Great Britain).

Diese Anfrage sollte Folgendes enthalten:

- Verweis auf Messe in Stockholm im April
- Überlegung, 1.000 unserer vor 1920 gebauten Altbauwohnungen mit diesem Regler auszustatten, um so eine Privatisierung voranzutreiben
- Produktanforderungen:
- wartungsfrei
- leicht zu bedienen
- tagesgenaue Programmierung
- 24-Stunden-Funktion
- Garantie?
- Anfrage nach Energieeinsparmöglichkeiten?
- Preisnachlass wegen großen Auftragsvolumens
- Hinweis: bei günstigem Angebot sind Folgeaufträge wahrscheinlich

One week later your boss sends you a short email with Energy Technolgy's answer to your letter.

Heute war in der Post die Antwort auf die Anfrage, die Sie an Energy Technology verfasst haben. Können Sie mir bitte eine kurze deutschsprachige Zusammenfassung dieses Briefes schreiben?

Energy Technology Ltd
10-16 Squires Walk, Lowestoft
NR32 4LA
Great Britain

Gemeinnützige Wohnungsbaugesellschaft Bochum
Kellerstraße 35-39
48456 Bochum
Germany

Dear Mr Witte,

your enquiry for digital thermostats

Thank you very much for your enquiry we received today. In turning to us you have chosen Britain's leading producer of heating technology.

We are pleased that we can offer you our new digital thermostat VPRO800 and are sure that this product will meet all of your requirements.

Our newly developed VPRO800 is absolutely effortless to use. Its logic and menu-driven programming respond to your choices and schedule for optimal comfort and energy savings. Moreover, this state-of-the-art product comes along with touch screen interaction, a real-time clock and a large, easy-to-read backlit display. Its easy-to-follow menu assists you in programming each day separately with no need to copy multiple days. All programming can be done on one screen.

Our research in our own laboratories has shown average energy savings of up to 33% on annual heating and cooling costs. As we are entirely convinced of the quality of this product, we offer a warranty of 5 years.

The list price of this product is € 68.45. In view of the size of this order, we are ready to grant you a discount of 25%. Of course we would also be prepared to send you a sample which you could test.

Please let us know if you would be interested in an installation of these devices by our technicians. In that case, we could surely make you a very favourable offer for both the thermostats and the installation. In view of any possible future business contacts, I would surely be prepared to come to Bochum and discuss this matter with you personally.

Let me end by drawing your attention to the fact that we are also well-known for the production of highly-efficient boiler systems which are computerised and also significantly add to saving energy-costs. As I believe that you are planning a retrofitting of some of your buildings, you might want to consider this option as well. Please let me know if you would like Energy Technology Ltd. to come up with a comprehensive offer for an entire refurbishment of the heating system in the above-mentioned properties including new computerised, energy-efficient boiler systems, digital thermostats which would of course be installed to match the exact performance of the new heating system, and the installation of these devices.

Should you have any further questions, please do not hesitate to contact my by mail, phone or fax.

Looking forward to hearing from you.

Yours sincerely,

Glyn Hodges

Managing Director

Discuss:

Do you think GW BO should modernise the heating system in 1,000 of its properties which were built before 1920?

Before you start your discussion in class, collect some arguments.

NO, we should not modernise...	YES, we should modernise ...

Waste separation

Have a look at the following wordlist having to do with these pictures.

Arrange the words in categories of your choice. Decide on meaningful terms to describe these categories. These categories might be: people, containers, activities, synonyms, places, American and British English etc.

However, each word can only be used once!

garbage collector	garbage collection	refuse collection
garbage	rubbish	waste management firm
refuse	garbage bag	waste disposal
refuse dump	refuse lorry	rubbish dump
waste	rubbish container	garbage truck
pile of rubbish	refuse bin	waste disposal site
refuse bag	rubbish bag	garbage can
garbage container	garbage man	refuse collection vehicle
landfill	rubbish tip	dustbin
illegal dumping	to fly-tip	

THE SCOTSMAN
SCOTLAND'S NATIONAL NEWSPAPER ONLINE

Fri 10 Mar 2006

MAN FINED £50 FOR PUTTING LITTER IN WASTE BIN
JOHN INNES

A MAN was fined £50 for throwing away two pieces of junk mail in a street litter bin.
Andy Tierney, 24, of Hinckley, Leicestershire, dumped the unwanted mail in a bin on his way to work but council officers tracked him down using the addresses on the envelopes to issue him with a fixed penalty.
They said he was being fined because "domestic refuse from your property was dumped into a street litter bin".
A spokesman for Hinckley and Bosworth Council said: "A fixed penalty notice is served to people who we believe have committed an offence."

Source: The Scotsman

What do you think? Should the man have to pay the fine? Did the council over-react?

Verfassen:

Senden | Kontakte | Rechtschr. | Anhang | Sicherheit | Speichern

Von:

An:

Betreff:

Normaler Text | Variable Breite

Die Beschwerden der Müllentsorgungsbetriebe häufen sich, dass in den Müllcontainern an unseren Häusern zunehmend falsch sortierter Müll eingeworfen wird. Aus diesem Grund habe ich veranlasst, dass kurze und übersichtliche Broschüren in den häufigsten Muttersprachen unserer Mieter erstellt werden, die die bei uns eingesetzten blauen, grauen und gelben Container erklären.

Bitte bereiten Sie ein entsprechendes Informationsblatt auf Englisch vor. Ich füge Ihnen eine englischsprachige Orientierungshilfe an.

Blue box/bin contents are recycled

food & drink cans and tins
Aluminium or steel can be recycled including food tins, drink cans & pet-food cans. Please rinse first before placing in your bin.

plastic bottles & containers
We can take plastic bottles which have HDPE or the number 2 on the bottom of the bottle. Types of bottle accepted include: milk, detergent, fruit juice, washing up liquid and fabric conditioner. We can also take 'PET' bottles with either 'PET' or the number 1 on the bottom.

paper & card
Leaflets and glossy pamphlets can be recycled, so can white paper. We can take all kinds of card including brown cardboard.

newspapers, directories & magazines
White telephone directories, magazines and catalogues can be recycled including yellow pages.

Some things that must NOT go in the Blue box/bin
Please NO polystyrene based products, NO foil items and NO plastic bin liners or thin plastic bags.

Brown bin — contents help us make compost

plants & leaves, green prunings, hedge clippings and grass mowings can all go in the brown bin
Hedge clippings are fine but not tree/thick branches or wood. For larger items please contact your local landscaping firm for shredding and/or removal.

pet straw, hay & sawdust will compost
Pet bedding is acceptable but not faeces.

Please contact us for the removal of poisonous plants.

Some things that must NOT go in the brown bin
Please NO meat or fish remains, NO cat/dog faeces, NO food items, NO plastic bags, NO metals, NO nappies, NO glass, NO textiles, NO stones/rubble, flower pots or soil.

For information about home composting click here.

Green bin — contents go to landfill

waste only
If anything can be recycled or reused then it shouldn't go in the green bin.

disposable nappies
If you cannot be part of a nappy recycling scheme, the green bin is the only one that takes nappies.

kitchen waste and household waste
Food and household waste (for which there is no recycling facility) goes into the green bin.

bin liners and thin plastic bags
The green bin is the place for these, they are not to be used in any other bin as they hinder the recycling process.

Some things that must NOT go in the green bin
Please NO hot ashes (they can damage the bin) and NO sharp objects without protective wrapping.

Choose the odd-one-out (i.e. the word that does not belong in that line) and explain your decision to your partner.

Make a sentence in which you include this word. e.g.

Rent	Electricity bill	Phone bill	Transport costs

- odd-one-out: rent; all other amounts can vary from month to month; the rent is usually fixed and written down in the tenancy agreement.
- word-in-context: In times of housing shortages, rents are more likely to go up.

gas	electricity	coal	water
property tax	rent	phone bill	cable TV
police	landlord	tenant	utility provider
bank	insurance company	housing company	postal service
lawyer	tenant's association	notary	court
attic	roof	penthouse	basement
garbage	waste	trash	sewage
furnished	unfurnished	fully-serviced	periodic
parking-space	common areas	laundry room	fitted kitchen
rent	taxes	maintenance costs	personnel costs
insulation	double-glazed windows	energy conservation	solar panels
power-cut	burst pipe	leaking roof	defect TV
wall	roof	socket	ceiling
restaurant	retail shop	warehouse	insurance agent

Talking about eviction

According to your knowledge, which of these reasons are the most common for landlords evicting tenants?

- rent arrears or breach of tenancy agreement
- nuisance or annoyance
- deterioration of the condition of house
- deterioration of furniture
- tenant has given notice to quit but does not leave
- subletting or assigning without permission
- accommodation required by landlord
- overcrowding

Given these reasons, why do landlords take this lengthy and sometimes costly step?

What could a landlord do before an eviction seems inevitable?

After five months in which you have never heard anything negative from the Bishops in Kolkstraße, you today find the following letter on your desk.

Dear Sir or Madam,

failure of heating system in our flat

As you will surely be aware, we are renting one of your flats in Kolkstraße. So far, we have always paid our rent in time and have never been a nuisance to anyone. But I am afraid that these times might be over now as I have to tell you that for four consecutive days our heating in our flat has not worked properly. In the tenancy agreement we signed your rights and obligations are stated as clearly as ours. So we ask you to accept this and behave accordingly.

The maximum temperature in all the rooms is 16 degrees, which – I am sure you will agree – is far too cold.

We are very surprised that so far you have done nothing to rectify this situation. Therefore we have decided to withhold our rent payments for the coming month as long as the necessary repairs works have not been carried out.

Yours faithfully

Michael Bishop

What is your first reaction?

Why do you think the Bishops react in this way?

How should you behave in a professional way?

Prepare a phone call in which you inform the tenants that you will send someone to repair the heating system.

Try to fill your role and include as many aspects as possible. This time, only very few cues are given to get you started.

Michael Bishop

- **you are very angry about the situation in your flat**
- **you repeatedly refer to the landlord's obligations as written down in the tenancy agreement**
- **you believe you are absolutely right to withhold the rent until the heating system will be repaired**
- **in the end, you agree on a date when the repair works can be carried out**

GW BO

- **you apologise for any inconvenience the Bishops had to experience**
- **show as much understanding as possible**
- **point out that they should have contacted you immediately**
- **explain that the tenant has no legal right to withhold the complete rent without having given the landlord enough time to solve the problem**
- **find a date when the heating system can be prepared**

Two months later you receive the following email from your accountant. It says:

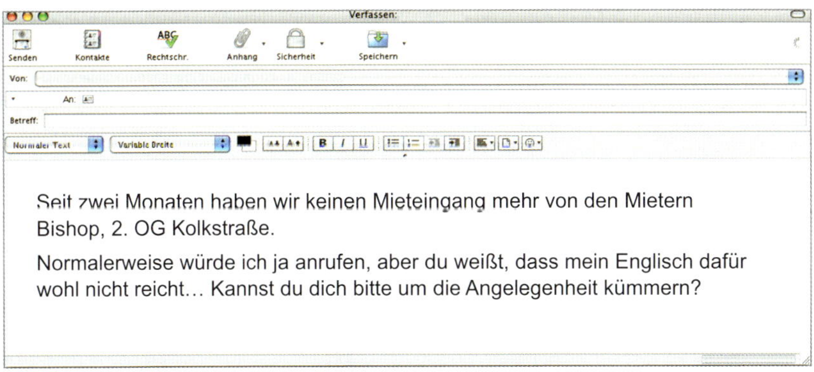

Seit zwei Monaten haben wir keinen Mieteingang mehr von den Mietern Bishop, 2. OG Kolkstraße.

Normalerweise würde ich ja anrufen, aber du weißt, dass mein Englisch dafür wohl nicht reicht... Kannst du dich bitte um die Angelegenheit kümmern?

You several times try to reach the Bishops but nobody answers the phone. You then call another tenant in that building who tells you that the Bishops still live in their flat.

You decide to write a letter which should cover the following aspects:

- brief explanation of situation
- last rent paid
- ask for explanation for non-payment
- list rent arrears
- ask for ways to solve situation
- also explain legal steps which might have to follow

Before you start writing your letter, you do some research on the internet and come up with the following text which you carefully read to collect all technical vocabulary that might be necessary:

How to deal with rent arrears

The collection of rent is a vital aspect of every housing company's business. This rental income makes it possible for them to provide their range of services to their tenants.

Therefore, checks on the payment of rent are usually run within short periods of time. Any subsequent action such as reminders, follow-up calls etc. will only be taken if a tenant's account is found to be overdue.

However, all housing providers know and understand that even their best tenants might run into financial problems from time to time – financial problems which might make it difficult or even impossible for the tenants to pay their rent in full and on time.

In order to avoid any legal conflicts possibly arising from rent arrears, housing companies offer a series of advice to their tenants on how to behave in situations like these. Here is a list of common advice provided:

- Talk to your housing company immediately once you know that you might find yourself in a difficult financial situation.
- Get benefits advice. Depending on the situation you find yourself in, you might be eligible for some benefit either by the council or by the state.
- Try to negotiate to pay back any outstanding rent in instalments, thus clearly indicating that you are trying your best to solve this difficult situation.
- Keep up the communication with your landlord showing that despite your financial situation you still want to be a reliable partner.

Usually any form of legal action will only be taken by a housing company, if the debts keep growing and if there is no communication between landlord and tenant whatsoever.

Once the housing company has decided to apply for costly and often time consuming legal action, they will contact the tenant and he or she will receive information from the court. In this case, it is important for the tenant to attend court to present their point of view. Even at this stage, the housing company will be glad to come to an agreement with their tenants in which the tenant might offer to pay instalments or even a lump sum if they do not want to lose their home.

The final and irrevocable stage in the legal process is the eviction of the tenant. This result will be the consequence if even though there is a court order to pay, the debts keep growing and the housing company sees no chance of getting their money back. At this stage, their prime interest will be the repossession of their property which means getting the tenant out of it.

Therefore, the housing company will ask for the Possession Order to be enforced. The court bailiffs will visit the tenant at home and let them know when they have to leave.

You wait for another two weeks but get no reply to your letter. When you contact the bookkeeping department, they tell you that no rent has been paid by the Bishops. You visit the flat in Kolkstraße to talk to the Bishops personally, but find the apartment completely empty. Your first quick inspection does not reveal any damages. A neighbour tells you that the Bishops moved out 10 days ago.

As you know that your boss now asks you to come up with a report explaining the situation, you try to remember how it all started.

Look at your notes again and complete the following diagram listing the steps you took for the flat 42 Kolkstraße.

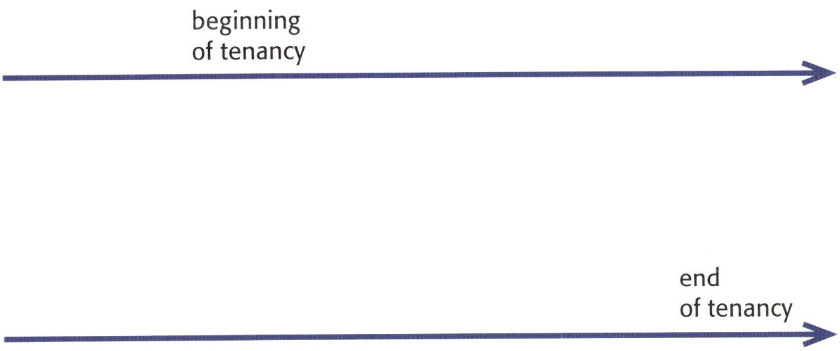

What is the financial picture for this flat?
Which are the next steps you should take?
Do you find any explanation for this situation?
Should you have behaved differently?

Discuss your answers in class.

Move-out procedures

Fill in the missing connectives and give the following letter a logical structure.

Bitte schreiben Sie Herrn Agali auf Englisch. Ich habe Ihnen alle relevanten Informationen hier zusammengestellt:

Wohnung Ringstraße 431 am 26. Juni mit Vater des Mieters abgenommen; er hat auch Übergabeprotokoll unterschrieben; bittet um Rückerstattung der Kaution von 650 €

- alle Schlüssel zurück;
- Wohnung abgenommen; folgende Mängel sind zu beseitigen:
  - Wohnzimmerteppich stark verschmutzt: weist Löcher auf, Beschädigungen gehen über normale Abnutzung nach zwei Jahren Mietzeit hinaus; Teppich wird von uns ersetzt und Kosten von Kaution einbehalten
  - im Schlafzimmerschrank: verschiedene Kleidungsstücke und Schuhe
  - Balkon: Fahrrad
  - Teppichboden im Schlafzimmer von Mieter eingebracht, da stark beschmutzt und unbrauchbar, muss er entfernt werden
  - ursprünglich installiertes Waschbecken im Badezimmer fehlt
  - Fliesen in der Küche stark verschmutzt
- falls Arbeiten nicht innerhalb der festgesetzten Frist ordnungsgemäß ausgeführt und Mängel beseitigt wurden, werden wir entstehende Kosten von der Kaution einbehalten
- Verweis auf Mietvertrag, in dem Vorgehen eindeutig geregelt und auch vom Mieter unterschrieben wurde
- Bitte, Angelegenheit kooperativ zu klären, damit es für ihn keine finanziellen Nachteile gibt und wir durch eventuelle Reparaturarbeiten Leerstand vermeiden können
- Bitte um Angabe der Bankverbindung, so dass wir eventuelles Guthaben überweisen können
- bei Rückfragen stehen wir unter der angegebenen Telefonnummer zur Verfügung

Mit freundlichen Grüßen

Dear Mr Agali,

move-out procedures / your flat Ringstraße 431

a) The carpet in the living room is heavily stained and shows various holes. This surely goes beyond a normal wear-and-tear after a two-year tenancy. ____________, we will replace the carpet and deduct the costs from your deposit.

b) ____________ I would like to confirm the receipt of all keys belonging to the flat you rented from us. On November 29th, I inspected the flat with your sister who also signed the move-out check list on your behalf.

c) Should you have any questions, please do not hesitate to contact us by phone or in writing.

d) I refer to the notice you have given and the final inspection of your flat after the termination of your tenancy agreement.

e) Should you fail to see to these aspects within the period mentioned above, we will be forced to deduct the costs from your deposit as well.

f) On that occasion, ____________, I noticed some defects which we have to hold you responsible for:

g) Please let us know your bank details so that we can transfer a possible deposit to you.

Looking forward to hearing from you soon,

Yours sincerely

h) This procedure is clearly expressed in the tenancy agreement which you signed on your move-in in 2001.

i) ____________, there are some aspects that still need to clarified before we will be in a position to refund any deposit. We ____________ ask you to make sure that you see to the following aspects within the next three days:

- Please remove the articles of clothing and the shoes from the wardrobe in the bedroom.
- Please remove the bicycle from the balcony.
- The carpet in the bedroom was brought in by you; as it is heavily soiled, it is of no further use, thus, it has to be removed as well.
- Please re-install the original hand wash basin in the bathroom.
- The tiles in the kitchen are extremely dirty, please clean them.

j) ____________, we ask you to solve this matter co-operatively, so as to avoid any financial disadvantages for you and a possible vacancy for us which would be caused by any repair works we need to carry out.

Talking about vacancies

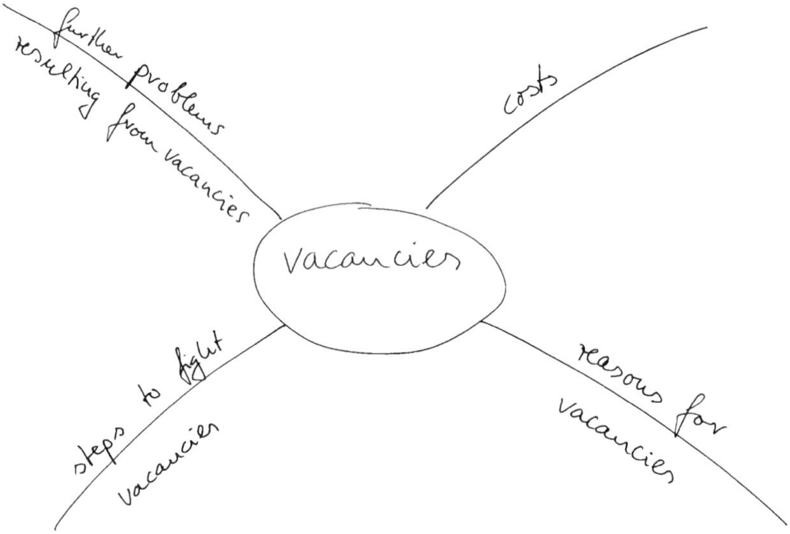

How Landlords Find Tenants In A Soft Market By David Schneider

What has happened to all the renters? Well, let's examine what has happened in the last few years in the housing markets.
First of all, interest rates have dropped to all time historical lows. This means that many renters have taken advantage of this and went out and bought a house. The second thing that has happened is that most real estate values throughout the country have gone up a lot in a short period of time. Because of this, many more people have decided to start to invest in rental real estate. More landlords and fewer renters equal a soft rental market.
When the market is soft, you have to be better at finding renters.
It's the mission of all businesses to get and keep customers. Well, the business of owning and managing investment real estate isn't any different. You must have a system and plan in place to find new tenants and keep your old tenants. Typically owners of small rental property only do one or two things to find tenants. They may run an advertisement in their local newspaper or they may put a sign on the property that says "FOR RENT". This is fine in a good rental market, but if you want to avoid vacancy you have to do more.
Here are five simple ideas to help keep those vacancies filled:

1. Put together a property feature sheet explaining the features and benefits of your property and distribute it to local real estate offices.
2. Offer bonuses and incentives to your other residents if they refer anyone to you that rents. As an example: gift certificates for a dinner out, tank of gas, microwave, etc.
3. Use the apartment rental services in your area. They can be found in your phone book and will list your property in their "properties for rent list" that they give to residents.
4. Make up some cards that say "Properties For Rent – Houses, Duplexes and Apartments. Call Me" and leave them all over. Put them in the envelope when you pay your bills, leave them at restaurants or post them on bulletin boards at stores. Leave them anywhere, be creative and get the word out.

5. Create a waiting list. Keep a list of all callers on any rental that you ever had available. When a new unit comes up for rent, notify the people on your list and see if they might have an interest. If you ever get calls from someone looking for a rental and you don't have any available now, put them on you waiting list.

Even though the above list is short, it should give you the idea that you need to have many ways to find renters. I'm sure that if you sat down and thought about it you could create a list of 50 –100 ideas. Once you have your list created, you should now test the ideas and see which ones gave you the best results. By doing this process you will fill your vacancies fast and have a constant stream of new tenants wanting to rent from you.

1. What, according to the text, characterises a soft market?
2. Would you say that there is a "soft" market in your part of Germany as well?
3. Which steps does the author of the article suggest to find tenants?
4. Do you believe these steps are appropriate for German housing companies as well? Give reasons.
5. If you do not agree with the advice given, what should German housing companies do to attract tenants in times of housing over-supply?

Talking about insurances

Have a look at the following words. Put them into a logical order and prepare a brief talk on the general idea of insurances.

compensation	claim	likelihood	damage	over-insured
situation	premium	contract	claims settlement	deductible
risk	insurance company	coverage	under-insured	insured against...
insurer	to take out an insurance	loss	adequately insured	sum insured
policy	beneficiary	compulsory	type of insurance	insurable

Why are insurances necessary for landlords and housing companies? Have another look at your list of words and find examples from your line of business.

Back at GW BO, you receive the following email:

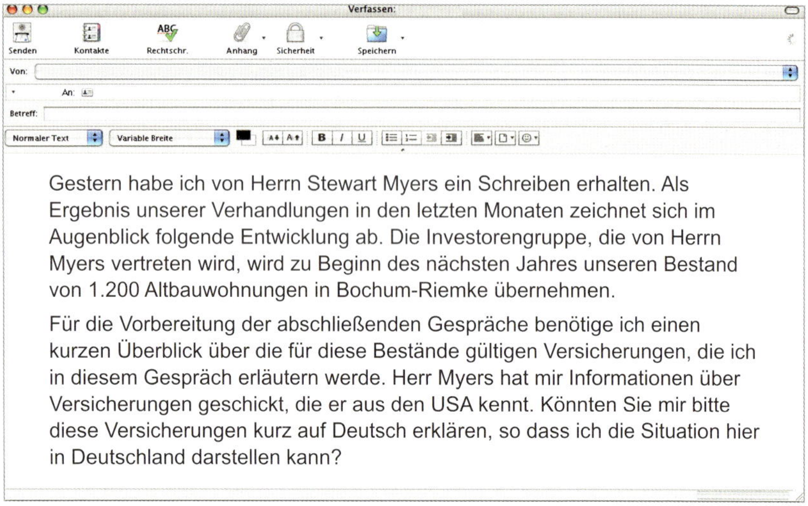

Gestern habe ich von Herrn Stewart Myers ein Schreiben erhalten. Als Ergebnis unserer Verhandlungen in den letzten Monaten zeichnet sich im Augenblick folgende Entwicklung ab. Die Investorengruppe, die von Herrn Myers vertreten wird, wird zu Beginn des nächsten Jahres unseren Bestand von 1.200 Altbauwohnungen in Bochum-Riemke übernehmen.

Für die Vorbereitung der abschließenden Gespräche benötige ich einen kurzen Überblick über die für diese Bestände gültigen Versicherungen, die ich in diesem Gespräch erläutern werde. Herr Myers hat mir Informationen über Versicherungen geschickt, die er aus den USA kennt. Könnten Sie mir bitte diese Versicherungen kurz auf Deutsch erklären, so dass ich die Situation hier in Deutschland darstellen kann?

PROPERTY DAMAGE - COMPULSORY COVER

Standard cover includes:

- Fire, Lightning, Explosion
- Aircraft
- Riot and Civil Commotion or Malicious Persons
- Earthquake
- Subterranean Fire
- Storm or Flood
- Escape of Water from any tank, apparatus or pipe
- Impact by any road vehicle or animal
- Theft
- Accidental Damage
- Subsidence

EXTENSIONS INCLUDED:

- **Sprinkler Installation Upgrade Costs**
  Additional costs of upgrading Sprinkler installations if required by us following a loss.
- **Alterations and Additions**
  Alterations, additions and improvements to existing premises or any newly acquired properties up to £2m or 20% of the total sum insured, whichever is the less.
- **Intention to Insure**
  Inadvertently omitted property up to an amount of £2m.
- **Removal of Debris**
  Cover extends to include irrecoverable costs in removing debris of tenants contents following damage up to an amount of £5,000.
- **Locks and Keys**
  The cost of replacing locks or keys following theft up to £5,000.
- **Landscaped Grounds**
  Damage to landscaped grounds as a consequence of damage to the property insured up to an amount of £25,000.
- **Metered Supplies**
  Loss of water, gas electricity or other supply charges up to a limit of £25,000.
- **Unauthorised Use of Supplies**
  The unauthorised use of electricity, gas, water or other metered supplies is covered up to an amount of £25,000.
- **Trace and Access**
  Costs incurred in tracing the source of damage to water pipes and underground services belonging to the property insured up to an amount of £10,000.
- **Tree Felling and Lopping**
  The cost of lopping or felling trees which are an immediate threat to life or damage to the property up to an amount of £5,000.
- **Removal of Wasps and Bees Nests**
  Cost of removing wasps or bees nests up to an amount of £500.
- **Alternative Residential Accommodation**
  The cost of providing alternative accommodation for residential portions of the premises. Up to 20% of the sum insured of the premises or portion of premises damaged.

LOSS OF RENTAL - OPTIONAL COVER

Loss of rental income following damage to the buildings and or contents, on an "All Risks" basis.

Extensions included:

- **Alterations and Additions**
  Increase in rental income following alterations, additions

and improvements or newly acquired premises up to £500,000 or 20% whichever is less.

- **Intention to Insure**
  Rent in respect of inadvertently omitted property up to an amount of £500,000 any one property.
- **Managing Agents Premises**
  Cover is given if there is interruption or interference to the business as a result of property damage at the premises of the managing agent. Limit 10% or £500,000 whichever is the less.
- **Denial of Access**
  Prevention of access to the premises.
- **Loss of Attraction**
  Loss of rental income resulting from the loss of potential tenants following damage to other premises in the vicinity. Limit 5% or £250,000 whichever is the less.
- **Supply Undertakings**
  Damage to premises where you obtain electricity, gas, water or telecommunications services.
- **Infectious and Contagious Diseases**
  Interruption to the business as a consequence of a Notifiable Disease. Maximum any one claim £250,000 subject to a 3 month indemnity period.
- **Book Debts**
  Cover is provided for outstanding debit balances that cannot be collected because the records have been damaged or destroyed. Limit £25,000.

Terrorism Cover

The cover given by this policy excludes cover in respect of damage or consequential loss caused by acts of terrorism. If you require cover in respect of Property Damage or Loss of Rent caused by acts of terrorism, please contact your insurance adviser.

PROPERTY OWNERS LIABILITY - OPTIONAL COVER

Provides cover in respect of all sums which you become legally liable to pay as compensation to third parties for accidental injury or damage.

Standard cover includes:

- **Standard Limit of Indemnity £2m**
- **Data Protection Act**
  Sums which you become legally liable to pay as compensation. Limit £250,000
- **Court Attendance Compensation**
  Covers attendance as a witness in connection with a claim. Compensation for each day of attendance:
  Director/partner £250
  Employee £150
- **Contractual Liability**
  Liability arising from your contractual obligations

EMPLOYERS LIABILITY – OPTIONAL COVER

Provides cover for damages, legal costs and expenses for which you are legally liable in respect of bodily injury or disease to employees.

Standard cover indudes:

- **Standard Limit of Indemnity £10m**
- **Health and Safety at Work - Legal Defence Costs**
  Cover is provided for legal defence costs
- **Court Attendance Compensation**
  Covers attendance as a witness in connection with a claim. Compensation for each day of attendance:
  Director/partner £250
  Employee £150

LEGAL EXPENSES

Provides you with advice and protection for the Professional costs and expenses of legal action which may arise.

Standard cover (compulsory) includes:

- **Legal Advice**
  Access to Lawphone which provides advice on all business related legal matters 24 hours a day, all year round.
- **Prosecution Defence**
  Costs of defending your legal rights after an event which results in criminal proceedings. Limit £50,000
- **Property**
  Payment of legal fees to pursue compensation for damage to your property. Limit £50,000.

Extensions available:

- **Employment Contract**
  Costs of defending your legal rights in a dispute with an employee over a contract of employment and any award the court or tribunal Orders you to pay as a result. Limit £50,000 (including up to £25,000 for the award)
- **Commercial Tenancy Disputes**
  Costs in taking legal action over a tenancy agreement - limit £50,000
- **Jury Service**
  Any shortfall in your salary or wages as a result of attending jury service. £100 per day maximum 20 days
- **Personal injury**
  Costs of taking legal action against another person who causes death or bodily injury to you.
- **Residential Lettings**
  Costs in respect of letting disputes for all residential properties. Limit £25,000.

Source: Property Cover – Allianz Cornhill, Commercial UK policy wordings

Commercial lettings

Listen to a recording about the development of commercial real estate in San Francisco after the crash of the dotcom market.

Pre-listening activity

Before you listen, what do you think was the effect of the dotcom-boom in the 1990s on the commercial real estate market? Who were the winners, who were the losers?

While-listening activity

Outline the development of commercial property in SF as presented in the recording.

Who are the winners, who are the losers of this development?

Post-listening activity

Imagine you had a stock of office space. Due to a sudden boom in one particular business segment, more or less over night there is a huge demand for office space in your area. All your properties are rented, however you would have the chance to end the tenancy agreements rather soon.

Discuss: Would you give notice to long-term tenants who pay a lower rent to be able to get new tenants who pay much higher rents even if you are not sure how long this new boom will last?

Collect some arguments and also explain what you would do in detail.

ALTERNATIVE 1: Keep long-term commercial tenants	**ALTERNATIVE 2:** Choose new tenants who pay much higher rents

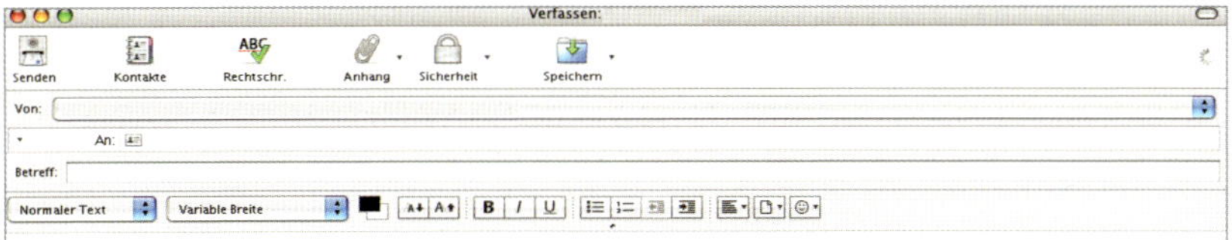

In einer unserer Gewerbeeinheiten (Huestraße Bochum Stadtzentrum; zurzeit Spielwarenhandlung in Mehrfamilienhaus mit dazugehörigen Lagerräumen im Keller) läuft der Pachtvertrag zum Ende des Jahres aus. Der jetzige Pächter gibt aus Altersgründen sein Geschäft auf und will sich auch nicht um die Nachfolge bemühen. Wir haben bereits eine Anzeige in der Zeitung geschaltet. Bisher haben wir nur die folgende englische Anfrage. Bitte erledigen Sie die entsprechenden Arbeiten und stellen mir das Ergebnis dann vor.

FineHats Limited
34-38 Bristol Square
B64 6AG Birmingham

Gemeinnützige Wohnungsbaugesellschaft Bochum
Kellerstraße 35-39
48456 Bochum
Germany

Dear Sir or Madam,

your advertisement for retail space

In yesterday's edition of the WAZ I read that you are offering retail space in the city centre of Bochum.

We at FineHats are an expanding chain-store operating throughout Europe planning to extend our business activities in Germany as well. At present, we operate stores in Hamburg, Frankfurt and Munich.

Should your property meet the needs of a modern fashion shop and should you be interested in a long-term tenancy agreement, we would very much like to discuss these matters with you in a personal conversation. Could you please be so kind as to prepare a brief property description including relevant details about the city of Bochum?

Thank you very much for your efforts.

Yours faithfully

Eudora M. Foster
European Sales Coordinator

In order to prepare the required dossier, you do some research on the internet and find the following property description: Study it carefully to decide on the structure you would like to give your description. Which technical terms do you need?

Property Type	Retail; Traditional Shop Unit
Age Band	Pre 1960's
Area	Total Area 2,679 Sq Feet
Availability Detail	For Lease Current Rent £ 62,500 pa The premises are held on a 25 year full repairing and insuring lease from 17 November 1981, expiring 6 November 2006. The current passing rent is £62,500 per annum. It should be noted that the landlord has indicated a willingness to enter into a new long lease over the premises. Each party will bear their own legal costs incurred in this transaction, however, the ingoing tenant will be responsible for extract copies, Stamp Duty Land Tax and VAT thereon. As the staff are currently unaware of the impending disposal of this unit, all viewing is via the agent. Further details are available upon application to the marketing agents.
Further Details	1 Trading Floor 2 Total Floors
General Comments	The premises comprise the ground and basement floors of a three storey and attic, sandstone mid-terrace building, under a pitched, slate clad roof. The premises have been extended to the rear to provide a single storey, ground floor and basement section, under a flat roof. The City of Edinburgh, Scotland's Capital City, is situated on the East Coast of Scotland, on the Firth of Forth. The M8, M9, A1 and A90 link the City to the trunk road network and motorway network beyond. Edinburgh's own airport, at Turnhouse, is located only 15 minutes drive from the City centre, and offers connections to UK, European and international destinations. Edinburgh is also well served by both rail and bus services, with Waverley Railway Station and St Andrews Bus Station situated in the New Town area and Haymarket in the city centre. The premises are located on the south side of Shandwick Place to the west end of Princes Street, Edinburgh's principal retailing pitch. The surrounding area is home to a large number of national retailers and substantial office occupiers. Nearby traders include Boots, Habitat, Pret a Manger, Somerfield and many others.

Parts	1,469 Sq Feet	Total Area Of Ground Floor
	1,210 Sq Feet	Total Area Of Basement Floor
	2,679 Sq Feet	Total Floor Area Of Retail Unit

After a week, you receive a phone call from Ms.Foster in which she thanks you for your information and suggests an appointment to discuss the matter in more detail.

Work in groups and role-play the following negotiation. Here are some prompts to organise your arguments. You might, however, be ready to find a compromise if your ideas do not seem to correspond with your business partner's ideas!

You represent two managers of FineHats.

You are interested in GWBO's property as it seems ideally located in the heart of the Ruhr district in the middle of a shopping precinct.

Here's your list of things you would like to achieve in your negotiation:

- **suitable equipment for fashion store, paid by landlord (list details)**
- **maximum tenancy period at this stage: two years;**
- **however, option to renew the tenancy on the same terms after 15 months**
- **parking space for employers (minimum 5)**
- **installation of customer WCs**
- **burglar alarm and rolling grill**
- **You would like to come to a definite decision in today's meeting.**
- **Anything else you consider important**

You represent two managers of GW BO.

You would like to let your property to FineHats.

Here's your list of things you would like to achieve in your negotiation:

- **five-year tenancy agreement;**
- **rent excluding any utility costs**
- **option to renew the tenancy on the same terms after 15 months**
- **you offer to install some equipment necessary for fashion store which you could use in further lettings (toilets etc.)**
- **deposit of 3 months' rent**
- **rent per month € 4,700**
- **You would like to come to a definite decision in today's meeting.**
- **Anything else you consider important**

Collect the various results you reached in your groups and discuss them in class. Are all your agreements good ones for GW BO?

Commercial Properties

Q	L	J	C	G	N	Q	Y	R	P	T	U	X	W	H	T	Q	D	L	F	N	I	K	R	K	Z	X	E	L	U
W	D	D	C	Z	Y	O	O	U	D	C	R	I	D	R	N	M	N	L	Q	Q	A	Y	G	U	V	Y	G	D	W
V	V	S	H	D	J	A	C	Y	L	T	H	L	C	I	E	G	A	R	A	G	B	Y	L	B	R	S	I	B	H
O	H	A	Y	D	B	O	F	Z	U	P	P	O	B	T	M	F	M	B	P	N	N	S	X	T	G	H	G	A	V
I	U	O	B	J	P	K	T	V	B	V	H	F	S	B	P	U	E	N	N	V	D	J	J	W	J	O	L	J	M
Z	J	P	B	P	Y	W	L	I	J	A	W	Y	J	R	I	R	D	F	F	W	W	L	T	O	F	I	C	N	C
A	Z	W	E	W	O	E	O	H	Z	D	S	B	P	W	U	N	H	K	M	T	K	Y	O	F	G	T	R	M	O
K	I	Z	C	W	A	C	K	K	J	Y	K	R	B	T	Q	I	V	V	T	J	C	Q	I	R	S	R	K	U	L
D	K	V	V	X	K	D	L	A	T	Z	L	O	C	H	E	T	W	N	B	N	J	C	L	C	D	H	Y	A	Z
S	J	G	N	N	Q	C	O	I	B	L	L	U	H	T	Z	U	A	F	A	P	E	B	O	J	K	N	W	M	A
D	T	M	P	H	T	P	R	P	F	K	R	G	X	Q	T	R	Y	C	A	Q	S	M	F	I	J	T	U	P	C
T	U	A	Z	Z	F	U	N	E	B	T	E	N	S	P	U	E	A	R	P	Y	P	J	T	K	T	P	R	O	N
W	M	I	T	R	C	Y	A	S	S	V	Z	Y	O	A	W	V	T	F	M	A	P	C	R	S	S	H	N	V	D
A	U	Z	B	E	G	H	B	A	H	Z	K	E	T	I	Q	I	D	R	N	P	H	A	O	W	E	B	C	Z	D
O	E	K	S	J	O	Q	R	E	P	R	E	S	E	N	T	A	T	I	V	E	P	O	P	L	I	V	L	A	E
R	B	K	C	K	V	F	U	L	L	Y	E	Q	U	I	P	P	E	D	N	R	H	S	B	Q	F	G	N	T	Z
Z	W	T	N	A	N	E	T	V	K	R	M	N	O	W	Z	S	E	E	A	S	G	B	V	O	Z	D	V	I	B
G	K	G	J	I	R	Z	I	H	T	R	G	N	T	M	Q	C	T	C	W	Q	U	O	Y	Q	I	J	V	A	E
C	F	K	V	E	C	P	R	N	E	N	W	F	M	B	N	T	I	A	E	B	W	R	X	V	H	V	Z	C	H
O	R	U	W	O	S	R	E	T	R	A	U	Q	D	A	E	H	H	H	F	R	Q	O	A	L	R	G	A	N	A
M	L	O	A	M	N	C	D	T	L	L	R	M	R	T	E	D	V	H	W	F	J	L	V	N	O	M	P	D	O
A	S	W	O	N	L	E	G	L	I	P	B	T	Y	Z	U	W	O	D	L	R	A	R	N	U	C	Z	A	Z	H
D	U	F	A	L	X	N	S	U	O	N	N	Z	W	A	R	K	L	W	P	N	W	W	G	S	T	E	V	V	X
R	V	R	A	I	F	T	J	T	L	E	G	K	I	I	L	Q	P	E	G	I	I	U	G	A	H	Y	X	Y	F
O	H	C	F	J	J	R	T	W	M	P	N	Q	E	M	J	J	O	R	U	B	Q	F	G	V	C	S	H	I	A
V	N	S	T	O	R	A	G	E	Z	O	J	L	Y	D	W	E	G	A	C	D	Q	J	U	Z	R	U	J	F	O
W	W	M	P	E	X	L	S	S	W	H	U	E	V	C	R	V	B	B	B	K	Q	U	W	Y	G	N	Y	E	L
M	X	H	N	C	P	A	Q	I	O	S	X	U	V	L	L	Z	G	Q	T	N	G	Q	T	W	P	X	H	K	S
Q	D	A	V	S	B	Z	O	F	V	Z	Q	S	B	I	W	N	L	C	A	C	B	L	P	O	D	A	W	E	M
O	Q	B	K	S	Y	E	H	J	G	U	E	V	O	Z	S	I	J	H	N	Z	L	G	B	F	O	X	Q	B	K

STEP 1 Work on your own.
Find the hidden terms. How many can you find?
Copy them in a list making sure your partner cannot see your collection of terms.

STEP 2 Work with your partner.
Take it in turns. Form logical and grammatically correct sentences dealing with commercial properties for which you use your words from your list. Each word can only be used once by every player and must then be deleted from your list. For every word which is used in a correct sentence you get one mark (i.e. In some CITIES, the rent for RETAIL space is calculated on the basis of the TURNOVER the TENANT produces. = 4 marks).
Whoever gets most marks in the end, is the winner.

WEB UNIT: Sustainable waste management in a closed loop materials economy:

Before you do this web unit, please copy the following pages so that you can easily fill in the gaps and answer the questions. In this web unit you will come across many words you have not heard of before. It is not always necessary that you learn them, but you should have a dictionary at hand so that you can look up what they mean. If, however, you prefer to use an online dictionary, go to **www.quickdic.org** *or* **www.leo.org.**

Pre-net activities

What do you already know about sustainable closed loop recycling management in the country?

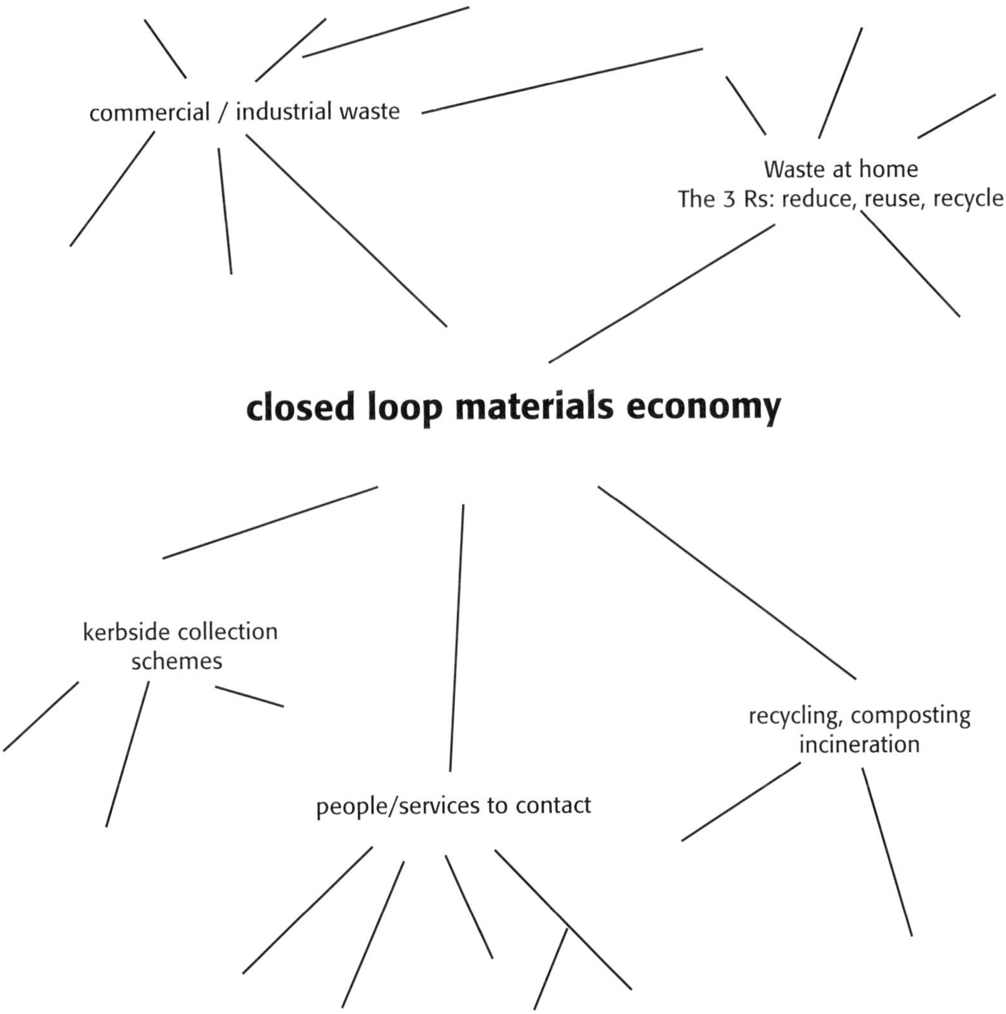

WEB UNIT: Sustainable waste management in a closed loop materials economy

In order to prepare your net-use activities, please write a short text about what you understand by a closed loop materials economy. Why is it so important to wonder whether waste is really waste? Why is recycling so important? Do you think there could be a world without any waste?

Net-use activities

Your own housing association is very much concerned about the ever increasing costs of your municipal waste management, and you are seeking best practices in order to reduce those costs. In order to increase your tenants' awareness for the 3 Rs (reduce, reuse, recycle), you are planning an information campaign about sustainable waste management in a closed loop materials economy.

Click on:
www.epa.gov/etop/forum/problem/waste_gas.html

1. **Have a look at the following URL and write down a couple of reasons why it is so important to reduce, to reuse and to recycle any kind of commercial, industrial and domestic waste.**

Here are two reasons to start with:

- Waste is a residual raw material resource after the use of an initial product. It can be used to manufacture new products.
- Waste has an impact on the environment.
-
-
-
-
-
-

WEB UNIT:
Sustainable waste management in a closed loop materials economy

2. Look at the following pie graph and explain in a few words, how the mentioned sorts of waste are collected in your own municipality. Explain the kerbside collection scheme.

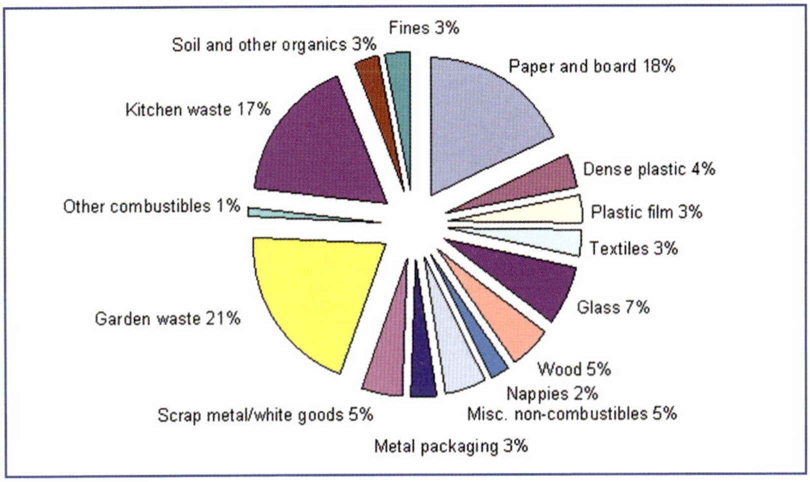

Source: Waste Watch, London, United Kingdom

3. Please click on the following URL and read the text.

Describe with your own words what can be recycled.

Click on: www.wasteonline.org.uk, then click on "recycling for householders" under "highlighted documents".

4. "Throw away the throwaway society!" This is the message you wish your tenants to understand. You decide to use a common mass product, i. e. scrap, to explain, how valuable waste can be.

Please write down the various sources of scrap and the activities of its recycling:

Click on: www.mtlm.com/services/recycling . Then click on "Ferrous".

WEB UNIT: Sustainable waste management in a closed loop materials economy

5. Briefly explain to your tenants the "dos and donts" in connection with the German system "Der Grüne Punkt":

THE DOS	THE DONTS

Click on: www.gruener-punkt.de, then click on "English", then on "Journalist Service", then on "All about DSD GmbH read more", then on "Separating waste properly - …"

6. "Measure the Treasure": Waste is not only money! It also drives technological development. And it is a real job creation machine.

Please study the following URL and explain briefly in your own words the tremendous economic potentials of the environmental technologies and services (ETS) sector:

Click on: www.envirolinknorthwest.co.uk
Click on "The Environmental Technologies Market" and then, subsequently on "Introduction", "Market Overview" and "ETS Subsectors".

Post-net activities

Please draft a brochure of 4 pages explaining to your tenants why they should and how they can reduce, reuse and help to recycle their own domestic waste.

UNIT 4

Aspects of letting

Vokabeln

A	account	Konto
	additions	Anbauten
	adjacent	angrenzend
	adjacent property	angrenzende Immobilie
	allocate (verb)	zuteilen
	alter (verb)	ändern, verändern
	alterations	Änderungen, Umbauten
	alternative residential accommodation	alternative Wohnversorgung
	annoyance	Beeinträchtigung, Belästigung
	arrears	Rückstände
	ash	Asche
	attic	Dachgeschoss
B	backlit display	beleuchtetes Display
	basement	Keller
	basin	Becken
	belongings	persönliches Eigentum
	beneficiary	Begünstigter
	bill of utility costs	Nebenkostenabrechnung
	bin liner	Müllbeutel
	boiler	Warmwasseraufbereiter
	booze	Alkohol, alkoholische Getränke, Sauftour
	breach	Bruch
	burst pipe	Rohrbruch
C	cable TV	Kabelfernsehen
	ceiling	Decke
	chain store	Einzelhandelskette
	charge (verb)	belasten
	chattel	bewegliches Gut
	chimney	Kamin
	civil commotion	Bürgerkrieg
	claim	Forderung
	cleanliness	Sauberkeit
	closed-loop	geschlossener Kreislauf
	closet	Toilette, Wandschrank
	coal	Kohle
	collateral	Pfand, Sicherheit
	commercial tenancy disputes insurance	Vermieterrechtsschutz-versicherung
	common areas	Gemeinschaftsanlagen
	compensate (verb)	kompensieren, ausgleichen, entschädigen
	compensation	Ausgleich, Entschädigung
	compulsory	verbindlich
	condensing gas boiler	Brennwertkessel
	conservation	Schutz, Naturschutz
	consumer protection and food safety acts	Verbraucherschutz- und Lebensmittelreinheitsgesetz
	contagious disease	ansteckende Krankheit
	contractual liability	vertragliche Haftung
	court attendance compensation	Verdienstausfallregulierung für Zeugenaussagen bei Gericht
	court possession order	gerichtliche Anordnung
	crowd	Menge, große Anzahl an Personen
	crucial	wesentlich
D	damage	Schaden
	damage following theft	Diebstahlfolgeschäden
	data protection act	Datenschutzgesetz
	day one reinstatement	Neuwertversicherung
	deduct (verb)	abziehen
	deductible	Eigenanteil
	deed	Urkunde
	defect	Defekt, Mangel
	defective premises act	Gebäudehaftpflichtgesetz
	deposit / security deposit	Kaution
	deterioration	Verschlechterung, Wertminderung, Schädigung
	disability	Behinderung
	divorce	Scheidung
	dossier	Akte
	dotcom market	IT-Markt
	drains	Abwasserrohre
	drug-related	mit Bezug zu Drogen
	duplex	Zweifamilienhaus
E	earthquake	Erdbeben
	electric meter box	Stromzähler
	electrical appliances	Elektrogeräte
	electricity	Elektrizität
	electricity meter	Stromzähler
	emergency	Notfall
	enable (verb)	befähigen
	energy savings	Energieeinsparungen
	eviction	Zwangsräumung
	exclusion	Ausschluss
	expire (verb)	ablaufen
	explosion	Explosion
F	faeces	Kot
	faucet	Wasserkran
	felling and lopping of trees	Fällen und Zurückschneiden von Bäumen
	fiancé	Verlobter
	fire	Brand
	fire extinguisher	Feuerlöscher
	fitted kitchen	Einbauküche
	fixed-term tenancy agreement	befristeter Mietvertrag
	floating floor	schwimmender Estrich
	flood	Überflutung
	floor	Fußboden
	fly-tip (verb)	illegal Müll abladen
	furnished	möbliert
	furniture	Möbel
G	garbage can	Mülleimer
	garbage truck	Müllwagen
	garden upkeep	Gartenpflege
	gas	Gas
	gas meter	Gaszähler
	gas meter box	Gaszähler
	green prunings	Gartenabfälle
	gutter	Dachrinne
H	hay	Heu
	health and safety at work	Arbeits- und Gesundheits-schutz
	hole	Loch
	housing benefit	Wohngeld, Subjektförderung
	humidity	Feuchtigkeit
I	incentive	Anreiz
	incineration	Verbrennung
	increase	Steigerung
	index linking	indexiert (mit Inflations-anpassung)
	inevitable	unvermeidlich
	infectious disease	Infektionskrankheit
	insulation	Isolierung
	insured	versichert
	insurer	Versicherer
K	kerbside collection scheme	Müllabfuhr
	key	Haupt-
L	landfill	Abfalldeponie

	landlord	Vermieter
	laundry facilities	Waschküche mit Waschmaschine
	leak	Leckage
	leaking roof	undichtes Dach
	legal action	Gerichtsverfahren
	legal expenses insurance	Rechtsschutzversicherung
	legal requirements	rechtliche Anforderungen
	light	Licht
	light bulb	Birne
	lightning	Blitzeinschlag
	lock	Schloss
	lump sum	Pauschalbetrag
M	mailbox	Briefkasten
	maintained	instand gehalten
	maintenance	Wartung
	maintenance cost	Wartungskosten
	maintenance-free	wartungsfrei
	marital status	Ehestand
	market niche	Marktnische
	menu-driven	menügesteuert
	move-in	Einzug
	move-in check list	Wohnungsübernahmeprotokoll
	move-out	Auszug
	move-out check list	Wohnungsübergabeprotokoll
N	nappy	Windel
	notary	Notar
	notice to quit	Aufkündigung des Pachtvertrages
	notify	benachrichtigen
	nuisance	Beeinträchtigung
O	occupancy	Belegung
	odour of gas	Gasgeruch
	open-ended lease	unbefristeter Mietvertrag
	outstanding financial obligations	Außenstände
	overcrowding	Überbelegung
P	parking-space	Pkw-Einstellplatz
	periodic tenancy agreement	unbefristeter Mietvertrag
	personnel costs	Personalkosten
	pet	Haustier
	pipework	Verrohrung
	plaster (verb)	verputzen, vergipsen
	power-cut	Stromausfall
	precaution	Vorkehrung
	premises	Örtlichkeiten, Grundstück
	preventive	präventiv, vorbeugend
	prior notice	vorherige Benachrichtigung
	privacy	Privatsphäre
	property damage insurance	Gebäudehaftpflichtversicherung
	property tax	Grundsteuer
Q	query	Abfrage
R	race	Rasse
	Ratio Utility Based Systems RUBS	Betriebskostenermittlung basierend auf Verteilungsschlüssel
	refrain	unterlassen
	refund (verb)	erstatten
	refuse	Müll, Abfall
	refuse collection	Müllabfuhr
	reinstate (verb)	wieder einsetzen, wieder in Kraft setzen, wieder einstellen
	removal of debris	Schuttentfernung
	removal of wasps and bees nests	Entfernen von Wespen- und Bienennestern
	rent arrears	Mietrückstände
	rent recovery	Eintreiben der Miete
	repair	Reparatur
	rights and obligations	Rechte und Pflichten
	riot	Aufstand
	roof	Dach
	roof tile	Dachziegel
	rubbish	Abfall
S	sawdust	Sägespäne
	scratched	verkratzt
	sewage	Abwasser
	sewerage	Abwassersystem, Kanalisation
	share	Teil, Anteil, Aktie
	smoke detector	Rauchmelder
	socket	Anschlussdose, Steckdose
	stairwell, staircase	Treppenhaus
	standard limit of indemnity	Standardversicherungssumme
	storage space	Lagerraum
	storm	Sturm
	straw	Stroh
	street cleaning	Straßenreinigung
	street litter bin	öffentlicher Abfallkorb
	sublet (verb)	untervermieten
	sub-meter	separater Zähler
	subsidence	Absenken
	sustainable	nachhaltig
	sweep (verb)	fegen, z. B. Kamin fegen
T	tenancy agreement	Miet-, Pachtvertrag
	terrorism cover	Deckung bei Schäden in Folge von terroristischen Anschlägen
	theft	Diebstahl
	thermostat	Thermostat
	timely	rechtzeitig
	toolbox	Werkzeugkasten, Instrumentarium
	touch screen	Touchscreen
	trade fair	Handelsmesse
	trunk road network	Fernstraßennetz
U	unlawful	gesetzeswidrig
	unpaid rent	Mietrückstand
	urgent	dringend
	utility bill	Nebenkostenabrechnung
	utility charges	Nebenkosten
	utility provider	Versorgungsunternehmen
V	vacancy loss	Verlust aus Leerstand
	vacate (verb)	räumen, überlassen
	variable service charges	variable Mietnebenkosten
	VAT (Value Added Tax)	MwSt.
W	waste	Abfall
	wasteful practice	Verschwendung
	water consumption	Wasserverbrauch
	wear and tear	Abnutzung, Verschleiß
	window frame	Fensterrahmen
	withhold rent payment	Mietminderung

SELF-ASSESSMENT GRID AFTER UNIT 4

Gehen Sie die einzelnen Abschnitte des gerade abgeschlossenen Kapitels noch einmal durch und überprüfen Sie sich selbstkritisch. Was haben Sie gelernt? Was sollten Sie wiederholen bzw. vertiefen? Was bereitet Ihnen Schwierigkeiten? Schreiben Sie kurze Kommentare in die Kästchen, die Ihren Lernzuwachs für Sie selbst erläutern. Arbeiten Sie nach eigenen Prioritäten Unterpunkte nach, wenn Sie mehrheitlich Ihre Kommentare in der rechten Spalte gesetzt haben.

Was ich in diesem Kapitel gelernt habe…	**Wie ich meinen Fortschritt einschätze**		
	Ich fühle mich beim Sprechen/Schreiben und beim Hören bzw. Lesen zu diesem Aspekt insgesamt sicher und verstehe einen Großteil der Informationen bzw. kann einen Großteil der Informationen wie beabsichtigt weitergeben; auch wenn ich Fehler mache, habe ich insgesamt Vertrauen in meine Sprachbeherrschung.	Ich kann vieles von dem, was für diesen Aspekt wichtig ist, mündlich und schriftlich ausdrücken bzw. beim Hören und Lesen verstehen; allerdings fehlen mir einige Fachvokabeln und auch die grundsätzliche Sicherheit, mich frei über diesen Aspekt auszutauschen.	Ich habe zu diesem Aspekt einige Fachbegriffe und Redewendungen gelernt und verstehe auch Informationen; jedoch erschließen sich mir noch nicht alle Zusammenhänge; sowohl die Textrezeption (Hören und Lesen) als auch das Sprechen und Schreiben bereiten mir noch Probleme; ich weiß, dass ich einige Aspekte nacharbeiten sollte.
den Fachwortschatz zur Beschreibung von Rechten und Pflichten von Mietern und Vermietern anzuwenden.			
die wesentlichen Bestandteile eines Mietvertrags und der Miete darzustellen und zu erläutern.			
grundlegende Aspekte der Betriebskosten zu erläutern.			
die Fachtermini zur Beschreibung einer Wohnung in einem Wohnungsübergabeprotokoll anzuwenden.			
die Grundzüge einer Hausordnung darzustellen.			
den Fachwortschatz, um Informationen und Tipps zum Energiesparen und zur Müllentsorgung zu geben.			
Leerstand und mögliche Ursachen zu beschreiben.			
den Fachwortschatz zu relevanten Versicherungen anzuwenden.			
Anbahnung und Abschluss eines Pachtvertrages für eine Gewerbeimmobilie darzustellen.			
die Anwendung und Erarbeitung des Fachwortschatzes „Mülltrennung“ in einer Web-Unit zu Abfallmanagement.			

UNIT 5 Talking about construction

In dieser Unit lernen Sie:

- den grundlegenden Fachwortschatz zur Beschreibung der wesentlichen Bauphasen anzuwenden
- den grundlegenden Fachwortschatz zur Bezeichnung der am Bau Beteiligten
- die Arbeit der verschiedenen am Bau beteiligten Gewerke zu beschreiben
- den grundlegenden Fachwortschatz zur senioren- bzw. behindertengerechten Ausstattung einer Wohnanlage anzuwenden
- grundlegende Merkmale von Solar- und PV-Energie darzustellen
- den grundlegenden Fachwortschatz zu den häufigsten Baumaterialien anzuwenden
- Kriterien für die Auswahl eines Baugrundstücks basierend auf dessen Beschreibung anzuwenden

Have a look at the following stages in the construction process of a house. Decide on a logical order of these stages and number them accordingly.

The construction process

STAGE	ACTIVITIES IN THE CONSTRUCTION PROCESS
	Landscaping. This stage marks the beginning of the end. The yard is formed including any driveways or walkway. To finish it all off, plantings such as trees, shrubs, and grass are added.
	Closing. Before you can own the home, you'll be walked through the house and have mechanical systems and appliances explained to you. Use this time to ask questions about how the home operates. Minor repairs, such as paint touch-ups can also be requested in this stage. A few days after the walk-through you'll sign papers and the house will be yours!
	Pre-closing. While the landscaping is being finished, final inspections are being conducted. If any problems are found, they are repaired before entering the next stage. Once any repairs are made all remaining construction materials are removed, and the home is cleaned and ready for the closing.
	Pre-construction. Still in the beginning stages, you will finalize design selections and pre-order all major materials, such as lumber. You will receive a tentative construction schedule to keep you involved in the process.
	Exterior finishes. This stage is just what it sounds like, finishing the exterior of your house. From the outside, your house is beginning to look like a home – but inside there's more work to be done!
	Interior finishes. This is likely to be an exciting stage for you, as it's when the house really starts to look finished. Your walls and ceilings are filled in; interior doors are installed along with shelving, cabinets, countertops, mirrors, and flooring. The plumbers and electricians return to finish their jobs, installing registers, faucets, and light fixtures and appliances.
	Insulation and air sealing. This stage is designed to keep you and your family comfortable in the house. Gaps are sealed and insulation is added to keep outside air outside and the inside temperature to your liking.
	Foundation. Make sure you're happy with the layout of your house, because after this stage it's literally set in stone. The foundation stage is devoted to the construction of the foundation of your home.
	Sales agreement. In this first stage you and the builder sign the sales agreement.
	Mechanicals. At this stage mechanical aspects such as wiring and plumbing are completed. The pipes and wires are still exposed at this stage; there are a few more stages before the interior is complete.
	Framing. This is the skeleton of your home. Floors, walls, stairs and the roof are constructed but your home isn't closed in just yet.

Use the information provided and prepare a talk on construction in Germany.

Make sure to include the following beginnings of sentences in any order of your choice:

- Compared to Spain and Portugal, the German construction industry...
- In Europe, 7% of all people employed...
- In 2003, in the EU-15...
- The building completions of multi-family houses in Germany...
- The number of building permits for new single homes...
- In 2005, non-residential construction in Germany...
- Compared to 2003, residential construction in Germany...
- By 2020, the renovation potential will...
- Until 1994, the construction volume for new buildings...
- In 1995, the building completions in Eastern Germany...
- The regeneration of many urban areas in Europe...
- In the new member states,...

The construction sector is strategically important for Europe providing building and infrastructure on which all sectors of the economy depend. With 11.8 million operatives directly employed in the sector, it is Europe's largest industrial employer accounting for 7% of total employment and 28% of industrial employment in the EU-15. It is estimated that 26 million workers in the EU-15 depend in one way or another on the construction sector. About 910 billion Euro was invested in construction in 2003, representing 10% of the GDP and 51.2% of the Gross Fixed Capital Formation of the EU-15.

Construction is also an important sector of the economy in new Member States. In Poland, the Czech Republic and Hungary alone, the turnover was about 38 billion Euro in 2003 and the market is estimated to be growing significantly at an average rate of +4.2% per year.

Moreover, the relationship between construction activities, and the built environment on the one hand, and sustainable development on the other, is both significant and complex. Construction uses more raw materials than any other sector, and the creation and operation of the built environment accounts for an important consumption of natural resources. There is also a pressing need to address the regeneration of many urban areas of Europe, in particular in the newly acceded countries, and the realisation of major trans-European infrastructure works.

UNIT 5

Talking about construction

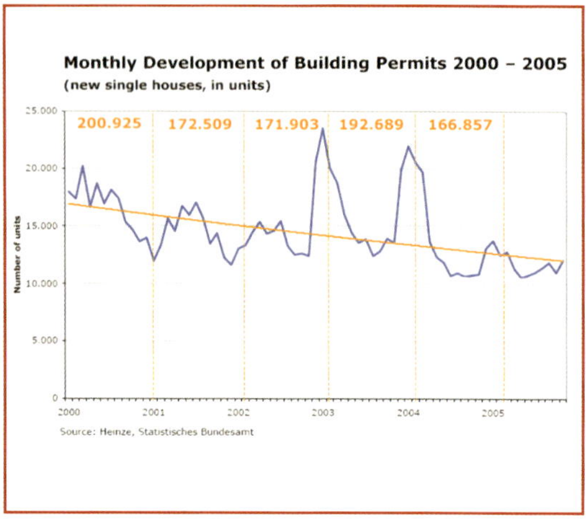

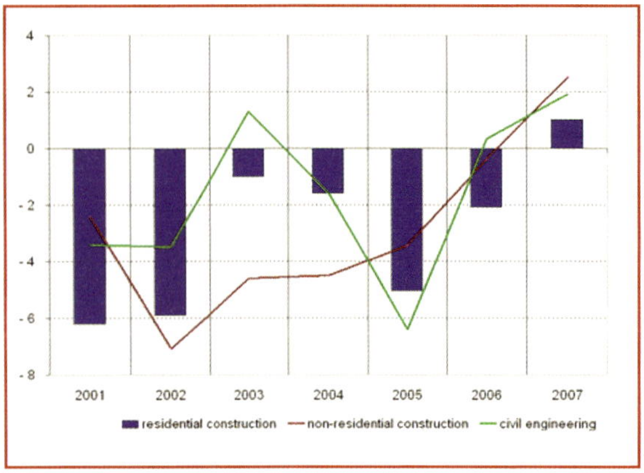

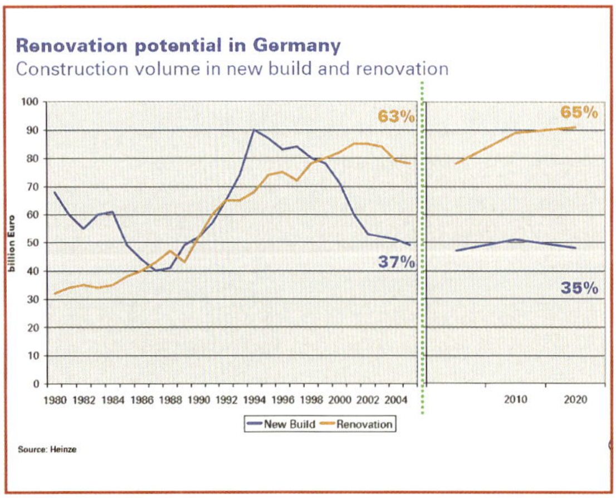

Source: European Commission

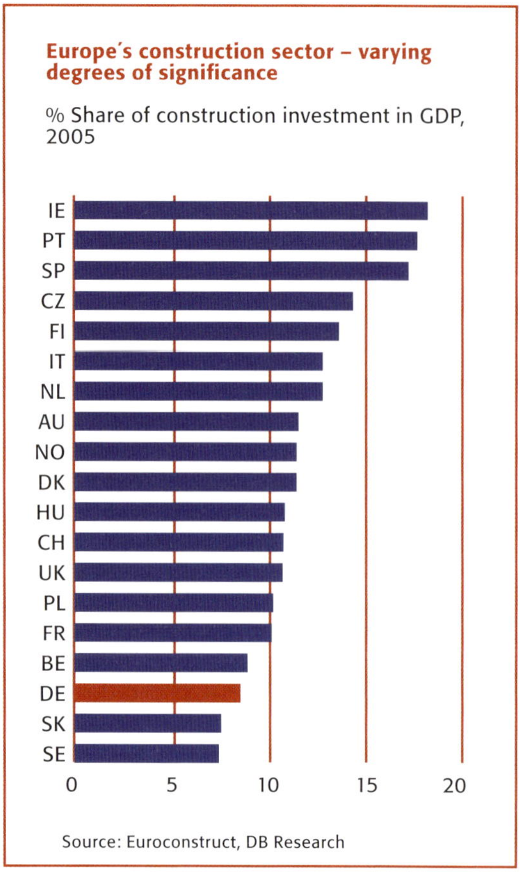

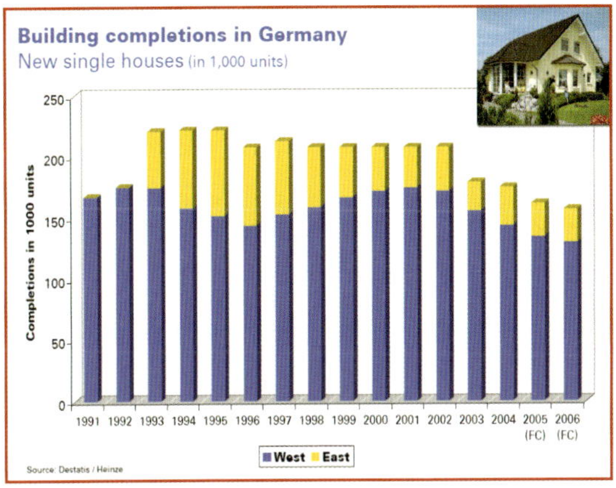

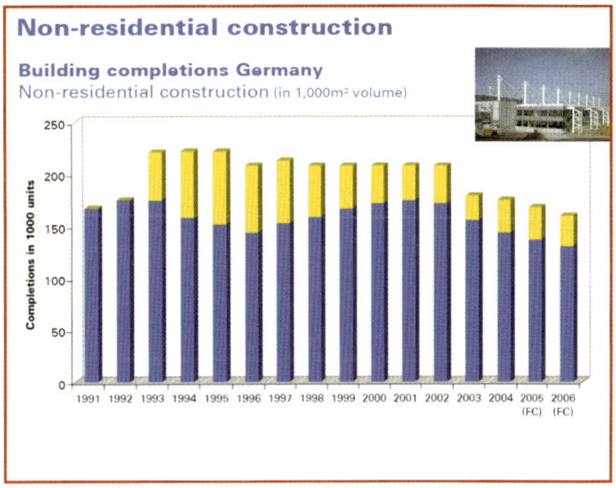

Source: European Commission

Grammatik wiederholen und lernen

Nach fast 5 Kapiteln in diesem Buch haben Sie sicherlich festgestellt, dass Grammatikübungen hier nicht zu den Standardaufgaben gehören. Dies bedeutet keinesfalls, dass wir eine Beherrschung von Grammatikregeln nicht wichtig finden, aber wir glauben auch, dass Sie Ihre individuell verschiedenen Grammatiklücken alleine auffrischen können/sollten.

Hierbei helfen Ihnen einige Lernstrategien:

- Lassen Sie sich nicht aus Angst davor, Grammatikfehler zu machen, vom Sprechen abbringen. Natürlich wäre es ideal, wenn Sie keinen einzigen Fehler in der englische Sprache machten, aber erst einmal ist es wichtiger, dass Ihr Gesprächspartner Sie versteht.
- Gelangen Sie über den Wunsch und das Bedürfnis, in der englischen Sprache zu kommunizieren, zu dem Wunsch, Grammatik zu wiederholen. Sagen Sie nie: Ich fange erst an, die Sprache frei zu benutzen, wenn ich weiß, dass ich keine Grammatikfehler mache.
- Lernen Sie Grammatik nie kommunikations- und themenunabhängig. Übungen wie „Schreiben Sie beliebige 10 Sätze im Passiv" sind nicht dazu angetan, dass sich die korrekten Sprachmuster bei Ihnen einprägen. Wiederholen Sie ausgehend von einer Kommunikationssituation und einem bestimmten Thema. Wollen Sie beispielsweise einen Fragebogen zur Mieterzufriedenheit erstellen, müssen Sie sich zwangsläufig mit den Regeln zur Fragenbildung im Englischen beschäftigen. Lernen Sie nicht alle möglichen Grammatikaspekte am Stück. Wenn es keine kommunikative und thematische Verknüpfung zwischen beispielsweise dem Present Perfect und den Prepositions gibt, werden Sie diese Regeln wieder schnell vergessen.
- Grammatikwiederholung ist sehr individuell. Bei allen von Ihnen sind unterschiedliche Lücken aufgetreten, die Sie am besten einzeln erarbeiten und schließen können. Nutzen Sie auf dem Markt befindliche Kurzgrammatiken (auch die aus der Schulzeit erfüllen ihren Zweck) oder auch sehr gut gemachte Seiten im Internet. Auf diesen zum Teil auch interaktiv gestalteten Seiten werden Ihnen z. B. häufig sofort die korrekten Antworten angezeigt.

UNIT 5

Talking about construction

Jobs and trades in construction

Work in pairs. Have a look at the following job descriptions. Choose various jobs in turns and describe the activities which are linked to this job. Make sure that you do not mention the term used for this job. Your partner will have to guess which job you are talking about.

The role of a **ceiling fixer** usually involves fitting suspended ceilings, often in big modern buildings like shops, offices and hospitals.

Stonemasons and bricklayers are often called on to produce both interesting and decorative effects. Bricklayers also use a variety of specialist tools to spread and joint mortar and cut bricks or blocks to size.

Not all finishes applied to walls and ceilings are 'wet', like plaster. 'Dry' finishes, such as plasterboard and wallboard, can be fixed up, joined together and decorated instead. A **dry lining operative** is the skilled worker who carries out this job.

Felt **roofers** apply felt to a roof, usually in several layers bonded together, to form a watertight covering and keep the interior of the building dry.

General construction operatives have a wide range of skills. They can be involved in tasks as diverse as concreting, formworking or timbering.

Bench joiners prepare and assemble doors, windows and staircases, ready for installation. They also create fitted furniture, such as wardrobes and cupboards for buildings.

Timber is an essential part of just about every structure, and it's the **carpenter and joiner**'s job to prepare it and put it into place. It's a skilled job that utilises special tools, and often involves many different kinds of wood.

Glazing is a highly skilled job that involves cutting glass – as well as other window materials – the right size and fixing them in place.

Town planners oversee the development of an entire town or region. They must understand the needs of a local environment, economy and population and how to make it into a pleasant place to live and work.

Roof sheeting and cladding is a lightweight covering that's attached to a building's structure. It's made in large units using metal, plastic or fibre cement. **Roof slaters and tilers** create a waterproof covering for a building by applying individual slates or tiles to a basic timber framework, such as the roof of houses.

Formworkers make temporary structures out of wood or metal. These moulds then have wet concrete poured into them and, when the concrete is hardened, the structures are removed to reveal perfectly shaped pieces.

Mastic asphalt is the material made from a mixture of limestone and bitumen. When it is heated up it can be spread and formed, returning to its original state as it cools down again.

A **shopfitter**'s job is to plan, build and finish the shop interior. Starting with an empty room, they choose, cut and shape the materials that give a shop its own look and style.

The role of a **painter and decorator** in the construction industry is normally more involved than simply decorating a room in a house. For example, oil rigs, bridges and steelwork all need heavy-duty coatings.

Most people know one part of the plasterer's work: applying wet finishes to walls, ceilings and floors. This is called solid **plastering**. There's also fibrous plastering, which involves making ornamental plasterwork in a workshop or on site - that's the kind you see on the ceilings of decorative buildings.

Wall and floor tiling may sound straightforward, but it can be a complex job, using coloured and textured tiles to decorate the inside of a building.

Demolition is one of the most highly skilled jobs in construction. It can also be very dangerous if the right precautions are not followed, especially with operations carried out by hand. Demolishing bridges and buildings involves plant machinery, careful planning, and high levels of safety. Once the structure has been demolished, the site is cleared, and the materials are often recycled.

It's the **land surveyor**'s job to measure, record and visually present features of the landscape all around us.

Project managers are in charge of the overall planning, management, co-ordination and financial control of a project.

A **structural engineer** makes sure that a building's shape, design and the materials it is made from are strong enough to withstand the forces of nature. In the UK this might not seem quite so radical but in areas prone to earthquakes, it can make the difference between life and death.

CAD technicians use computer generated drawings to prepare the information needed for a construction job. This can involve working across a wide range of fields, including architecture, building services, building, civil and structural engineering.

Scaffold is usually made of metal tubes, fittings and metal or timber platforms, put together by **scaffolders** so that workers can reach the parts of the structure they're working on. Safety is paramount, both for the people working on the scaffold and those below.

Renderers work on new buildings or on the extension or maintenance of existing buildings, and provide an attractive finish to the outside. Two coats are applied, and different finishes can be applied to give different textures, such as pebbledash.

The role of a **plumber** is highly varied and ranges from installing systems to new buildings to the maintenance of existing ones. Installation work includes central heating systems, sanitary systems, drainage and guttering. Heating systems may be powered using electricity, gas, oil, solids fuel, or even solar energy. Maintenance work includes routine servicing and emergency repairs. In addition, much of the work involves finding faults and carrying out repairs.

The job of the **building engineer** is an important and varied one. It incorporates all activities involved in the creation and maintenance of the built environment, ranging from site investigations, building inspections and surveys to project design, cost evaluations, and deciding on appropriate construction methods.

There are also **civil engineering technician** roles to consider. These technicians work in constructing roads, bridges, tunnels and other major construction projects.

Landscape architecture is really a combination of architecture and horticulture. Working with plants, shrubs and trees, they develop the spaces between buildings. Of course, plants and trees also grow, so the landscape architect must be able to visualise how they will look a few years down the line.

It's the **planner**'s job to make sure that a project is completed with the right resources, and to ensure that they're all delivered safely, on time, and in the right amount and quality.

Steel erectors install the prefabricated structural steel frames of buildings such as warehouses, industrial units and multi-storey buildings. Work can be on both new buildings and the extension or adaptation of existing buildings.

Source: CITB-ConstructionSkills

Stages in construction

Look at the various construction stages and building activities given in the boxes below. Decide where to place them on the timeline to finish your building as soon as possible. From your list of jobs in construction, add the professionals carrying out these tasks as well. Of course, you may want to do some steps parallel.

decision to build

- obtain planning and building permission
- find suitable plot
- talk to an architect
- specify what you want to build
- specify how much land you need
- coordinate the various stages of construction and crafts involved
- find contractors
- find builders
- installation of windows and doors
- siding
- rough HVAC
- insulation
- painting
- finish electrical
- finish plumbing
- tiling
- carpet and flooring
- finish HVAC
- hook-up to water main
- hook-up to sewer
- bathroom and kitchen counters and cabinets
- bare brickwork
- final inspection and acceptance of construction work
- answer all questions having to do with the financing of the project
- drywall and interior fittings
- roofing
- grading and site preparation
- foundation construction
- rough electrical
- rough plumbing
- trimming

Construction and DIY

Do homebuilders need the services of professionals in the building trade?

Before you have a look at the following texts, brainstorm advantages and disadvantages of do-it-yourself in building. Are there more pros or cons?

Now have a look at this German text and summarise the main points in clear statements.

DIY IN CONSTRUCTION
DIY can save you a lot of money – however you should carefully consider what you can really do yourself and where you should rather employ professionals.
...

Mit Eigenleistung Geld sparen

Wer am Bau selbst Hand anlegt, kann sich eine Stange Geld sparen. Man sollte allerdings gut abwägen, wofür das eigene Know-how ausreicht – und was man lieber den Profis überlässt.

Von Andrea Nasemann

„Wer sich am Bau zu viel vornimmt, kann sich schnell übernehmen", ist die Erfahrung von Bernhard Riedl vom Verband Privater Bauherren in München. Zwar können Eigenleistungen die Kosten beim Bau des Eigenheims senken. Mehr als zehn Prozent Ersparnis ist allerdings für Berufstätige nicht realistisch. Da selbst handwerklich geschickte Bauherren annähernd doppelt so lange für die Arbeiten benötigen wie Profis, können leicht 1.000 Arbeitsstunden auf der Baustelle zusammenkommen. Bevor man Eigenleistungen ins Kalkül zieht, sollte man sich daher gut überlegen, ob man sowohl das fachliche Know-how als auch ausreichend Zeit und Tatkraft einbringen kann.

Sich selbst nicht überfordern

Vernünftigerweise plant man nur solche Jobs in Eigenregie, die keine hohen fachlichen und technischen Anforderungen stellen, also Malen und Tapezieren, Bodenbeläge und Außenanlagen. Wer sich an Fliesenarbeiten und Dachausbau wagt, sollte schon über entsprechende Erfahrungen verfügen. „Trotz allem sollte man sich vorher bei Kollegen oder Bekannten über die notwendigen Arbeiten informieren. Wer zum Beispiel das Dach selber ausbauen will, muss die bauphysikalischen Zusammenhänge kennen sowie sicherstellen, dass die Wärmedämmung ausreicht und das Dach luft- und dampfdicht ist", rät Bernhard Riedl.

Klare Vereinbarungen

Schon vor dem Vertragsabschluss sollte man sich von der Baufirma eine Aufstellung der Material- und Lohnkosten für die Eigenleistungen unterbreiten lassen. Meist können die Firmen die Baustoffe günstiger beziehen. Dies sollte man in seiner Kalkulation berücksichtigen. Grundsätzlich sollte man nur solche Tätigkeiten übernehmen, die sich von den Vertragsleistungen der Hausbaufirma oder des Bauträgers konkret abgrenzen lassen. Um den vertraglichen Fertigstellungstermin einhalten zu können, sollte man den eigenen Einsatz mit dem Architekten, der Hausbaufirma oder dem Bauträger genau abstimmen. Die vereinbarte Eigenleistung und die damit verbundenen Gutschriften sollte man in den Vertrag aufnehmen lassen. Am meisten spart derjenige, der Arbeiten mit hohem Lohnkostenanteil übernimmt.

Faktor Sicherheit

„Im Vertrag sollte man sich auch überlegen, wer für die Planung und Koordination der Eigenleistungen verantwortlich ist", empfiehlt Bernhard Riedl. Nachbarn, Freunde und Verwandte, die auf der Baustelle mit anpacken, muss der Bauherr bei der Berufsgenossenschaft der Bauwirtschaft (BG BAU) innerhalb einer Woche nach Beginn der Bauarbeiten anmelden. Dies gilt unabhängig davon, ob mithelfende Personen unentgeltlich arbeiten oder gegen Bezahlung. Das kostet den Bauherren regional unterschiedlich zwischen 1,73 und 2,21 Euro pro Helfer und Arbeitsstunde.

Die Beitragspflicht entfällt bei kurzfristigen Gefälligkeitsleistungen von Verwandten oder wenn alle Helfer zusammen nicht mehr als 39 Stunden arbeiten. Wer der Melde-, Nachweis- und Aufzeichnungspflicht nicht nachkommt, riskiert ein Bußgeld bis zu 2.500 Euro. Der Bauherr ist auch für die Sicherheit auf der Baustelle verantwortlich: Die Baustelle muss mit Gerüsten abgesichert sein und die Helfer müssen Schutzkleidung tragen.

Für Schäden, die der Bauherr selbst verursacht hat, übernimmt der Bauträger keine Gewährleistung. Hat ein Handwerker gepfuscht, kann dieser zur Kasse gebeten werden. Allerdings treffen den Bauherren, soweit er die Arbeiten fortführt, Prüf- und Hinweispflichten. Es kommt dann darauf an, ob er den Mangel erkennen konnte, beziehungsweise ob er ihn rechtzeitig gerügt hat.

Source: Andrea Nasemann, Süddeutsche Zeitung vom 28.10.2005

Now have a look at the English text and complete your table of arguments for and against DIY-building.

TextTextText
TextTextText
TextTextText
ARBEIT
TextTextText
TextTextText

theguardian

A firm foundation for your D-I-Y building

Emma Tyrrell; Saturday June 15, 2002; The Guardian

Tens of thousands of people every year dream of finding the perfect plot of land and building a home. But for many, that dream plot is more likely to be found on the site of an old ice-cream factory or builder's yard, than on an undeveloped piece of green.

Recent Government figures show that three out of every five new homes built last year were on previously developed land, and through the conversion of existing buildings. But while the hassle of knocking down derelict buildings, and clearing possibly contaminated land, may not appeal to the dreamers, many can see the benefits.

"In many ways it is easier to work with a brownfield site," says Sam Malcolm of specialist self-build services company BuildStore.

"Planners will generally be restrictive on how much you can increase the footprint of the previous building, but a major advantage is that your services – gas, electricity and water – are likely to be there."

According to the Council of Mortgage Lenders, self-build is the fastest growing area of the property market.

An estimated 20,000 people each year succumb. Few do all the building work themselves, preferring to employ builders and architects. Even then, the average saving is around 20 per cent - if everything goes to plan.

In areas where land is cheaper, savings can obviously be higher. Build It magazine found that self-builders in Shropshire could save nearly half the cost of a new home. But in areas like Surrey and Sussex, the savings can be small. According to Buildstore, which examined 11,000 advertised plots, the average cost in the UK is £76,342.53. But within this, there are huge variations - from a 0.75-acre site on the outskirts of Kingston at £1.5million, to £5,000 for a 2,529 sq metre site on the Isle of Skye in Scotland.

Self-built homes account for around 13 per cent of new builds, and an astonishing one in four of all new detached houses. But the real problem is finding the right plot. "Some people search for years," Mr Malcolm says. "Our internet service, Plotsearch, lists around 6,000 sites but that includes renovations, conversions and a lot of brownfield sites."

The internet can save on wasted trips by showing pictures and allowing searchers to weed out unsuitable sites. [...]

Plots listed as "building plots" should already have outline or detailed planning permission, but it is essential to check any restrictions on the land. Cutting down certain trees, for example, could make a plot unsuitable for the size and shape of the house you have in mind. Access, boundaries and the cost of clearing a brownfield site should also be checked.

In expensive areas, such as the south-east and London, it is important not to get carried away and end up paying more than you can afford. Overpaying for land could mean you are left without the cash to build the house. Daunting as the task of finding the perfect plot at the right price may be, there are thousands who do manage it.

Mr Bradshaw says the key is to stay determined and keep plodding on until you achieve your dream.

Keeping an open mind to previously-used sites is also key; knocking down the old buildings on his land cost between £2,000 and £3,000, but added roughly ten times more to the value.

"There are queues of people ready to tell you that you'll never find what you're looking for," he says. "Well, stuff them, because you'll get there in the end."

Determined to get the green light

Although most new homes nowadays are supposed to be built on brownfield land, many enthusiastic and determined self-builders still manage to find their plot of green - at least after a lengthy and exhaustive search. [...]

As so many other determined self-builders have discovered "finding a plot of land was definitely the hardest thing about self-build", particularly if you have a fixed view of what you are looking for. [...]

Get together in groups of seven. Each of you takes one of the following roles and prepares arguments to put forward in the discussion. The topic to be discussed is: **The ultimate way to your dream house is self-build.**

- Stuart Lowry, Association of Builders
- Fiona Hodges, Federation of Architects
- Peter Clifton, SelfBuild
- Norman Taylor, United Building Trades
- Sarah Peters, Association of Real Estate Agents
- Hugh Prescott, successful and satisfied selfbuilder
- Your name, moderator of the discussion

Pre-reading activity

Hurricanes Katrina and Rita destroyed tens of thousands of buildings in the US. Which in your opinion are the effects on construction costs and availability of buildings materials?

Wanted: A Project That Meets Budget: Supply shortages, rising prices of building materials force facility planners to adapt.

Insurance adjusters hadn't even finished processing claims from hurricanes Katrina and Rita when sharply higher bills for construction projects started reaching the desks of corporate facility planners.

While building material prices and availability fluctuated constantly in the months following the storms that ravaged the Gulf Coast, the net effect of these changes is certain to impact a wide range of construction projects through most of 2006. Real estate executives can now expect to face higher costs to build virtually any type of commercial structure and longer lead times on quotes and construction.

Industrial asset managers, in particular, are having to adjust to the aftermath of America's worst hurricane season on record.

Consider how much these building materials increased in price, from late August to mid-December 2005: concrete, up 20 percent; lumber, up 30 percent; plywood, up 30 percent; plastics, up 7 percent; PVC pipe, up 50 percent; insulation, up 8 percent; gypsum, up 25 percent; copper, up 17 percent; and brass, up 12 percent.

With price hikes like these, builders and clients alike were left scrambling to fill supply orders and cope with the sudden, unexpected strain on their budgets.

"If it used to take days to get a construction quote on a building project, it now takes weeks," says Sean Nugent, executive director of Pfizer Global R&D's Global Strategic Facilities Planning in New London, Conn. "If it used to take weeks, it could now take months."

Nugent is not alone. Site Selection interviewed a wide range of corporate real estate directors, site selection consultants, brokers and builders and found that nearly all of them had been affected in some form by either building material shortages or construction cost increases since August 2005. While the impact varies from region to region throughout North America, several trends have taken hold throughout the industry:

- Delays in securing construction quotes are now the norm, rather than the exception, as building-material prices in some regions keep rising sharply and seldom stay put for long.
- Overall project costs from building start-up through completion are now considerably higher than they were a year ago; total cost increases of 25 to 50 percent, depending upon facility type, are common.
- Existing buildings have moved to the top of the list for site selectors when considering a new plant location, as costs to rehab a facility are usually lower than constructing a new one on a greenfield site.
- A wave of new building-material-plant construction is cropping up to meet the demand for everything from cement and concrete pipe to plastics and lumber.

Arthur Murray, associate broker for Lavista Associates Inc. in Norcross, Ga., says he has been shocked recently to see construction quotes for projects in metropolitan Atlanta.

"I have actually seen quotes that are 100 percent higher for the exact same type and size of building that was built only three or four years ago here in Atlanta," says Murray, who sells and leases large industrial facilities throughout the metro area.

Most experts who track construction costs and material prices do not expect these costs to stabilize until December 2006.

Source: Ron Starner

What – according to the text – is the effect of the hurricanes on the general situation in the building industry?

How do many site selectors react?

Make a list of technical terms having to do with construction and group them in the following categories:

land	professions	buildings	building material	economical/ financial aspects

UNIT5

Talking about construction

Have a look at the following list of terms used for construction. Find between 3 and 5 categories of your choice and group the terms accordingly.

air conditioning
alternating current
appliances
attic
balcony
basement
bathroom products
boiler room
bricking
carpet
ceiling
cement, concrete and mortars
ceramic
chimney
circulating pump
cladding & siding
coatings, laminates
cold bridge
communication systems
concrete slab
condensing boiler
conduit pipe
door frame
door opener
doorbell
doors
downpipes
drainage course
ductwork
electric installation
electrical outlets & cable
ducting
fans, ventilation & airconditioning
fences & exterior work
fire door
fire staircase
fittings
floating floor screed
floor covering
floor heating
flooring
flush-mounted
fresh water
frost resistant

garage door
gateway
glass
granite
granite, marble, stone, slate
gutter
handrail systems
heater
heating circuit water
heating, insulation
hinge
inner wall
insulating covering
insulation
intercom
joinery, doors & windows
kitchens
landing
laundry room
letter box
lifts & escalators
lightning
locks
loggia
mailboxes
main entry
main fuse
mains
marble
mortar
motion detector
on-wall
outer wall
paint
panels & linings
parquet
partition
partitions, screens
paving
pipes
plaster
power supply
pumps
push switch
PVC
railing
ramp
reinforced concrete
rising mains
roller shutter

roof beam
roof covering
roof garden
roof tile
roof sealing strip
roofing
roofing & roof drains etc
sanitation
scrap chute
sealing
seam
security & safety
sewer system
shop fittings
shutter
sink
skirting board
skylight
socket
stainless
staircase
stairs & balustrades
statics
steel
subsonic noise insulation
supply pipe
swimming pools, spa pools, saunas
switches
tap
telephone wall jack
temperature sensor
thermostat
timber products
toilet
toilet tank
towel rail
truss
vent pipe
ventilation
wall light
wall tiles
walls
water heaters
water meter
window frame
window sill
windows
wire & wrought iron work
zink

Talking about construction

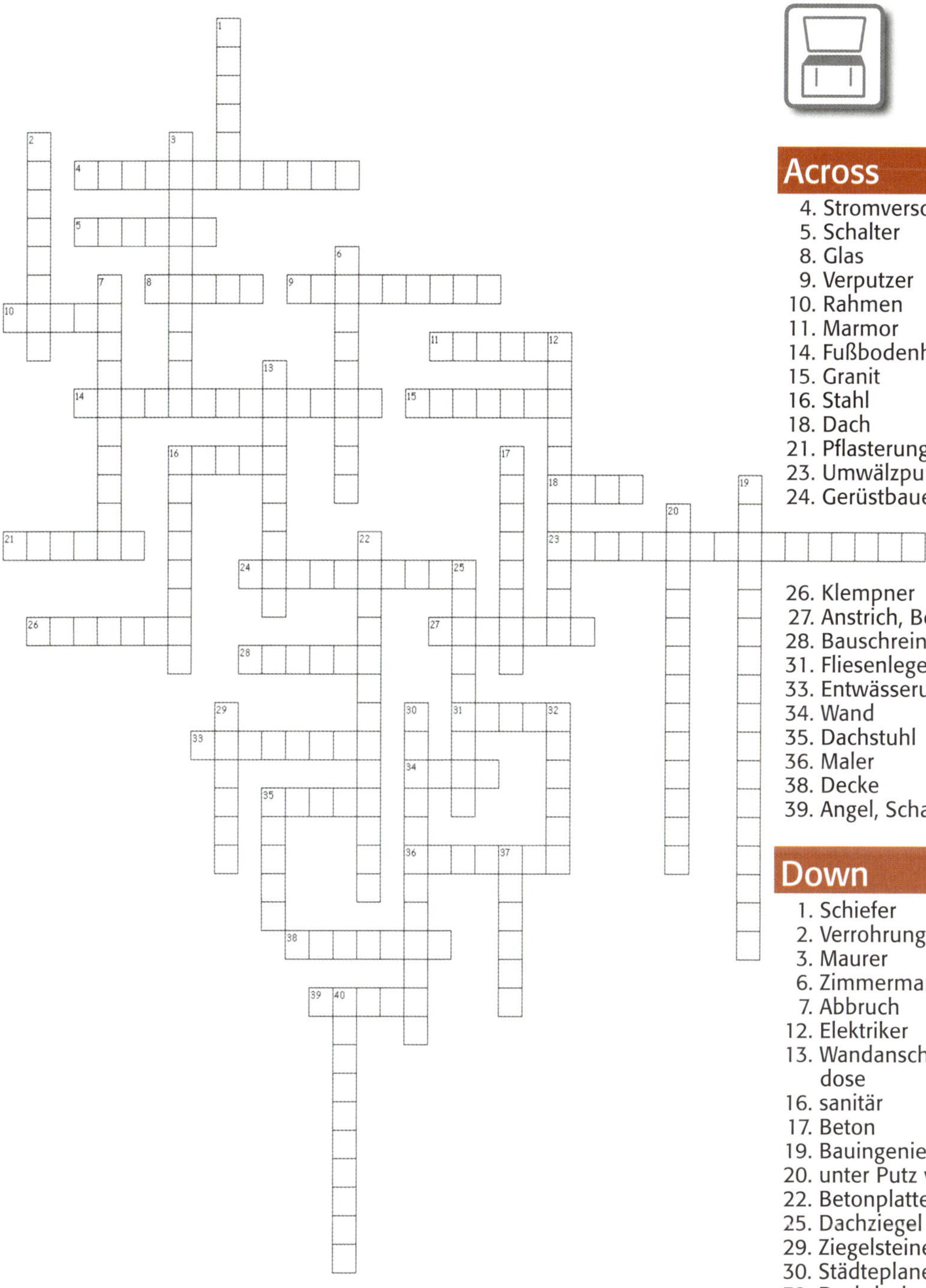

Across

4. Stromversorgung
5. Schalter
8. Glas
9. Verputzer
10. Rahmen
11. Marmor
14. Fußbodenheizung
15. Granit
16. Stahl
18. Dach
21. Pflasterung
23. Umwälzpumpe
24. Gerüstbauer
26. Klempner
27. Anstrich, Belag
28. Bauschreiner
31. Fliesenleger
33. Entwässerung
34. Wand
35. Dachstuhl
36. Maler
38. Decke
39. Angel, Scharnier

Down

1. Schiefer
2. Verrohrung
3. Maurer
6. Zimmermann
7. Abbruch
12. Elektriker
13. Wandanschluss-dose
16. sanitär
17. Beton
19. Bauingenieur
20. unter Putz verlegt
22. Betonplatte
25. Dachziegel
29. Ziegelsteine
30. Städteplaner
32. Dachdecker
35. Fliesen
37. Bauholz
40. Isolierung

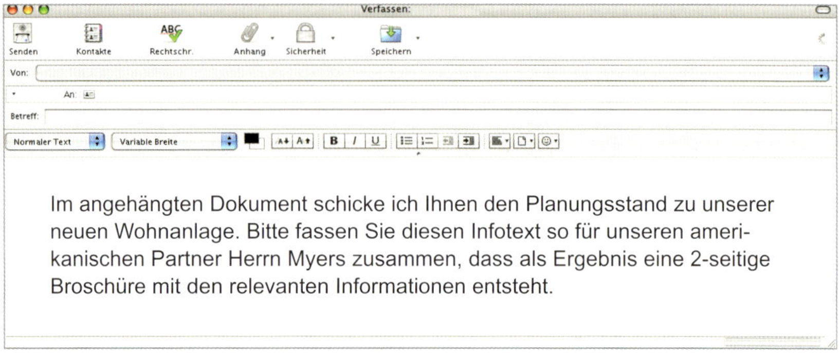

Planung und Errichtung einer Anlage Integriertes Wohnen

Die GW BO hat sich nach den zurückliegenden erfolgreichen Geschäftsaktivitäten mit der Investmentgruppe von Herrn Myers entschlossen, für ein Neubauprojekt in Deutschland eine gemeinsame Tochterfirma zu gründen. In enger Abstimmung mit dem von Herrn Myers eingesetzten kaufmännischen Geschäftsführer der neuen Unternehmung ConceptInvest GmbH, Floyd Brandis, soll als Pilotprojekt zusammen mit der Stadt Bochum eine Anlage integrierten Wohnens in Bochum entstehen. Die Gründe für diese Art der Immobilie liegen maßgeblich in der aktuellen Mieterstruktur der GW BO begründet. Eine Mieterbefragung auf freiwilliger Basis und eine parallel durchgeführte Portfolio-Analyse ergaben, dass augenblicklich in den zu Beginn der 1970er Jahre gebauten (und noch nicht modernisierten) 3-Zimmer-Wohnungen (ca. 640) über 50 % von zwei Personen und mehr als 30 % von nur noch einer Person bewohnt werden. Die Altersstruktur in dieser Mietergruppe stellt sich wie folgt dar:

Zwischen 50 und 60:	37 %
Zwischen 60 und 65:	29 %
Zwischen 65 und 75:	23 %
Über 75:	11 %

Die befragten Mieter zahlen augenblicklich eine Miete zwischen 380 € und 420 €.

Besonders aus den letzten beiden Altersgruppen gaben in der Befragung mehr als die Hälfte an, dass sie ihr Leben in der eigenen Wohnung als „eingeschränkt gut" (65 %) bzw. „gar nicht mehr gut" (32 %) einschätzen. Analog zu diesen Angaben äußerten mehr als 80 % dieser Gruppe, dass sie lieber in einer deutlich kleineren Wohnung leben möchten.

Aus diesem Grund sieht die GW BO besonders in dieser Mietergruppe eine klar definierte Zielgruppe, so dass bei den jetzigen Überlegungen bereits zu Erstbezug von einer Vollbelegung der Anlage ausgegangen werden kann. Berücksichtigt man auch die für die Stadt Bochum prognostizierte demographische Entwicklung, kann zu dem jetzigen Zeitpunkt davon ausgegangen werden, dass ein solches Pilotprojekt auf hohe Akzeptanz stoßen wird.

Die Gesamtplanung soll in Bochum erfolgen, über die unterschiedlichen Schritte und Entscheidungen wird Herr Myers entsprechend informiert.

Bisherige Kernpunkte der Überlegungen sind:

Planung und Errichtung einer Anlage zum integrierten Wohnen, bestehend aus:

- ca. 35 seniorengerechten/behindertengerechten Wohneinheiten (von ca. 36 m^2 bis 68 m^2)
- ca. 8 Gewerbeeinheiten (Arztpraxis, Friseursalon, Fußpflege, Lebensmittel o. Ä. mit wohnnahen Dienstleistungen)
- entsprechend der Anzahl der Gewerbeeinheiten Wohneinheiten für die jeweiligen Pächter (Größen von ca. 72 m^2 bis 92 m^2)
- alle Wohn- und Gewerbeeinheiten sollen vermietet werden, über eine Veräußerung von einzelnen WE kann zukünftig nachgedacht werden
- Innenhofgestaltung: Parkbänke, Blumenbeete, Rasen, Springbrunnen, kleiner Wasserlauf
- Portierservice am Eingang
- Sicherheitssystem zur Überwachung des Hauptzugangs und des Innenhofs
- Tiefgarage mit Möglichkeit der Stellplatzvermietung (insgesamt ca. 40 Stellplätze)
- Grundstück innenstadtnah
- benötigte Grundstücksfläche ca. 4.000 m^2
- enge Planungskooperation mit der Stadt Bochum
- über besondere Umsetzungsformen zur Energieeinsparung und Nachhaltigkeit beim Bau wird zurzeit entschieden

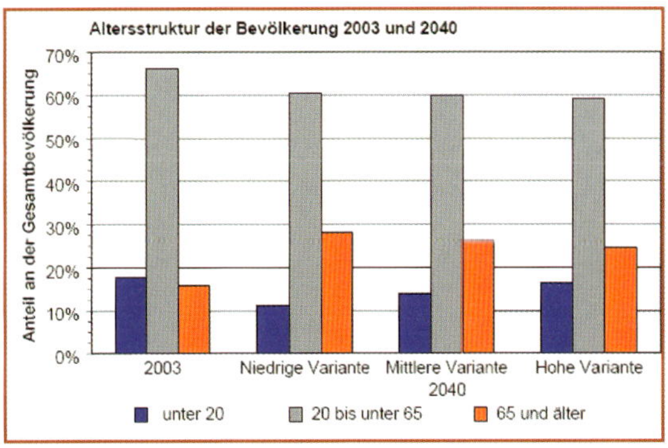

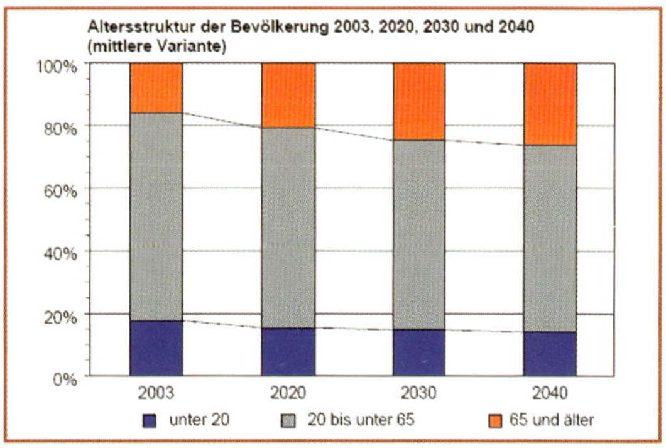

Solar energy

Before you have a look at the text, brainstorm your ideas and knowledge on this renewable energy. Include aspects such as efficiency, price, location, maintenance etc.

Now have a look at the following text on solar energy and photovoltaic technology. Carefully read through the text so that you have got a detailed understanding of its contents. When you have finished, no longer look at the text and answer the questions below.

Alternative electricity supply: Photovoltaic Technology

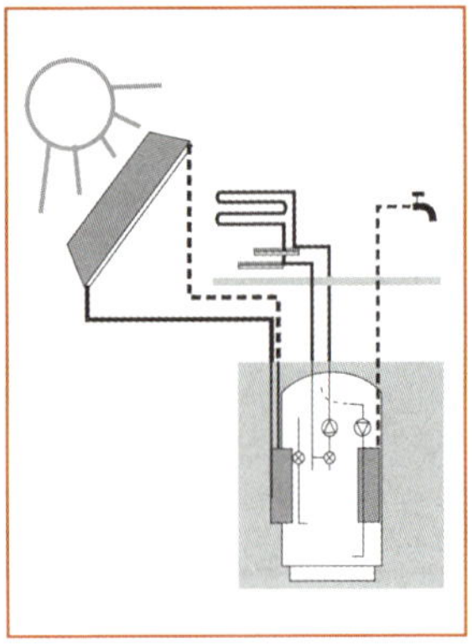

Photovoltaic systems are solar systems that produce electricity directly from sunlight. Photovoltaic systems produce clean, reliable electricity without consuming any fossil fuels. They are being used in a wide variety of applications, from providing power for watches, highway signs, and space stations, to providing for a household's electrical needs.
The number of photovoltaic powered households is increasing. Typically there are two types of photovoltaic technology used for household applications: Stand Alone and Grid-connected systems. Stand-alone PV systems are typically referred to as autonomous photovoltaic systems that operate independently from any electricity grid. This system generates electricity to run the application and store any extra energy in batteries. The batteries take over whenever the solar power cannot sustain the need of the application. Conversely, if there is an excess of solar power and the batteries are full, this power is lost. Grid-connected photovoltaic systems are directly connected to the electricity grid. The system can supply any surplus of energy to the grid, or extract energy if the generator does not meet the demand. In Germany, any excess of electricity on the grid can be sold back to the open market, which dictates prices based on the electricity provider. Grid-connected photovoltaic systems can be used if the house is very close to an electric grid. Otherwise, under the assumption that the building is located in a remote area, where distribution lines are difficult and inefficient to use, stand-alone photovoltaic systems are better suited. Since PV systems are installed by modules, the entire system itself can be constructed to any size based on the energy requirement. Hence, the energy extracted from the sun can be used to supply all a household's electricity needs, or synergize with other forms of electric generation to reduce costs and to increase conservation. The application of a photovoltaic home is very ideal for Europe, because the photovoltaic home is relatively inexpensive to construct, very energy efficient, and requires little maintenance and can save up to 95 percent of energy used and consequently leads to reduced charges found on the typical electricity bill. Furthermore, it contributes to reduce the emission of greenhouse gas.

Source: Dr. Peter Catania

Questions on the text:

STATEMENT	TRUE	NOT IN THE TEXT	WRONG, IN THE TEXT IT SAYS THAT…
PV systems can be autonomous.			
Maintenance is complicated and rather expensive.			
A photovoltaic home is relatively inexpensive to construct.			
The electricity produced comes directly from the sunlight.			
The system can save up to 55 percent of energy used.			
Any excess of electricity on the grid can be sold back to the open market in all European countries.			
One disadvantage is that this electricity does not synergise with other forms of electricity.			
Excessive energy can be stored in batteries.			
These batteries only work when there is enough sunlight.			
A PV system for a traditional detached house costs between € 25,000 and € 35,000.			
In theory, you do not need to be connected to the electricity grid if you have a PV system in your house.			

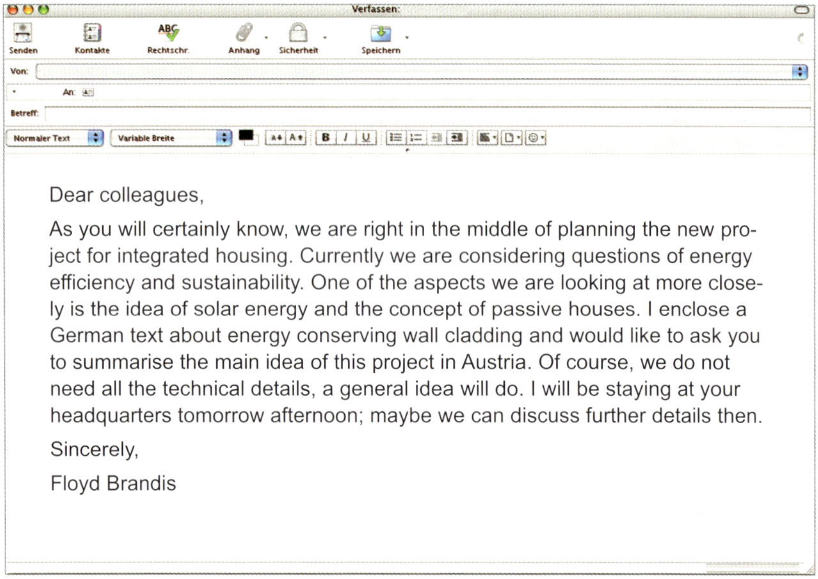

Dear colleagues,

As you will certainly know, we are right in the middle of planning the new project for integrated housing. Currently we are considering questions of energy efficiency and sustainability. One of the aspects we are looking at more closely is the idea of solar energy and the concept of passive houses. I enclose a German text about energy conserving wall cladding and would like to ask you to summarise the main idea of this project in Austria. Of course, we do not need all the technical details, a general idea will do. I will be staying at your headquarters tomorrow afternoon; maybe we can discuss further details then.

Sincerely,

Floyd Brandis

Bauen im Passivhausstandard – über die Hülle effizient realisierbar

In der solarCity bei Linz wachsen interessante Energiespargebäude derzeit wie die sprichwörtlichen Pilze aus dem Boden. Darunter befinden sich zwei Passivhäuser mit einer gap-Solarfassade zur Wärmedämmung. Eines der beiden Wohnhäuser unterschreitet die Anforderungen an den Passivhausstandard gar um 50 %.

Die Stadt Linz verzeichnete Anfang der 90er Jahre etwa 12.000 Wohnungssuchende. Da die Niedrigenergiebauweise zu dieser Zeit im sozialen Wohnungsbau etabliert werden sollte, entschlossen sich die Verantwortlichen, die Aufgabe konsequent in Form eines neuen Stadtteils im Süden von Linz umzusetzen. Die Idee für den Bau einer solarCity war geboren. Derzeit entstehen mehr als 1.300 Wohnungen von 12 beteiligten Wohnbaugenossenschaften im Baugebiet der solarCity.

Das Passivhaus 1 der GIWOG soll hier näher vorgestellt werden. Es handelt sich dabei um einen Baukörper in Mischbauweise. Eine Besonderheit stellt die solare Hülle dar. Dabei wird hinter Glas eine eingefärbte Solarwabe aus Zellulose eingesetzt.

Das 0,7-Liter-Haus

Herausragend ist der jährliche Heizwärmebedarf von Haus 1. Mit einem Wert von 7,3 kWh/m²a (Berechnung mit dem Passivhaus Projektierungspaket) werden die Anforderungen an Passivhäuser um 50 % unterschritten – neuer Bestwert in Österreich! Im Vergleich zum Neubaustandard der 90er Jahre, der pro Jahr umgelegt etwa 10 Liter Heizöl/m² zur Deckung der Raumwärme benötigte, beträgt der Bedarf von Haus 1 lediglich 0,7 Liter Heizöl. Dieser Quantensprung wird durch die optimierten Dämmwerte der Bauteile in Kombination mit einer entsprechend abgestimmten Haustechnik (Lüftungsanlage mit Wärmerückgewinnung) möglich. Die solare Hülle schafft eine Ausgangsbasis, die einfache Haustechnikkonzepte ermöglicht.

	Charakteristik Passivhaus 1
Außenwand Süd/Nord (von außen nach innen)	• Glas ESG Float 6 mm • Luftebene 30 mm • Solarwabe aus Karton 50 mm • Paneelrückwand 4 mm • Ausgleichsdämmung 40 mm • Gipsfaserplatte 15 mm • Holzrahmenkonstruktion mit Zellulosedämmung 180 mm • OSB-Platte 18 mm • Installationsebene gedämmt 80 mm • GK-Platte 12,5 mm
Außenwand Ost/West Solarwand vor Ziegel (von außen nach innen)	• Glas ESG Float 6 mm • Luftebene 30 mm • Solarwabe aus Karton 50 mm • Paneelrückwand 4 mm • Ausgleichsdämmung 40 mm • Weichfaserplatte 15 mm • Holzrahmenkonstruktion mit Zellulosedämmung 140 mm • OSB-Platte 18 mm • Hochlochziegel 300 mm • Innenputz
Fenster	Passivhausfenster Holz/Alu
Oberste Decke	Eckwohnungen 40 cm Dämmung Mittelwohnungen 28 cm Dämmung
Kellerdecke	30 cm Dämmung auf Kellerdecke
Energiekennzahl nach PHPP	7,3 kWh/m²a
Wohnungsanzahl	24
Geschosse	4
Wohnungsgrößen	durchschnittlich 78 m²
Baubeginn	3/2003
Fertigstellung	9/2004

Anzumerken ist, dass für die Bauten in der solarCity Anschlusszwang an das Fernwärmenetz bestand. Daher wird für die beiden Passivhäuser die Warmwasserbereitung und der Restwärmebedarf mittels Fernwärme abgedeckt.

Solare Hülle im sozialen Wohnbau

An eine Gebäudehülle werden viele Anforderungen gestellt. Die „Intelligenz" einer Fassade zeichnet sich nicht in erster Linie durch besonders komplexe Technik aus, sondern durch größtmögliche Nutzung von natürlichen Energiequellen mit einem Minimum an technischem Aufwand. Das System muss so aufgebaut sein, dass die einzelnen Bestandteile auswechselbar und wiederverwertbar sind. Der Gehalt an „grauer Energie" (Herstellungsenergie) muss möglichst gering sein.

Der Bauherr erhält die komplette Hülle aus einer Hand. Ein bequemer und schneller Ablauf ist die Folge. Zudem steigt die Qualität. Der Krieg der Gewerke ist beendet!

Ökologische, ökonomische und energetische Gründe legen Systeme für Gebäudehüllen nahe, die Solarenergie nutzen. Dabei zeigt der Markt, dass sich nur einfache „LOW-TECH-Systeme" in der Breite durchsetzen. Da sich ein Gebäude meist über die Hülle definiert, werden hohe Anforderungen an die architektonischen Möglichkeiten gestellt. Energiesparen muss schön sein.

Industrielle Vorfertigung von Hüllen

Was in der Autoindustrie seit Jahrzehnten Standard ist, muss auch im Baubereich Eingang finden. Die Effizienz einer Gebäudehülle wird künftig auch an der raschen Verfügbarkeit und Integration ins Gebäude gemessen werden. Die Leichtbauweise birgt hier ein Potenzial, das bisher nur die Fertighausindustrie zum Teil erkannt hat. Das Baustellenfoto zeigt die Montage einer vorgefertigten Wand mit den Abmessungen von 10 x 3 Metern. Die dezentralen Lüftungssysteme mit Wärmerückgewinnung sind in der Wand bereits integriert, ebenso die Fenster mit den Rollos.

Source: gap-solar GmbH

Pre-listening activity

In how far could a roof garden be an idea to consider for the Bochum project?

Do you see a relation between roof gardens and energy consumption?

Now listen to the recording on rooftop gardens and make notes on their main advantages.

Post-listening

Discuss: Should we have a rooftop garden at our integrated housing project?

Choosing the right site

Have a look at the following texts about plots and building sites and read them carefully. Working on your own at first, come up with a total of nine questions on aspects and information given in the text.

Put your questions into three categories:

easy = 1 point;
more difficult = 2 points;
difficult = 3 points.

Of course you should know the answers to your own questions.

Now work with a partner and ask him/her your questions, answering his/her questions. You can choose from which category you would like to be asked a question. However, you are not allowed to have a look at the text. Whoever has scored most points when all questions have been used, is the winner.

How to choose the suitable building plot?

The decision is taken, you want to become a homeowner. Build, not buy the future home for yourself, your wife, your children, actually a brand-new real family-home.

Then, one of the most important questions is: Where do you want to live?

Unless you intend to move to the Taymir-Central Siberian tundra, the choice in Central Europe isn't as big as you might think.

There are a couple of limiting personal factors: Where do you work, where does your partner earn his / her money, how many cars can you afford, to which kind of school do you want to send your children, is your personal life-style compatible with such remote holiday-like areas like the German Allgäu, do you fancy the peal of cowbells or do you rather feel deaf when you don't hear the sirens of police cars, the squeaking sound of sluggish trams over the rails and the honking of car-horns for a couple of seconds?

Basically, you will be torn between three alternatives:

- find a nice plot of land in the **city**. The dream of young urban professionals is surely the bungalow-style handsome cottage in front of Saint-Martin-in-the-Fields in the very heart of London. Forget about it. It is either physically not available or financially not affordable. Most of the real estate transactions in big cities are, nowadays, sales and purchases of condo flats.

- Given the tremendous price and the threatening scarceness of fossil fuels, it might be a proof of your common sense to reduce the distance between your new home and your workplace as much as possible. This will encourage you automatically to look for your plot of land in the **suburban tissue around the city-centre**, where land is still affordable and where you can take full profit of the vicinity of urban infrastructures.
- Freelancers, nature lovers, people suffering from claustrophobia and persons of independent means who do not have to care for public transportation, may like the idea of living only a five minutes foot walk away

from their favourite golf court. They always do their shopping by car, they do never feel like running into the next pub around the corner to have a pint and talk to completely unknown people and they fancy the Goethe-style "On the lake"-romanticism: "The Nature is so kind and good / That to her breast clasps me!" If you belong to this category of people, helping yourself more with your own top-opening freezer instead of strolling between the market stands bending under the load of fresh oriental fruits and vegetables, then you will surely buy your vast plot of land in the countryside in **rural areas**.

Once you have made up your mind, where you and your family want to live, make sure you check a certain number of indispensable prerequisites of your future happiness: Make sure that you will not have to deal with legacies, such as old and inherited pollution, that your new home far outside the city centre is not built directly underneath the entry lane of the close-by international airport, that National Rail hasn't yet decided to build a high-speed railway line behind your garden fence, that you will have sympathetic neighbours, if any, etc.

And do never ever forget to read and understand the "zoning ordinance" or "land-use plan" of the local municipality that is eager to welcome you as a new tax-payer and often frenetically striving to constrict your personal wishes and expectations.

What Is a Zoning Ordinance?

Zoning ordinances are specifications or written policies that limit the use of the site. Before a potential homeowner hires an architect, he needs to go online or to the local building department to find out what zone the home will be in and what ordinances are relevant to the site. All the building department will need is the address of the lot.

The ordinances exist to protect the quality of the neighbourhood.

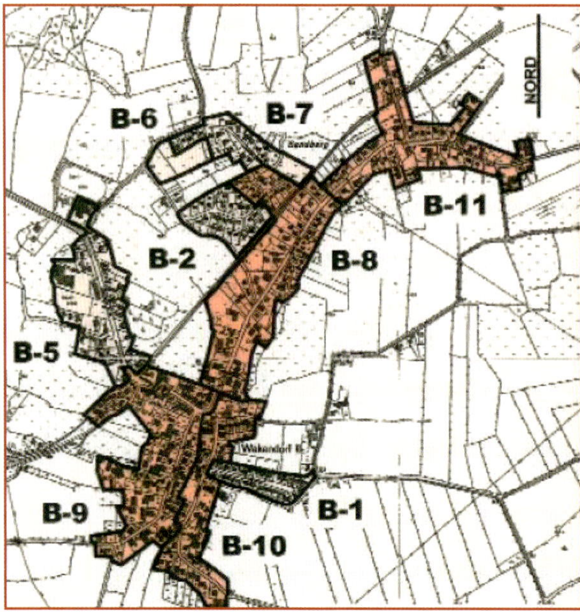

What Is a Covenant?
A covenant (also called land-use plan) is a "more-specific" guideline or regulation that limits what a property owner can build into or in conjunction with their home.

For example, a covenant may restrict the homeowner to only build a side-low garage, which can affect the width of the house. A covenant can put limits on everything from the size of your pool to whether or not you can have a pet kangaroo.

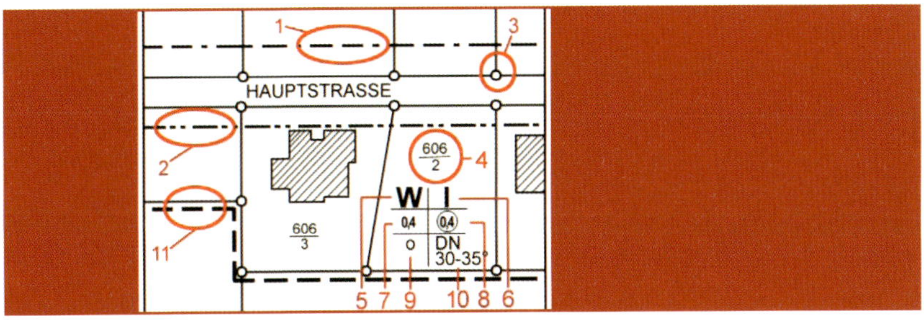

You've found the site, picked the house plans and met the team of people who will build your home – now it's time to find out about the building permit.

What Is a Building Permit?

A building permit is the document you receive from your local building department that actually "allows" you to do construction. Once you have a site, a house plan and a builder in place, your builder will then apply for a building permit, which is needed before construction can start.

How to Get a Building Permit
Here are the steps your contractor must go through in order to secure a building permit:

1. The contractor will talk with local officials to discuss the plans of your house, and the experts will advise him or her of any revisions that need to be made to the plan.
2. Submit the application to local officials for formal review. This review will determine if the proposed house meets with local code. For example, does the plan have adequate infrastructure, fire protection to service the area, etc. This can take as short as a couple of weeks to as long as a couple of months.
3. The following is needed for a building permit –
   - House plans, including the foundation elevation and framing considerations.
   - Sign-offs from the architect and engineer.
   - Soil reports showing the condition of your site. This is important in rural areas where an additional septic permit may be needed.
   - Approvals and reports from other agencies requested by the permitting office.
4. Once the application is approved you'll be asked to pay a fee based on the project size, and once payment has been received your builder can pick up the permit from the local city or county building department.
5. Once the permit is received it must be hung up at the property site.

Talking about plots

Across

2. Zugang
3. Bauland
4. Infrastruktur
5. Nachbarschaft
7. Antrag
9. städtisch
11. erschlossen
13. Bauamt
14. Baugenehmigung
15. Einschränkungen, Auflagen

Down

1. Bebauungsplan
6. Baustelle
8. ländlich
10. Flächennutzungsplan
11. Gebiet
12. vorstädtisch

Bitte erstellen Sie anhand der von Herrn Myers zugesandten Kriterienkiste (finanzielle Aspekte bleiben aufgrund der laufenden Verhandlungen mit der Stadt Bochum ausgeklammert) eine Empfehlung für eine Standortwahl. Ich habe Ihnen die kurzen Grundstücksbeschreibungen als Dokument angehängt.

Bitte bereiten Sie eine ausführliche Begründung vor, die Sie dann in einem Gespräch mit Herrn Brandis auf Englisch darstellen können.

Bochum Project:

SITE SELECTION CRITERIA

- Does the general shape of the plot correspond with the building plans so far?
- Is there any existing structure or property that needs to be demolished before we can start building?
- Taking into consideration possible future growth or expansion, is it possible to purchase adjoining sites?
- Does the site provide enough parking space in front of or next to the building? How much parking space will be needed at all?
- Which outdoor facilities (e.g. the court) will be needed? Are there any special requirements that have to be met?
- Does the site offer enough remaining open space?
- Is the site close to public parks or green areas?
- Are there any non-usable areas on the site (wetlands, flood plains, etc.)
- Does the site offer proper access to roads?
- Is the site relatively level with adequate drainage or very hilly requiring substantial earthwork grading?
- What are the building plans for the adjoining plots?
- Does the site provide access to public transport? If not, how can that be arranged?
- Is the quality of the soil good enough to provide adequate foundation-bearing capacity for the building?
- Is the building site likely to be contaminated?
- Are there any noise and air pollution sources known to be nearby?
- Are all necessary utilities needed for sanitary sewer service, drinking water, sprinkler systems, fire hydrant flows, electrical requirements, telephone, and information services available?
- Does our building fit into the neighbourhood?
- Which previous developments, buildings or foundations can be found or suspected on the site?

GRUNDSTÜCK 1

Zentral gelegen im Bochumer Vorort Riemke, ehemaliges Deutsche-Bahn-Grundstück; Grundstücksgröße 6.000 m^2; an 2 Grundstücksseiten von Industriebrachland umgeben, Eigentümer Nachfolge DB; unebenes Gelände, bewachsene Hügel und Schotterflächen; Bodendichte aufgrund Nachbarbebauung vermutlich unproblematisch; nächste Bebauung Gewerbegebiet (Möbelhaus und Autowaschanlage), Stichstraße zu Hauptverkehrsstraße ca. 3 Minuten; da Anschluss an ÖPNV (Bochum Stadtmitte mit U41 8 Minuten); Autobahnauffahrt A43 und A40 ca 4 Minuten; unerschlossen; Entfernung zu Riemke Ortskern ca. 5 Minuten zu Fuß; Einkaufsmöglichkeiten und Einrichtungen täglichen Bedarfs.

GRUNDSTÜCK 2

Bochum Stadtmitte; Nähe Stadtpark; jetzige Bebauung Hotelgebäude (Bj. 1972) mit Tiefgarage; muss abgerissen werden; Gesamtgrundstücksfläche 4.100 m^2; inmitten von Wohngebiet, sehr ruhige Wohnlage; Nachbargrundstücke mit älterem Wohnhausbestand in Privatbesitz; Anschluss an Straßenbahn (2 Minuten Fußweg); voll erschlossenes Grundstück.

In your group, have a look at your checklist for the site selection. Decide on eight criteria you consider most important. Give each criterion a factor of importance, making sure that all factors add up to 100. Then agree on how much this plot fulfils your individual criteria. Choose from 5 (absolutely) to 0 (not at all). The sum for weighting then tells you how many marks you give to this plot. In the end, add up your points for the two plots. Which one is your favourite?

Value benefit analysis

Issue to be decided

SITE SELECTION		**PLOT 1**		**PLOT 2**	
criteria	importance	factor	weighting	factor	weighting
SUM	100				
RANKING					

Ten principles of architecture

Have a look at these ten principles. Do you agree with them? What do they mean in detail for GW BO's project? What are your ideas and the requirements that should be met? Discuss your ideas in class.

Architecture is the art and science of designing buildings and structures.

"RESPECT THE LAND"

"ARCHITECTURE IS LIKE A LANGUAGE"

"BUILDINGS MUST RELATE FIRST OF ALL TO HUMAN PROPORTIONS"

"THE PLAYING TOGETHER OF THE PARTS"

"AN ELEMENTARY IDEA WITH A THOUSAND VARIANTS"

"LET WHERE IT IS BE WHAT IT'S MADE OF"

"A BARE OUTLINE WON'T DO; GIVE US THE DETAILS"

"ART SHOULD ALWAYS BE AN ORGANIC AND INTEGRAL PART OF ALL GREAT NEW BUILDINGS"

"DON'T MAKE RUDE SIGNS IN PUBLIC PLACES"

"LET THE PEOPLE WHO WILL HAVE TO LIVE WITH WHAT YOU BUILD HELP GUIDE YOUR HAND"

UNIT 5

Talking about construction

Fill in the gaps.

scope	materials	cadastral	brickwork
utilities	architect	beams	foundation
tenders	registry	built	specifications
contractors	trade	construction	building
bearing	static	openings	thickness
interior	floor	size	swing
trim	thermostats	lintels	switches
electrical	sides	electricians	on-wall
pitch	attachments	heights	

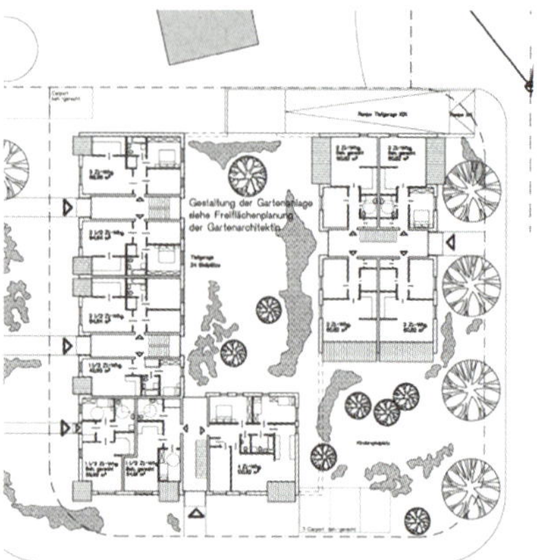

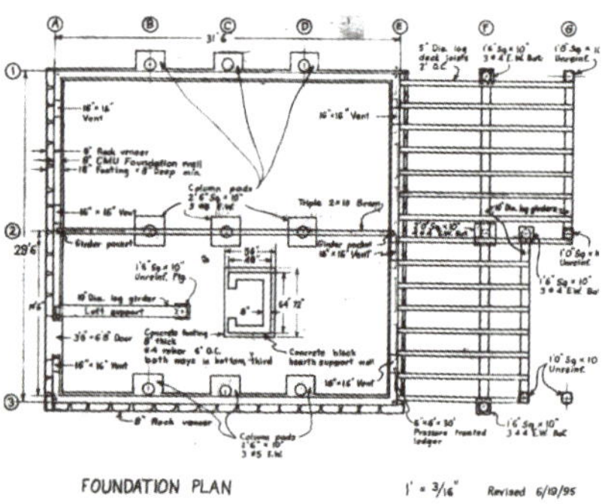

Before the ____________ works as such can start, a lot of paperwork has to be done; several plans have to be obtained from the land ____________ or have to be produced by the ____________.

Based on the official ____________ map a site plan of your building land will show the legal description of your plot, any existing ____________, the exact site dimensions, the topographical features and the proposed ____________ location.

Of course, the builder and the ____________ need several plans and a lot of paperwork to exactly carry out the specified works as planned by the architect. For each ____________, these specifications have to be very clear in defining the ____________ of work to be carried out and also have to state precisely what is to be ____________ and which ____________ should be used. Based on these ____________, the contractors usually submit their ____________.

The foundation plan is important for the building shell and

the __________. It should show the footings and locations for __________ walls, piers and columns. __________ such as windows, doors, sleeves and vents have to be defined. For __________ reasons, the positions of steel __________ and pilasters as well as the load __________ walls have to be very accurate. Of course, the __________ of walls, their depths and the position of drains should be given, too.

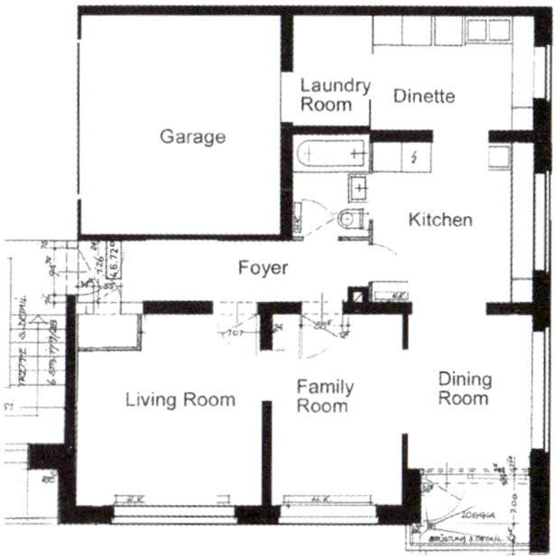

There should be a detailed floor plan for each __________. It should show both exterior and __________ walls, window and door locations (including their __________ direction) and the exact position of the __________. Each room should be identified and named; its appliances and permanent fixtures should be shown. The __________ of the room and the type of ceiling, flooring and __________ (plaster, headers etc.) are given as well.

The elevation plan shows at least four __________ of the building. It informs about the roof (__________ and type, chimney) and the floor and ceiling __________. Windows and doors are shown as well; furthermore exterior walls are described (i.e. clinker brick, wood panel etc.). Any __________, terraces, porches or garages are included, too.

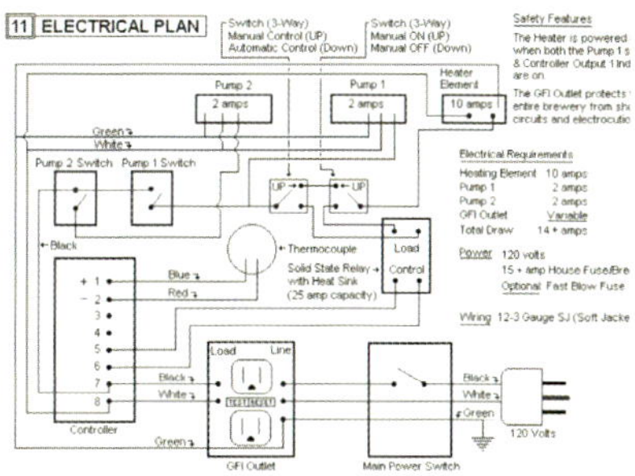

For any __________ works to be carried out, there needs to be one electrical plan for each floor plan. Sometimes, however, these specifications are included in the floor plan. Anyhow, __________ need to know exactly about the locations of all __________, outlets, phone jacks, and __________. Recessed lights and any further appliance outlets need to be included to avoid __________ mounting later on. Electrical plans often show HVAC plan outlets as well.

Adaption of housing for disabled and senior citizens

Die grundlegenden Entscheidungen mit den beteiligten Architekten und Herrn Brandis bezüglich der Anlage integrierten Wohnens sind getroffen.
Der Planungsstand so weit:

- Errichtung von 37 seniorengerechten Wohnungen, davon 12 behindertengerecht ausgestattet
- Größe: 12 zu 68 m^2, 19 zu 36 m^2, 6 zu 47 m^2
- die 12 Wohnungen zu 68 m^2 sollen behindertengerecht ausgestattet werden, alle anderen erhalten eine seniorengerechte Ausstattung
- Errichtung von 7 Gewerbeeinheiten im Erdgeschoss (angeboten werden: Vermietung einer Arztpraxis, eines Friseursalons, einer Apotheke, eines kleinen Lebensmittelgeschäftes, Kiosk mit Zeitungen, Bankautomat und Postfiliale; Maniküre-/Pediküresalon; kleines Café mit Außenfläche)
- 7 Wohneinheiten für die Pächter; davon 4 zu 92 m^2, 2 zu 72 m^2

Bitte bilden Sie zwei Projektgruppen, die Herrn Brandis Vorschläge zu

- den grundsätzlichen Bodenbelägen in den Wohnungen
- Elementen der senioren- bzw. behindertengerechten Ausstattung der Wohnungen

machen.

Auch wenn Herr Brandis durch seine Tätigkeit bei der ConceptInvest GmbH mittlerweile gute Fortschritte bei seinen Deutschkenntnissen gemacht hat, bittet er Sie, diese Ausführungen auf Englisch vorzubereiten und auch vorzutragen.

Projekt 1: Bodenbeläge
Bitte schlagen Sie für die verschiedenen Wohnräume Bodenbelagsarten (keine ins Detail gehenden Dekorempfehlungen) vor und begründen Sie für den entsprechenden Raum, warum Sie diesen und keinen anderen Bodenbelag für passend halten. Bitte bedenken Sie hier immer auch die Zielgruppe und die normale Nutzung der Wohnung.

Projekt 2: Elemente der senioren- und behindertengerechten Ausstattung der Wohnungen
Bitte schlagen Sie Ihrer Meinung nach sinnvolle Ausstattungen vor, indem Sie zwischen seniorengerecht und behindertengerecht unterscheiden. Bitte bedenken Sie auch Fragen der Handhabbarkeit, Sicherheit, Wartung etc.

Flooring materials

When considering which flooring material (i.e. the permanent cover of the floor) you choose for your home, various aspects should be considered. For many people, the final look the flooring material gives to your home is one of the most important criteria. Among others, you might want to consider questions like costs, wear, maintenance and comfort.

Of course the flooring material you choose, largely depends on the function of the room you want to use it in. Naturally, a carpet makes more sense in a living room than in a bathroom.

Those who consider wooden flooring (e.g. parquet and hardwood floors) praise its quality because of its naturalness. This refers to its organic origin but also to the choice of natural-looking designs which are available and which add soft and warm colours. Thus, many believe that wood is one of the most decorative building materials available.

Wood is a rather poor heat conductor which means that it provides warmth in the winter and cool temperatures in the summer. But on the other hand this also means that you should get expert advice before you decide to use it with floor-heating as not all types of wood are suitable for this. Its sound-insulating properties reduce indoor and outdoor noises and thus create silent and comfortable environments.

Due to their greater hardness and resistance to wear, wooden floors guarantee a long life. It has been proven that hardwood and parquet floors will last up to two or three times longer if they are regularly cleaned and maintained.

Parquet floorings, for example, can easily be brought back to their original condition by planing the surface. Cleaning and maintenance are rather easy, even the replacement of broken or damaged pieces often does not cause high costs.

Floor tiles are another flooring material representing durability and resistance to wear. Tiles are one of the earliest manmade building materials and are available in countless options, patterns, colours and textures. They are frequently used in kitchens and bathrooms because they are nearly impervious to water. Unglazed tiles provide a warmer, earthy look, whereas glazed tiles look much brighter. However, glazing tiles can also make them slippery, so you should take care that you choose the right texture for the right room. The harder the tiles, the easier it is to clean them or keep them clean. Unlike other flooring materials, tiles are quite cold underfoot. Of course this is a great advantage in hot summers, but in winter times some people may want to have underfloor heating installed below their floor tiles.

Whatever quality you choose: carpets are comfortable, quiet, warm and quick to install. These are the major reasons why many people prefer this flooring material in their living rooms and bedrooms.

Like nearly all other flooring materials, they are available in countless colours and styles. Hence, there is a wide price range from very affordable to quite expensive. Carpet flooring is warm and comfortable underfoot, but it is less durable than other materials. Furthermore, it might be more difficult to clean carpet floors once they are heavily soiled.

Some people see cork flooring as a good compromise between carpet flooring and wooden flooring. Cork is warm underfoot, natural in appearance and is an environmentally sustainable material. Unlike carpets, cork floors do not retain dents caused by furniture as easily. Due to their surface structure, cork floors resist wear and are easy to maintain and clean. Another distinguishing feature is an excellent insulation, both thermal and acoustic.

In recent years, the quality of laminate flooring has increased considerably. These flooring materials mostly imitate the structure and look of wooden floors. Mostly they are glued or snapped together; a foam pad underneath provides a cushioning effect and a moisture barrier. Thus, laminate flooring causes a floating floor. Without underfloor heating, laminate can be cold underfoot, as it looks like wood but does not have its qualities.

Laminate needs to be cleaned regularly (often sweeping or vacuuming will do for loose dirt) as otherwise ground-in dirt might cause scratches to the surface. When mopping the floor for more in-depth cleaning, make sure that you do not allow any water to stand on the floor.

Linoleum flooring (a floor covering made from solidified linseed oil in combination with wood flour or cork dust over a burlap or canvas backing) is an excellent choice for kitchens, children's rooms and bathrooms. It is water repellent and has a natural resistance to bacteria. Linoleum floors can be cleaned easily and do not show wear that easily. However, deeper cuts might well destroy the flooring. Genuine linoleum floors can be quite expensive.

For many, vinyl floorings represent the affordable alternative to linoleum floors. Like linoleum, vinyl is comfortable underfoot, easy to clean, quite durable and slip-resistant. Depending on the quality you choose, vinyl can be scratched, burned and dented without ruining your entire floor covering.

Apart from the wide range of technical equipment of flats for the elderly or handicapped people which can be found on the market, there are various aspects which can be realised easily and do not cost a lot of money.

- Within walking distance of the flat there should be enough shopping facilities, doctors, and also pharmacies.
- There should also be bus stops or tram stops nearby.
- Are the sidewalks or ways leading to the flat or building well-lit and safe to use?
- The main entrance to the building should be well lit; there should not be any steps.
- Furthermore, there should be as many lifts as necessary so that all flats can be reached without having to climb stairs.
- The front door should have an automatic door opener; the entire area leading to the building should be roofed over.
- The house number should be large enough and well lit so that emergency services can find the address quickly.
- In the building there should always be one contact person available in case of problems and emergencies etc.
- The staircase should have handrails on both sides; the stairs themselves should have nonslip covers.
- The corridors should be wide enough and there should be enough light which is turned on by movement detectors.
- All potential risks of stumbling should be eliminated both in all common areas and in the flat itself.
- All rooms should be equipped with height-adjustable amenities such as counter tops, wash basins, cupboards etc.
- In the bedroom, light switches should be within reach of the bed.
- There should also be ample space around the bed.

In the year 2050, about 70 percent of the population in most of the OECD-countries will be 60 years and older, which means that maintaining people in their traditional dwellings will be a major objective for the housing sector.

Nowadays, elderly people usually are fit and healthy, but exposed also to a certain number of risks and limitations. Therefore, they often need special equipment in their flats in order to prevent falls and related injuries.

This equipment will help them to live comfortably in a safe flat, thus giving them a high degree of independence, self-confidence and self-esteem.

In order to maintain their own mobility, flexibility and full independence, they may need special wall tracks, handrails, height adjustable sinks, safe lifting and handling devices, special toilet seats, shower chairs, etc.

Their flats should be made easily accessible, especially when they depend on a wheelchair. Bathrooms, toilets and all other rooms, including the basement, have to be barrier free.

Last but not least, it is becoming more and more popular, as the elderly often have no relatives nearby, to install special emergency call systems in all rooms of their flat, so that they can call for help as soon as they feel they would have to do so.

Integrated housing

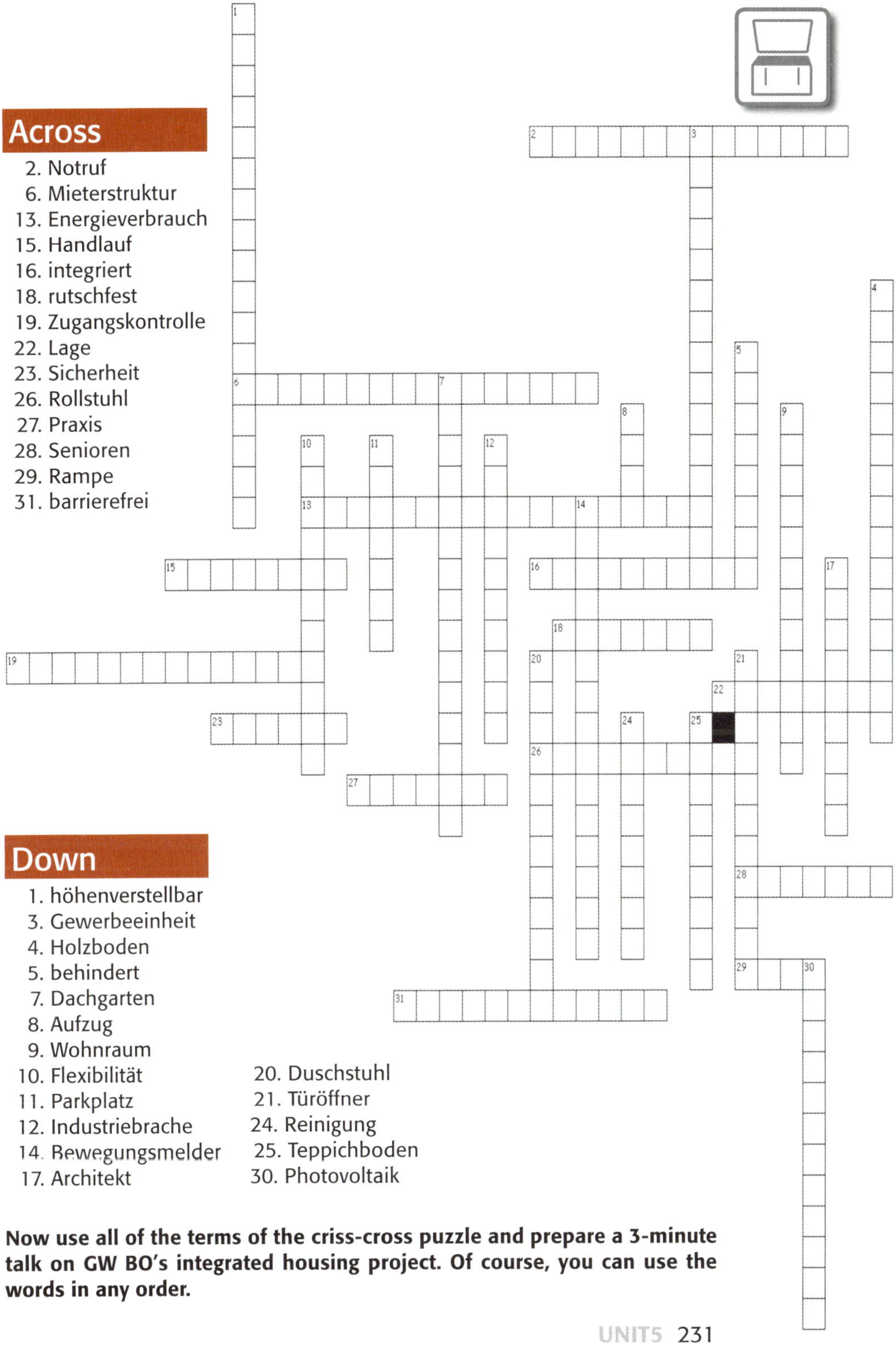

Across

2. Notruf
6. Mieterstruktur
13. Energieverbrauch
15. Handlauf
16. integriert
18. rutschfest
19. Zugangskontrolle
22. Lage
23. Sicherheit
26. Rollstuhl
27. Praxis
28. Senioren
29. Rampe
31. barrierefrei

Down

1. höhenverstellbar
3. Gewerbeeinheit
4. Holzboden
5. behindert
7. Dachgarten
8. Aufzug
9. Wohnraum
10. Flexibilität
11. Parkplatz
12. Industriebrache
14. Bewegungsmelder
17. Architekt
20. Duschstuhl
21. Türöffner
24. Reinigung
25. Teppichboden
30. Photovoltaik

Now use all of the terms of the criss-cross puzzle and prepare a 3-minute talk on GW BO's integrated housing project. Of course, you can use the words in any order.

Contract a building

Work in teams. Each team decides on one project they want to develop and later on present to the others.

Your task: Construct a building or change an existing building. You should include both residential and commercial aspects in your plans, i.e. you have to produce living space for a certain target group but must also plan any kind of unit in your building which produces income. The smaller unit of both (residential and commercial) must occupy at least 30% of the entire floor space. Make sure that all assumptions (e.g. rental income etc.) are realistic. You are the future owners of that building, but do not have to live in it.

All teams are given the following:

- a plot (450 sqm) which does not have to be paid for
- the sum of € 250,000 can be used
- the following requirements have to be met:
- each building must produce an annual income of at least € 8,000
- modern heating technologies and means of energy conservation must be used
- an ecologically sound building
- a very general outline for the income producing unit for the next 10 years

In your presentation, you are expected to explain the future use of the building, the space created and used; the main layout of the floor plan and further characteristic features, which give this building a specific note. Have a look at the checklist below which will be used by all the groups during the presentations to find out the best project.

Here are four projects to choose from:

PROJECT 1

Urban plot, situated directly at the historical market square in the city of Unna; existing building three-story art-nouveau building (1902) with three separate flats; planning and building permission for three-storey building given; total living space 362 sqm (2 x 140sqm, 1 x 82 sqm); 5 garages at the rear of the building; building refurbished in early 1970s; no further modernisation;

PROJECT 2

Fully developed building site, popular suburb in the south of Dortmund, residential neighbourhood; building permission for 2-family house; last plot in a fully developed estate;

PROJECT 3

Well-established small hotel (9 rooms) in the centre of Bochum-Stiepel, very good traffic connections, but quiet location; has been a family business for the last 70 years; very traditional equipment; simple facilities; (hotel rates from € 35/single room to € 65/double room); own restaurant (traditional German kitchen; about 10 regular guests every lunchtime; not popular in the evenings) last modernisation in 1975;

PROJECT 4

Old farmhouse; rural area 15 km outside Bremen; total living space 280 sqm; farmland sold 10 years ago, no more agriculture; new housing estate to be built in 2 years time; planning and building permission for one- or two-storey building;

If you do not like any of the projects suggested and think you have got a better idea, you can also come up with something completely different. Remember, however, that all criteria apply to you as well.

Now follow the presentations by the other groups and complete one checklist for every project. Agree on a total result from your group. Which of all the projects presented gets the highest marks?

PROJECT CHECKLIST

ASPECT	MARKS OUT OF 10
Is the general idea of the project convincing?	
Does it meet the requirements of living space and income producing unit?	
Is there enough potential for the income producing unit?	
Does it offer enough energy-saving technology?	
Can it be considered a "green" building?	
Does it have unique characteristics?	
How much did we like the presentation as such?	

UNIT 5

Talking about construction

Vokabeln

A	air sealing	Abdichtung gegen Luftzug
	appliance	Gerät
	approval	Genehmigung
	architect	Architekt
	attachment	Anbau
	attic	Attika, Dachboden, Dachgeschoss
B	backrest	Rückenlehne
	bamboo flooring	Bambusboden
	barrier-free	barrierefrei
	beam	Balken, Träger
	bench joiner	Tischler
	bitumen	Teer
	boiler room	Heizungskeller
	brass	Messing
	bricklayer	Maurer
	brickwork	Rohbau
	bridge	Brücke
	brownfield	Industriebrache, Altlast
	builder	Bauherr, Bauunternehmer
	building completion	Baufertigstellung
	building engineer	Bauingenieur
	building inspection	Bauaufsicht
	building permit	Baugenehmigung
	building plot	Baugrundstück
C	cabinet	Wandschrank
	cadastral	kataster-
	CAD technician	Berechnungsingenieur
	carpenter	Schreiner
	ceiling	Decke
	cement	Zement
	central heating system	Zentralheizung
	circulating pump	Umwälzpumpe
	civil engineering	Bauingenieurwesen, Hoch- und Tiefbau
	cladding	Fassadenverkleidung
	coat	Schicht, Farbanstrich
	coating	Anstrich, Belag
	concrete	Beton
	concrete slab	Betonplatte
	condensing boiler	Brennwertkessel
	construction material	Baumaterial
	construction operative	Bauarbeiter
	construction sector	Baubranche
	construction volume	Bauvolumen
	contractor	Bauunternehmer
	copper	Kupfer
	cork flooring	Korkboden
	cost evaluation	Kostenauswertung
	countertop	Arbeitsplatte
	craft	Gewerk
D	decorator	Dekorateur
	demolition	Abriss
	detergent	Reinigungsmittel
	door-opener	Türöffner
	drainage	Abfluss
	driveway	Zufahrt, Auffahrt
	drywall	Trockenausbau
	ductwork	Verrohrung
E	earthwork	Erdarbeiten
	electrical plan	Elektroplan
	electrician	Elektriker
	electricity grid	Stromnetz
	elevation plan	Aufrissplan
	environment	Umgebung / Umwelt
	exterior finish	Außenarbeiten, Außenwandgestaltung
F	faucet	Wasserkran
	fence	Zaun
	fibrous	Faser-
	final inspection	Endabnahme
	flat roof	Flachdach
	floating floor	schwimmender Estrich
	floor heating	Fußbodenheizung
	flooring	Fußbodenausbau
	flush-mounted	unter Putz
	formworking	Verschalung
	fossil fuel	fossiler Brennstoff
	foundation	Fundament
	foundation plan	Fundamentplan
	frame	Rahmen
	framing	Rohbau
	fuse	Sicherung
G	gap	Lücke, Kältebrücke
	GDP = gross domestic product	BIP = Bruttoinlandsprodukt
	glazing	Verglasung
	grading	Begradigung, Stufung
	grass	Gras
	greenfield	auf der grünen Wiese
	grid-connected	ans Elektrizitätsversorgungsnetz angebunden
	gutter	Dachrinne
	gypsum	Gips
H	handrail	Handlauf, Geländer
	heating circuit water	Heizwasserkreislauf
	height	Höhe
	height adjustable	höhenverstellbar
	hinge	Angel, Drehkreuz
	house plan	Bauplan
	HVAC = heating, ventilation, air conditioning	Heizung, Lüftung, Klimatechnik
I	insulation	Isolierung
	intercom	Gegensprechanlage
	interior finish	Innenausbau
L	laminate	Laminat
	landscaping	Landschafts- und Gartengestaltung
	lead sheeting	Blechverkleidung
	lift	Aufzug
	light fixture	Lampeninstallation
	linoleum	Linoleum
	lintel	Fenster-, Türsturz
	load-bearing wall	tragende Wand
	low-energy house	Niedrigenergiehaus
	lumber	Bauholz
M	mailbox	Briefkasten
	marble	Marmor
	mastic asphalt	Gussasphalt
	mechanicals	Schlosserarbeiten
	mirror	Spiegel
	mortar	Mörtel, Speis
	motion detector	Bewegungsmelder
N	natural resources	natürliche Ressourcen
	noise insulation	akustische Isolierung

O	on-wall mounting	Auf-Putz-Installation
	outdoor facilities	Außenanlagen
P	paint touch-ups	Malerausbesserungsarbeiten
	painter	Maler
	parquet	Parkett
	photovoltaic technology	Photovoltaiktechnologie
	pier	Pfeiler
	pipe	Rohr(-leitung)
	pitched roof	Steildach
	plantings	Bepflanzung
	plaster	Gipsputz
	plasterboard	Rigipsplatte
	plot	Grundstück
	plumber	Installateur
	plumbing	Sanitärinstallationsarbeiten
	plywood	Sperrholz, Schalungsplatte
	power-supply	Stromversorgung
	prefabricated house	Fertighaus
	principal	Bauherr
	project manager	Projektleiter / Bauleiter
	property site	Baustelle
	PVC pipe	PVC-Rohr
Q	quote	Angebot
R	recycle (verb)	recyclen
	register	öffentliches Verzeichnis
	reinforce (verb)	stärken, verstärken
	renovation potential	Renovierungspotenzial
	retaining wall	tragende Wand
	road	Straße
	roof	Dach
	roof garden; roof-top garden	Dachgarten
	roof pitch	Dachneigung
	roof plan	Dachplan
	roof slater / tiler	Dachdecker
	roofer	Dachdecker
	roofing	Dacheindeckung
	rural	ländlich
S	sales agreement	Kaufvertrag
	sanitary	Sanitär-
	sanitary system	Sanitärinstallationen
	savings	Ersparnisse
	scaffold	Gerüst
	scaffolder	Gerüstbauer
	scope	Umfang
	self-esteem	Selbstachtung, Selbstwert-gefühl
	shelving	Regalbau
	shop fitter	Inneneinrichter
	shrub	Strauch, Bodendecker
	site plan	Grundstücksplan, Lageplan
	skeleton	Rohbau
	slab	Platte, Decke (Rohbau)
	slate	Dachschiefer
	soil report	Bodenanalysebericht
	solar energy	Sonnen- / Solarenergie
	solid fuel	fester Brennstoff
	stairs	Treppen
	steel beam	Stahlträger
	steel erector	Stahlbauer
	stonemason	Maurer

	structural engineer	Bauingenieur, Statiker
	suburban	Vorort-
	supply pipe	Versorgungsrohr
	supply shortage	Lieferengpass
	surveyor	Sachverständiger
	suspended ceilings	abgehängte Decken
	switch	Schalter
T	telephone wall jack	Telefonanschlussdose
	temperature sensor	Temperaturfühler
	tender	Angebot auf eine Ausschreibung
	tentative	provisorisch
	thickness	Dicke
	tile	Dachziegel
	tiler	Fliesenleger
	timber	Bauholz, Balken
	towel rail	Handtuchhalter
	town planner	Stadtplaner
	tree	Baum
	truss	Dachstuhl
	tunnel	Tunnel
U	urban	städtisch, urban
	urban regeneration	Stadterneuerung
V	vinyl	Vinyl
W	walk-through	Begehung
	walkway	Fußweg
	wall	Wand
	wall / floor tiling	Fliesen legen, Fliesenbelag
	watertight	wasserdicht
	wheelchair	Rollstuhl
	window sill	Fensterbank, Fensterbrett
	wire	Draht
	wiring	Verdrahtung, Verkabelung
	wrought-iron	schmiedeeisern
Y	yard	Hof, Lagerplatz, als Längenmaß Yard: 91,44 cm
Z	zoning ordinance *oder* land use plan	Flächennutzungsplan

SELF-ASSESSMENT GRID AFTER UNIT 5

Gehen Sie die einzelnen Abschnitte des gerade abgeschlossenen Kapitels noch einmal durch und überprüfen Sie sich selbstkritisch. Was haben Sie gelernt? Was sollten Sie wiederholen bzw. vertiefen? Was bereitet Ihnen Schwierigkeiten? Schreiben Sie kurze Kommentare in die Kästchen, die Ihren Lernzuwachs für Sie selbst erläutern. Arbeiten Sie nach eigenen Prioritäten Unterpunkte nach, wenn Sie mehrheitlich Ihre Kommentare in der rechten Spalte gesetzt haben.

Was ich in diesem Kapitel gelernt habe…	**Wie ich meinen Fortschritt einschätze**		
	Ich fühle mich beim Sprechen/Schreiben und beim Hören bzw. Lesen zu diesem Aspekt insgesamt sicher und verstehe einen Großteil der Informationen bzw. kann einen Großteil der Informationen wie beabsichtigt weitergeben; auch wenn ich Fehler mache, habe ich insgesamt Vertrauen in meine Sprachbeherrschung.	Ich kann vieles von dem, was für diesen Aspekt wichtig ist, mündlich und schriftlich ausdrücken bzw. beim Hören und Lesen verstehen; allerdings fehlen mir einige Fachvokabeln und auch die grundsätzliche Sicherheit, mich frei über diesen Aspekt auszutauschen.	Ich habe zu diesem Aspekt einige Fachbegriffe und Redewendungen gelernt und verstehe auch Informationen; jedoch erschließen sich mir noch nicht alle Zusammenhänge; sowohl die Textrezeption (Hören und Lesen) als auch das Sprechen und Schreiben bereiten mir noch Probleme; ich weiß, dass ich einige Aspekte nacharbeiten sollte.
den grundlegenden Fachwortschatz zur Beschreibung der wesentlichen Bauphasen, der am Bau Beteiligten und der Baumaterialien anzuwenden			
die Arbeit der verschiedenen am Bau beteiligten Gewerke zu beschreiben.			
den grundlegenden Fachwortschatz zur senioren- bzw. behindertengerechten Ausstattung einer Wohnanlage anzuwenden.			
grundlegende Merkmale von Solar- und PV-Energie darzustellen.			
Kriterien für die Auswahl eines Baugrundstücks basierend auf dessen Beschreibung anzuwenden.			

Vokabeln Englisch-Deutsch

A	abbreviate (verb)	abkürzen
	abbreviation	Abkürzung
	abolish (verb)	abschaffen
	abolition	Abschaffung
	abusive	missbräuchlich, beleidigend
	accession countries	Beitrittsländer
	accommodation	Unterbringung
	account	Konto
	accounting	Buchhaltung, Bilanzbuchhaltung
	achieve (verb)	erreichen, erzielen
	acknowledgement	Anerkennung, Bestätigung
	acquire (verb)	erwerben
	acquisition	Erwerb
	acre	Fläche von 4.047 m^2
	add on	Erweiterung, Zusatz, Zugabe
	additions	Anbauten
	adjacent	angrenzend
	adjacent property	angrenzende Immobilie
	advance payment for service charges	Nebenkostenvorauszahlung
	advertise (verb)	werben, Anzeigen schalten
	advertisement	Werbung
	advice	Beratung, Ratschlag
	affiliated service	mieternahe Dienstleistung
	affordable	erschwinglich, bezahlbar
	agent	Makler
	agreement	Einigung, Vertrag
	air (verb)	lüften
	air conditioning	Klimaanlage
	air sealing	Abdichtung gegen Luftzug
	airfield	Flugfeld, Flugplatz
	airport	Flughafen
	alert (verb)	alarmieren
	allocate (verb)	zuweisen
	all-time high / low	Allzeithoch / -tief
	alter (verb)	ändern, verändern
	alterations	Änderungen, Umbauten
	alternative residential accommodation	alternative Wohnversorgung
	amenities	Vorzüge, Annehmlichkeiten, Ausstattungsmerkmale
	amortisation	Tilgung
	annoyance	Beeinträchtigung, Belästigung
	answer phone	Anrufbeantworter
	apartment complex	Wohnimmobilie, Geschosswohnungsbau
	apologise (verb)	entschuldigen
	appliance	Gerät
	appointment	Verabredung
	appropriate	geeignet
	approval	Genehmigung
	architect	Architekt
	arrangements	Arrangements
	arrears	Rückstände
	Asbo	einstweilige Anordnung wegen antisozialen Verhaltens
	ash	Asche
	assault	Angriff, tätlicher Übergriff
	assume (verb)	annehmen, übernehmen, vermuten, unterstellen
	attach (verb)	anbauen, anbringen, anfügen
	attached	angebaut, angefügt
	attachment	Anbau
	attic	Attika, Dachgeschoss
	attire	Kleidung
	authorities	Behörden
	availability	Verfügbarkeit
	available	verfügbar
	average	Durchschnitt, durchschnittlich
B	back porch	Anbau, Windfang, Terrasse hinter dem Haus
	backlit display	beleuchtetes Display
	backrest	Rückenlehne
	bakery	Bäckerei
	balanced market	ausgeglichener Markt
	balcony	Balkon
	bamboo flooring	Bambusboden
	bank	Bank
	bar chart	Balkendiagramm
	barbecue	Grill
	barrier-free	barrierefrei
	basement	Keller
	basin	Becken
	bathroom	Badezimmer
	bathroom sink	Badezimmerwaschbecken
	beam	Balken, Träger
	be eligible for (verb)	einen Anspruch haben auf
	be subject to (verb)	Gegenstand von etw. sein
	bedroom	Schlafzimmer
	bed-sit	Zimmer, möbliertes Zimmer
	begging	Bettelei
	belongings	Besitztümer, Hab und Gut
	bench joiner	Tischler
	benchmarking	Benchmarking, Maßstab, Bezugsgröße
	beneficiary	Begünstigter
	bicycle stand, kick stand	Fahrradständer
	bid	Angebot
	bill of utility costs	Betriebskostenabrechnung
	bin liner	Müllbeutel
	biometric access control	biometrische Zugangskontrolle
	bitumen	Teer
	block of flats	Blockbebauung
	boiler	Warmwasseraufbereiter
	boiler room	Heizungskeller
	booze	Alkohol
	borough	Bezirk, Gemeinde
	bow	Bogen
	branch	Niederlassung
	brass	Messing
	breach	Bruch
	breach (verb)	brechen, verletzen, zuwiderhandeln
	breakdown	Betriebsstörung
	bricklayer	Maurer
	brickwork	Rohbau
	bridge	Brücke
	briefcase	Aktenkoffer
	broadband internet	Breitband-Internet
	brochure	Broschüre, Prospekt
	brownfield	Industriebrache, Altlast
	budget	Haushalt, Budget
	builder	Bauherr, Bauunternehmer

Vokabeln Englisch-Deutsch

building block for urbanism	Blockbebauung
building completion	Baufertigstellung
building engineer	Bauingenieur
building inspection	Bauaufsicht
building permission	Baugenehmigung
building permit	Baugenehmigung
building plot	Baugrundstück
built-in cupboard	Einbauschrank
bulb	Glühbirne
bungalow	Bungalow
burglar	Einbrecher
burglar alarm	Alarmanlage
burglary	Einbruchdiebstahl
burst pipe	Rohrbruch
business park, commercial area	Gewerbegebiet
business trip	Geschäftsreise
bust (verb)	sprengen
butchery, butcher's	Fleischerei, Metzger
buyer	Erwerber, Käufer
C cabinet	Wandschrank
cable TV	Kabelfernsehen
cadastral	kataster-
CAD technician	Berechnungsingenieur
campsite	Campingplatz, Stellplatz für ein Zelt
car parking space, car port	Einstellplatz
caretaker	Hausmeister, Hauswart
cargo	Fracht
carpenter	Schreiner
carpet flooring	Teppichbodenbelag
carpet, carpeted floor	Teppichboden
cash in (verb)	vereinnahmen
cash reserve	Liquiditätsreserve
cathedral ceiling	Gewölbedecke
ceiling	Zimmerdecke
cell phone	Handy
cellar	Keller
cement	Zement
central gas heating	Gaszentralheizung
central heating	Zentralheizung
central heating system	Zentralheizung
centralised	zentralisiert
century	Jahrhundert
certification	Zertifizierung
chain store	Handelskette
challenge	Herausforderung
chamber of commerce and industry	Industrie- und Handelskammer
charge (verb)	berechnen, in Rechnung stellen
chart	Chart, Diagramm
chattel	bewegliches Gut
children's room	Kinderzimmer
chimney	Kamin, Schornstein
chimney sweeper	Schornsteinfeger
circuitry	Kreislauf, Schaltkreis, Schaltschema
circulation pump	Umwälzpumpe
city council	Stadtrat
civil commotion	Bürgerkrieg
civil engineering	Bauingenieurwesen, Hoch- und Tiefbau
civil rights campaigner	Bürgerrechtler
civil servant	Beamter, öffentlicher Angestellter
civil service	öffentlicher Dienst
cladding	Fassadenverkleidung
claim	Anspruch
cleaning service	Reinigungsdienst
cleanliness	Sauberkeit
climax	Höhepunkt
climb (verb)	ansteigen
closed-loop	geschlossener Kreislauf
closet	Toilette, Wandschrank
clubhouse	Clubhaus
coal	Kohle
coat	Schicht, Farbanstrich
coating	Anstrich, Belag
collateral	Pfand, Sicherheit
colleague	Kollegin, Kollege
column	Säule, Kolonne, Rubrik
command economy	Planwirtschaft
commence (verb)	beginnen
commercial	gewerblich
commercial (real estate) property	Gewerbeimmobilie
commercial manager	kaufmännischer Geschäftsführer
commercial rent	Gewerbemiete
commercial tenancy disputes insurance	Vermieterrechtsschutzversicherung
commodity	Verbrauchsgut
common	gemeinschaftlich
common areas	Gemeinschaftsanlagen
common property	Gemeinschaftseigentum
community association	Eigentümergemeinschaft
community development project	Quartiersentwicklungsprojekt
community-owned	in Gemeinschaftsbesitz
compensate (verb)	entschädigen
compensation	Entschädigung, Wiedergutmachung
compete (verb)	konkurrieren
competition	Wettbewerb, Konkurrenz
competitive	wettbewerbsfähig
complaint	Reklamation, Klage
complimentary clause	Grußformel
comply (verb)	übereinstimmen mit
compulsory	verpflichtend, vorgeschrieben
computerised	computergesteuert
concrete	Beton
concrete slab	Betonplatte
condensing boiler	Brennwertkessel
condensing gas boiler	Brennwertkessel
condensing heating technology	Brennwerttechnologie
condo fee	Hausgeld (für Eigentumswohnungen)
condominium	Eigentumswohnung
conference centre	Konferenzzentrum
confirmation	Bestätigung

Vokabeln Englisch-Deutsch

congestion	Andrang, Verdichtung
conservation	Erhaltung, Naturschutz, Einsparung
conservatory	Wintergarten, Gewächshaus
considerable	beachtlich
consist of (verb)	bestehen aus
consolidate (verb)	konsolidieren
construct (verb)	bauen
construction	Bau
construction material	Baumaterial
construction operative	Bauarbeiter
construction sector	Baubranche
construction volume	Bauvolumen
consumer protection and food safety acts	Verbraucherschutz- und Lebensmittelreinheitsgesetz
consumption	Verbrauch
consumption goods	Verbrauchsgüter
contagious disease	ansteckende Krankheit
contractor	Auftragnehmer
contractor	Bauunternehmer
contractual liability	vertragliche Haftung
conversion	Umwidmung, Umwandlung
cooperative	Genossenschaft
copper	Kupfer
copper pipe	Kupferrohr
core business	Kerngeschäft
cork flooring	Korkboden
corner shop	Laden an der Ecke, Tante-Emma-Laden
corporate	Unternehmens-
cost control	Kostenmanagement
cost evaluation	Kostenauswertung
costly	teuer
countertop	Arbeitsplatte
court	Gericht
court attendance compensation	Verdienstausfallregulierung für Zeugenaussagen bei Gericht
court order	Gerichtsentscheidung, gerichtliche Mahnung
court possession order	gerichtliche Anordnung
courteous	höflich, zuvorkommend
craft	Gewerk
craftsman	Handwerker
craftspeople	Handwerkerschaft
crawl space	Souterrain
crowd	große Anzahl an Menschen
crucial	wichtig
cubic	Kubik-
cul-de-sac	Sackgasse
current	gängig, aktuell
customer	Kunde
D damage	Schaden, Beschädigung
damage following theft	Diebstahlfolgeschäden
data carrier	Datenträger
data protection act	Datenschutzgesetz
database	Datenbank
day one reinstatement	Neuwertversicherung
day-to-day operation	Tagesgeschäft
deadline	Termin
decade	Jahrzehnt
decentralised	dezentralisiert
deck	Dachterrasse
decorator	Dekorateur
decrease (verb)	abnehmen
deduct (verb)	abziehen
deductible	Eigenanteil
deed	Urkunde
default	schlecht, fehlerhaft
defect	Mangel, Fehler
defective premises act	Gebäudehaftpflicht-gesetz
delivery	Lieferung
demand-driven market	Nachfragemarkt
demolition	Abriss
deny (verb)	verneinen, verleugnen, bestreiten, dementieren
department store	Kaufhaus, Warenhaus
deposit	Kaution, Anzahlung
deposit / security deposit	Kaution
deprived area	Stadtteil mit besonderem Entwicklungsbedarf, sozialer Brennpunkt, benachteiligtes Quartier
destination, place of excursions	Ausflugsziele
detached house	frei stehendes Haus
deter (verb)	abschrecken, abhalten von
detergent	Reinigungsmittel
deterioration	Abnutzung, Verfall, Wertverlust
determine (verb)	bestimmen, festlegen
deterrent	abwehrend, abschreckend
develop (verb)	entwickeln
development	Entwicklung
diagram	Diagramm
dining room	Esszimmer
disability	Behinderung
disabled	behindert
disciplinary action	Disziplinarmaßnahme
discount	Rabatt
dishwasher	Geschirrspülmaschine
display	Display
disposition	Veräußerung
disturbance caused by animals	Störung durch (Haus-)Tiere
divorce	Scheidung
domestic violence	häusliche Gewalt
door chain	Türkette
door mat	Fußmatte
door opener	Türöffner
door viewer	Türspion
dossier	Dossier
dotcom market	IT-Markt
double glazed windows	Doppelverglasung
drain pipes	Entwässerungsrohre
drainage	Abfluss
drains	Abwasserrohre
dramatic	dramatisch
drastic	drastisch
draw up (verb)	anfertigen, aufstellen, entwerfen
dress code	Kleiderordnung
drip (verb)	tropfen

Vokabeln Englisch-Deutsch

dripping	tropfend
driveway	Zufahrt, Auffahrt
drop (verb)	(ab-)fallen
drug-related	drogenbezogen
dry cleaning	Reinigung
drywall	Trockenausbau
ductwork	Verrohrung
due	fällig
due diligence	Kauf- / Prospektprüfung
dues	Abgaben, Gebühren, Rechte
duplex	Zweifamilienhaus
duplicate (verb)	verdoppeln
dwelling	Wohnung
dwelling stock	Wohnungsbestand
E earthquake	Erdbeben
earthwork	Erdarbeiten
eat-in kitchen	Wohnküche
economy	Wirtschaft
electric meter box	Stromzähler
electrical appliances	Elektrogeräte
electrical plan	Elektroplan
electrician	Elektriker
electricity	Elektrizität
electricity grid	Stromnetz
electricity meter	Stromzähler
elevation plan	Aufrissplan
emergency	Notfall
employee	Angestellter, Arbeitnehmer
employer	Arbeitgeber
enable (verb)	in die Lage bringen, befähigen
enclose (verb)	beifügen
enclosures	Anlagen
end unit	Endreihenhaus
energy provider	Energieversorger
energy savings	Energieeinsparungen
enforce (verb)	in Kraft setzen, durchsetzen
enquiry	Anfrage
ensure (verb)	gewährleisten, sicherstellen
enterprise	Unternehmen
entire	gesamt
entity	Entität, Einheit
entrepreneur	Unternehmer
entrepreneurial	unternehmerisch
envelope	Umschlag
environment	Umgebung / Umwelt
environmentally friendly	umweltfreundlich
equipment	Ausstattung, Ausrüstung
erect (verb)	errichten
essential	wichtig, wesentlich
estate agent	Immobilienmakler
estate, housing estate	Wohngebiet
estimate	Kostenvoranschlag
etiquette	Etikette, Benimmregeln
EU member states	EU-Mitgliedsstaaten
eviction	Räumung
exactly (adv.)	genau, präzise
examine (verb)	untersuchen
exclusion	Ausschluss
executive	Führungskraft
existing	bestehend
expenditures	Ausgaben, Aufwand
expense	Ausgabe, Kosten
expire (verb)	auslaufen, zu Ende gehen
explode (verb)	explodieren
explosion	Explosion
exterior	Außen-
exterior finish	Außenarbeiten, Außenwandgestaltung
exterior walls	Außenwände
F face-to-face	gegenüber
facial expression	Gesichtsausdruck
facility	Facility, Einrichtung
faeces	Kot
fall (verb)	(ab-)fallen
fan	Ventilator
fashion boutique	Modeboutique
faucet	Wasserkran
faulty	fehlerhaft, defekt
favourable	günstig
felling and lopping of trees	Fällen und Zurückschneiden von Bäumen
fence	Zaun
fenced	eingezäunt
fiancé(e)	Verlobte(r)
fibrous	Faser-
fight fire (verb)	Brand bekämpfen
file	Akte, Datei
file (verb)	nachverfolgen, ablegen
final inspection	Endabnahme
financial operation	finanzielle Transaktion
financial statement	Geschäftsbericht
financing	Finanzierung
fire	Brand
fire brigade	Feuerwehr
fire extinguisher	Feuerlöscher
first-home buyer allowance	Eigenheimzulage
fitted	eingebaut
fitted kitchen	Einbauküche
fittings	Anschlüsse
fixed	befestigt
fixed-term tenancy agreement	befristeter Mietvertrag
fixture	fest eingebaute Armatur
flat roof	Flachdach
flat-bed scanner	Flachbettscanner
flat-screen monitor	Flachbildschirm
float-ball	Schwimmer
floating city	schwimmende Stadt
floating floor	schwimmender Estrich
flood	Überflutung
floor	Stockwerk
floor covering, flooring	Bodenbelag
floor heating	Fußbodenheizung
floor plan, layout	Grundriss
flooring	Fußbodenausbau
flooring material	Bodenbelag
flow chart	Ablaufdiagramm
flush-mounted	unter Putz
fly-tip (verb)	illegales Müllabladen
focus (verb)	Fokus, Hauptaugenmerk
follow up (verb)	nachverfolgen
footage	Länge, Gesamtlänge

Vokabeln Englisch-Deutsch

	formwork	Schalung
	fossil fuel	fossiler Brennstoff
	found (verb)	gründen, begründen
	foundation	Fundament
	foundation plan	Fundamentplan
	fraction	Bruchteil
	frame	Rahmen
	framing	Rohbau
	fringe	Brache, Rand-
	front window	Vorderfenster
	funding	Finanzierung
	furnace	Ofen
	furnished	möbliert
	furnishing house	Einrichtungshaus
	furniture	Möbel
	fuse	Sicherung
G	gap	Lücke, Kältebrücke
	garage	Garage
	garage	Werkstatt
	garbage	Müll
	garbage can	Mülleimer
	garbage truck	Müllwagen
	garden upkeep	Gartenpflege
	gardener	Gärtner
	garlic	Knoblauch
	gas	Gas
	gas heating	Gasheizung
	gas leak	Leck in der Gasleitung
	gas meter	Gasuhr
	gas meter box	Gaszähler
	gas provider	Gasversorger
	gate	Tor
	gather (verb)	versammeln
	GDP = gross domestic product	BIP = Bruttoinlandsprodukt
	German housing act of 1956	II. Deutsches Wohnungsbaugesetz von 1956
	German non-profit housing act	WGG, Wohnungsgemeinnützigkeitsgesetz
	German Tenants' Protection Association	Deutscher Mieterschutzbund
	gesture	Geste, Gebärde
	glazing	Verglasung
	governance	Führung, Steuerung
	government-funded	staatlich gefördert
	grading	Stufung, Begradigung
	grant (verb)	einräumen, gewähren
	grass	Gras
	green prunings	Gartenabfälle
	greenfield	auf der grünen Wiese
	grid-connected	ans Elektrizitätsversorgungsnetz angebunden
	grille	Gitter, Fenstergitter, Gittertür
	grooming guide	Knigge
	ground floor	Erdgeschoss
	grounds	(Außen-)Anlagen
	groundskeeping	Reinigung und Pflege von Außenanlagen
	grow (verb)	anwachsen
	growth	Wachstum
	guarantee	garantieren, gewährleisten
	guest toilet	Gäste-WC
	gutter	Dachrinne

	gypsum	Gips
H	half	halb
	hallway light	Hauslicht
	halve (verb)	halbieren
	handicapped-equipped bathroom equipment	behindertengerechte Badezimmerausstattung
	handle (verb)	handhaben
	handrail	Handlauf, Geländer
	hangar	Hangar
	haphazard	wahllos, willkürlich
	harassment	Belästigung
	hay	Heu
	head of	Chef, Leiter
	headquarter	Hauptsitz
	health and safety at work	Arbeits- und Gesundheitsschutz
	heating	Heizung
	heating circuit water	Heizwasserkreislauf
	heating costs	Heizkosten
	heating system	Heizung
	heating technology	Heiztechnologie
	height	Höhe
	height adjustable	höhenverstellbar
	hesitate (verb)	zögern
	high	Spitze, höchster Punkt
	hinge	Angel, Drehkreuz
	hold a conference (verb)	eine Konferenz abhalten
	hole	Loch
	holiday park	Ferienpark
	home-builder	Bauherr, Häuslebauer
	homeowner	Hausbesitzer, Eigentümer
	home-seller	Hausverkäufer
	hook-up	Zusammenschaltung, Anschluss
	hostel	Wohnheim, Herberge
	hostility	Feindlichkeit
	house plan	Bauplan
	household	Haushalt
	housing	Wohnungswesen
	housing association	gemeinnützige Wohnungsbaugesellschaft (britische Form)
	housing benefit	Wohngeld
	housing cooperative	Wohnungsbaugenossenschaft
	housing market	Wohnungsmarkt
	housing supply	Wohnversorgung
	humidity	Feuchtigkeit
	HVAC = heating, ventilation, air conditioning	Heizung, Lüftung, Klimatechnik
I	icon	Symbol
	improve (verb)	verbessern
	in charge	verantwortlich, zuständig
	incentive	Anreiz
	incineration	Verbrennung
	income limit	Einkommensgrenze
	income-producing	Einkommen schaffend
	inconvenience	Belästigung, Unbill
	incorporation	Eingemeindung, Gesellschaft (Unternehmensform)
	increase	Steigerung
	increase (verb)	wachsen, anwachsen, steigern, ansteigen

Vokabeln Englisch-Deutsch

indemnify (verb)	entschädigen
index linking	indexiert (mit Inflations-anpassung)
indispensable	unerlässlich
industrial park	Industriegebiet
industrialized building/ apartment block	Plattenbau
inevitable	unausweichlich
infectious disease	Infektionskrankheit
infrastructure	Infrastruktur
infringe (verb)	verletzen
inhabitant	Einwohner
inner courtyard, patio	Innenhof
insulation	Isolierung
insurance	Versicherung
insurance company	Versicherungsunternehmen
insurance premium	Versicherungsprämie
insured	versichert
insurer	Versicherungsnehmer
intercom	Gegensprechanlage
intercom system, interphone	Gegensprechanlage
interest rate	Zinssatz
interests	Zinsen
interior finish	Innenausbau
intimidation	Einschüchterung
in-tray	Posteingangskorb
investigate (verb)	nachforschen
investment opportunity	Investitionsmöglichkeit
issue	Thema
J janitorial	hausmeisterlich
jumbled	durcheinander, ungeordnet
jump suit	Overall, Trainingsanzug
jurisdiction	Rechtsprechung
K kerbside	Straßenrand, am Bürgersteig
key (adj.)	Haupt-
kitchen	Küche
kitchenette	Kochnische
L laminate	Laminat
land	Grund und Boden
land registry	Kataster
landfill	Abfalldeponie
landlord	Vermieter
landscaping	Landschaftsbau
landscaping	Landschafts- und Garten-gestaltung
laundry facilities	Waschküche mit Wasch-maschine
laundry room	Waschküche, Wäschezimmer
law	Gesetz
lawn	Rasen
lawyer	Rechtsanwalt
lead sheeting	Blechverkleidung
leading	führend
leak	Leckage
leaking roof	undichtes Dach
leaking toilet	laufende Toilette
lease (verb)	verpachten
lease agreement	Miet-, Pachtvertrag
lease expiration	Auslaufen des Mietvertrags
legacy	Altlast
legal action	Gerichtsverfahren

legal advice	Rechtsberatung
legal expenses insurance	Rechtsschutzversicherung
legal matter	Rechtsangelegenheit
legal requirements	rechtliche Anforderungen
legally binding	rechtsverbindlich
leisure	Freizeit
length	Länge
let (verb)	vermieten
letter head	Briefkopf
letting agent	Immobilienmakler (Vermietung)
liability	Haftung
liability insurance	Haftpflichtversicherung
lift	Fahrstuhl
light	Licht
light bulb	Birne
light fixture	Lampeninstallation
lighting system	Beleuchtungssystem
lightning	Blitzeinschlag
limited liability company	Gesellschaft mit beschränkter Haftung; GmbH
line graph	Liniendiagramm
line of business	Geschäftsaktivität, Geschäftssegment
linoleum	Linoleum
lintel	Fenster-, Türsturz
living room	Wohnzimmer
living space	Wohnraum
living standard	Lebensstandard
load-bearing wall	tragende Wand
loan	Darlehen, Baudarlehen
local authority	Kommunalbehörde
local budget	kommunaler Haushalt
local government	Stadt-, Gemeinderat
located	gelegen
location	Lage, Ort
lock	Schloss
lodger	(Unter-)Mieter
loft	Loft, Wohnung über zwei Etagen
long-term strategic financial planning	langfristige, strategische Finanzplanung
lot	Bauplatz, Baustelle
lottery license shop	Lottoannahmestelle
low	Tiefpunkt
low rent	niedrige Miete
low-energy house	Niedrigenergiehaus
low-income housing	Sozialwohnungsbau
lumber	Bauholz
lump sum	Pauschale
M mailbox	Briefkasten
maintain (verb)	unterhalten, beibehalten, instand halten, warten
maintained	instand gehalten
maintenance	Wartung, Instandhaltung
maintenance and repair	Wartung und Instandsetzung
maintenance bill	Rechnung für Wartung / Instandhaltung
maintenance cost	Wartungskosten
maintenance-free	wartungsfrei
mall	Einkaufszentrum, Promenade

Vokabeln Englisch-Deutsch

manage (verb)	managen, Geschäft führen
manners	Betragen, Benimm, Verhaltensweisen
manor house	Herrenhaus, Schloss
mansion	herrschaftliches Wohnhaus
manufacturer	Hersteller
marble	Marmor
marital status	Ehestand
market leader	Marktführer
market niche	Marktnische
market position	Marktstellung
mastic asphalt	Gussasphalt
means	Mittel (um etwas zu tun)
mechanicals	Schlosserarbeiten
medium-sized	mittelgroß
menu-driven	menügesteuert
mercantile	kaufmännisch
metal-grilled window	vergittertes Fenster
microwave	Mikrowelle
migrate (verb)	wandern, abwandern, ziehen, migrieren
migration	Migration
mirror	Spiegel
mismatch (verb)	nicht zusammenpassen
misuse	Missbrauch
mobile, mobile phone	mobil, Mobiltelefon
monitor (verb)	überprüfen, nachverfolgen
mortar	Mörtel, Speis
mortgage	Hypothek
mortgage bank	Hypothekenbank
motion detector	Bewegungsmelder
mould, mold (AE)	Schimmel
move-in	Einzug
move-in and move-out procedure	Verfahren bei Auszug / Einzug
move-in check list	Wohnungsübernahmeprotokoll
move-out	Auszug
move-out check list	Wohnungsübergabeprotokoll
multi-family	Mehrfamilien-
multi-family house	Mehrfamilienhaus
multi-storey	mehrgeschossig
multi-storey car park	Parkhaus
municipal	kommunal
municipality	Kommunalverwaltung
mutual	gegenseitig
N nappy	Windel
natural resources	natürliche Ressourcen
negotiate (verb)	verhandeln
negotiation	Verhandlung
neighbourhood	Nachbarschaft, Wohnviertel
net income	Nettoeinkommen
network	Netzwerk
noise insulation	akustische Isolierung
noise pollution	Lärmbelästigung
noisy	laut, lärmend
notary	Notar
notice to quit	Kündigung durch Vermieter
notify (Verb)	benachrichtigen
nuisance	Beeinträchtigung
O occupancy	Belegung
occupancy rate	Belegungsrate
occupied	belegt, genutzt
occur (verb)	auftreten, passieren, geschehen
odour of gas	Gasgeruch
offender	Angreifer, Straftäter
offer	Angebot
offer-driven market	Angebotsmarkt
on time	pünktlich
on-wall mounting	Auf-Putz-Installation
open-ended lease	unbefristeter Mietvertrag
open-plan living area	Wohnfläche
operating system	Betriebssystem
operation	Transaktion, Operation
option-to-buy	Vorkaufsrecht
oral communication	mündliche Kommunikation
order	Auftrag
ordinance	Anordnung, Verfügung
outbuilding	Außengebäude, Nebengebäude
outdoor facilities	Außenanlagen
outlet	Steckdose
outside lighting	Außenbeleuchtung
outside staircase	außen liegendes Treppenhaus
outskirt	Stadtrand
outstanding financial obligations	Außenstände
out-tray	Postausgangskorb
overcrowding	Überbelegung
overemphasize	überbewerten
overload	Überlastung
oversee (verb)	überblicken
oversupply	Überangebot
own (verb)	besitzen
owner-occupied house	selbst genutztes Wohneigentum
P paint touch-ups	Malerausbesserungsarbeiten
painter	Maler
pane	Glasscheibe
paragraph	Absatz
paramount	höchst, überragend, vorrangig, Haupt-
parking	Pkw-Stellplatz
parking-space	Pkw-Einstellplatz
parquet	Parkett
parquet flooring	Parkettfußboden
partition wall	Trennwand
patio	Patio, Innenhof
payroll	Gehaltsliste
peak	Höchstwert, Höchststand
percentage	Prozentsatz
performance	Leistung
periodic tenancy agreement	unbefristeter Mietvertrag
periodical report	Monats- / Quartalsbericht
periodically	periodisch
periphery	Peripherie, Stadtrand
permission	Genehmigung
perpetual, for an unlimited period	unbefristet
personnel	Personal
personnel costs	Personalkosten
pest-control	Kammerjäger
pet	Haustier

Vokabeln Englisch-Deutsch

photo shop	Fotogeschäft
photovoltaic technology	Fotovoltaiktechnologie
pie chart	Kuchendiagramm
piecemeal	stückchenweise, allmählich, nach und nach
pier	Pfeiler
pilot scheme	Pilotvorhaben
pipe	Rohr(-leitung)
pipework	Verrohrung
pitch	Steigung
pitched roof	Steildach
plantings	Bepflanzung
plaster	Gipsputz
plaster (verb)	verputzen
plasterboard	Rigipsplatte
playground	Kinderspielplatz
plot	Grundstück
plumber	Klempner, Installateur
plumbing	Installateurarbeit
plumbing	Sanitärinstallationsarbeiten
plummet (verb)	(ab-)stürzen
plywood	Sperrholz, Schalungsplatte
police	Polizei
pool	Swimmingpool
population	Bevölkerung
population density	Bevölkerungsdichte
porch	Portal, Veranda, Vorbau, Wintergarten
portfolio	Produktpalette, Bestand, Portfolio
postal worker	Postangestellter
potential	Potenzial
power-cut	Stromausfall
power-supply	Stromversorgung
preamble	Präambel
precaution	Vorkehrung
prefabricated house	Fertighaus
premises	Örtlichkeiten, Grundstück
premium	Prämie
preventive	präventiv
price list	Preisliste
principal	Bauherr
prior notice	vorherige Benachrichtigung
privacy	Privatsphäre
private housing company	privates Wohnungsunternehmen
privatisation	Privatisierung
privatise (verb)	privatisieren
professional housing provider	Wohnungsunternehmen
profitable	einträglich, profitabel
project manager	Projektleiter / Bauleiter
promote (verb)	fördern
property	Eigentum
property damage insurance	Gebäudehaftpflichtversicherung
property description	Immobilienexposé
property site	Baustelle
property tax	Grundsteuer
proportionate	proportional
prospective tenant	möglicher Mieter
provide (verb)	versorgen, bereitstellen
public interest group	öffentliche Interessengruppen
public utility company	Stadtwerke
public-sector corporation	öffentliches Unternehmen
pull-down stairs	ausziehbare Dachstuhltreppe
punctuality	Pünktlichkeit
punctuation	Interpunktion
purchase (verb)	kaufen, erwerben
purpose	Ziel, Zweck
PVC pipe	PVC-Rohr
Q query	Anfrage, Ersuchen
quirky	schnörkelig, schrullig, schrill, sonderbar
quote	Angebot
R race	Rasse
racist	rassistisch
range of products	Produktportfolio
ranking	Klassifizierung
rapport	Verbindung, Verhältnis
Ratio Utility Based Systems RUBS	Betriebskostenermittlung basierend auf Verteilungsschlüssel
real estate industry	Immobiliensektor
real estate investment	Immobilieninvestition
real estate property	Immobilieneigentum
real estate tax, tax on land and buildings	Grundsteuer
receiver	Empfänger (bei Geschäftskorrespondenz)
recommend (verb)	empfehlen
recreation park	Erholungsanlage
rectangular	rechtwinklig
recycle (verb)	recyclen
reduction	Verringerung, Reduktion
refrain	unterlassen
refrigerator, fridge	Kühlschank
refund (verb)	rückerstatten
refurbish (verb)	sanieren
refurbishment	Modernisierung
refuse	Abfall
refuse collection	Müllabfuhr
register	Zähler
regulation	Regelung, Rechtsvorschrift
reinforce (verb)	verstärken
reinstate (verb)	wiederherstellen, wiedereinstellen
reliability	Zuverlässigkeit
reliable	zuverlässig
remain (verb)	bleiben, verbleiben
reminder	Mahnung
removal of debris	Schuttentfernung
removal of wasps and bees nests	Entfernen von Wespen- und Bienennestern
renovation potential	Renovierungspotenzial
rent	Miete
rent arrears	Mietrückstände
rent collection	Vereinnahmung der Miete
rent excluding service charges	Kaltmiete
rent increase	Mieterhöhung
rent recovery	Eintreiben der Miete
rental	Miet-

Vokabeln Englisch-Deutsch

repair	Instandsetzung, Reparatur
repair jobs	Reparaturarbeiten
representative (adj.)	repräsentativ
representative	Vertreter
reputation	Leumund, Ruf, Reputation
request	Anfrage, Anforderung
request (verb)	nachfragen, fordern
requirement	Anforderung, Erfordernis
re-sale value	Wiederverkaufswert
resident	Anwohner
residential	wohn-
residential (real-estate) property	Wohnimmobilie
residential area	Wohngebiet
resolve (verb)	lösen, beschließen
responsibility	Verantwortung
restrictions	Beschränkungen
retail shop	Einzelhandelsgeschäft
retaining wall	tragende Wand
revenue	Einkommen, Ertrag
rights and obligations	Rechte und Pflichten
rigid	steif, starr
riot	Aufstand
rise (verb)	(an-)steigen
risk assessment	Risikobeurteilung
road	Straße
rogue	Schlingel, Spitzbub
rolling grill	durchgängige Rollläden
roof	Dach
roof garden; roof-top garden	Dachgarten
roof pitch	Dachneigung
roof plan	Dachplan
roof slater / tiler	Dachdecker
roof tile	Dachziegel
roofer	Dachdecker
roofing	Dacheindeckung
roughly	ungefähr, zirka
routine	Routine
routinely	routinemäßig
RSL = Registered Social Landlord	Sozialwohnungsunternehmen in Großbritannien
rubbish	Abfall
rude	grob
rundown	verwohnt, abgewirtschaftet, heruntergekommen
rural	ländlich
RV (Recreational Vehicle)	Wohnwagen, Campingmobil
S safety	Sicherheit
sales agreement	Kaufvertrag
sales floor, sales area	Verkaufsfläche
sales literature	Verkaufsprospekt
salutation	Begrüßung
sample	Muster
sanitary	Sanitär-
sanitary system	Sanitärinstallationen
satisfied	zufrieden
savings	Ersparnisse
sawdust	Sägespäne
scaffold	Gerüst
scope	Umfang
scaffolder	Gerüstbauer
scorecard	Berichtsbogen, Scorecard
scratched	zerkratzt
seafront	an der Küste
security	Sicherheit
segment	Segment, Abschnitt
self-contained central heating	Etagenheizung
self-esteem	Selbstachtung, Selbstwertgefühl
semi-detached	einseitig angebaut
service charges	Nebenkosten
service enterprise	Dienstleistungsbetrieb
service of condominium	WEG-Verwaltung
sewage	Abwasser
sewerage	Abwassersystem, Kanalisation
share	Anteil
shareholder	Aktionär
shed	Schuppen, Lagerhaus
shelf, shelves	Regal(e)
shelving	Regalbau
shop	Ladenlokal
shop fitter	Inneneinrichter
shopping centre	Einkaufszentrum
shopping park	Einkaufspark
shortage	Not, Mangel
short-term	kurzfristig
short-term lets	befristeter Mietvertrag
shower	Dusche
shower curtain	Duschvorhang
shower head	Duschkopf
showroom	Ausstellungsraum
shrub	Strauch, Bodendecker
sign (verb)	unterzeichnen
signature	Unterschrift
single family home	Einfamilienhaus
sink (verb)	absenken, absacken
site	Baustelle
site plan	Grundstücksplan, Lageplan
size	Größe
skeleton	Skelett
skylights	Dachluke, Dachfenster, Oberlicht
skyscraper	Wolkenkratzer
slab	Platte, Decke (Rohbau)
slate	Dachschiefer
sleek	geschmeidig, glatt
slightly	ein wenig
small business enterprise	Kleingewerbe
smell of gas	Gasgeruch
smoke detector	Rauchmelder
social commitment	Sozialengagement
social housing	sozialer Wohnungsbau
social housing, council housing, RSL housing	Sozialwohnung
social services department	Sozialamt
social, cultural, economic, ethnic mix	soziale, kulturelle, wirtschaftliche, ethnische Durchmischung
socket	Steckdose
soil report	Bodenanalysebericht
solar energy	Sonnen- / Solarenergie

Vokabeln Englisch-Deutsch

solicit (verb)	jmd. bitten, auffordern
solid	solide
solid fuel	fester Brennstoff
soot	Ruß
spare key	Ersatzschlüssel
specialist	Fachmann, -frau, Spezialist
sprawling	sich der Länge nach hinstrecken / ausdehnen
spreadsheet	Kalkulationsblatt, Tabellenkalkulation
spy (verb)	spionieren
square metre	Quadratmeter
staff	Personal
stagnate (verb)	stagnieren, stillstehen
stagnation	Stagnation, Stillstand
stairs	Treppen
stairwell, staircase	Treppenhaus
stalking	Stalking
stamp	Briefmarke
standard limit of indemnity	Standardversicherungssumme
stapler	Hefter
starched collar	gestärkter Kragen
state-of-the-art	auf dem neusten Stand
stationery	Briefpapier
steady	gleichmäßig, beständig, dauerhaft
steel beam	Stahlträger
steel erector	Stahlbauer
stipulate (verb)	festsetzen, niederlegen, vereinbaren, vorschreiben
stock	Bestand
stonemason	Maurer
stop	Stopp
storage facilities	Lagerräume
storage space	Lagerraum
store (verb)	speichern
storey	Stockwerk, Geschoss
storm	Sturm
straw	Stroh
street cleaning	Straßenreinigung
street litter bin	öffentlicher Abfallkorb
structural engineer	Bauingenieur, Statiker
student hostel	Studentenwohnheim
subdivision	Unterabteilung
subject line	Betreffzeile
sublet (verb)	untervermieten
sub-meter (verb)	einzeln ablesen (Energieverbrauch o. Ä.)
submit (verb)	vorlegen
subsidence	Absenken
suburb	Vorort
suburban	Vorort-
subway	U-Bahn
sudden	plötzlich
suit (verb)	passen, taugen, übereinstimmen
sun blinds	Sonnenblenden
supervise (verb)	überwachen, überprüfen
supplier	Lieferant
supplies	Lieferungen, Zubehör, Betriebsstoffe
supply	liefern
supply (and demand)	Angebot (und Nachfrage)
supply pipe	Versorgungsrohr
supply shortage	Lieferengpass
surgery	Arztpraxis, Behandlungsraum
survey	Erhebung, Gutachten, Studie
surveyor	Gutachter, Sachverständiger
suspended ceiling	abgehängte Decke
suspicious	verdächtig, suspekt
sustainable	nachhaltig
sustainable urban development	nachhaltige Stadtentwicklung, Stadtumbau
sweep (verb)	fegen
switch	Schalter
T table	Tabelle
takeaway bar	Lokal mit Speisen zum Mitnehmen
tap	Wasserkran
target	Ziel
target group	Zielgruppe
tax	Steuern, Abgaben
tea kitchen	Teeküche
telephone company	Telefongesellschaft
telephone wall jack	Telefonanschlussdose
television company	Fernsehgesellschaft
temperature sensor	Temperaturfühler
tenancy agreement	Mietvertrag
tenant	Mieter
tenant files	Mieterakten
tenants' association	Mieterbund
tenants' involvement	Mieterbeteiligung
tender	Angebot auf eine Ausschreibung
tennis court	Tennisplatz
tentative	provisorisch, vorläufig
tenure	Miet- / Pachtverhältnis
terminate (verb)	beenden, abschließen
termination-of-lease procedure	Beendigung des Mietvertrags
terms and conditions	Geschäftsbedingungen AGB
terrace	Häuserreihe, Terrasse
terraced house	Reihenhaus
terrorism cover	Deckung bei Schäden in Folge von terroristischen Anschlägen
theft	Diebstahl
thermal insulation	Wärmeisolierung
thermostat	Thermostat
thickness	Dicke
thorough	sorgfältig
tie	Krawatte
tie (verb)	(fest-)binden, festzurren
tile	Fliese
tile	Dachziegel
tiled	gefliest
tiled floor	Fliesenboden
tiler	Fliesenleger
timber	Bauholz, Balken
time switch	Zeitschaltung
timely	rechtzeitig
tobacco products	Tabakwaren
toilet bowl	Toilettenschüssel
toilet seat	Klobrille

Vokabeln Englisch-Deutsch

	tool	Werkzeug
	toolbox	Werkzeugkasten
	touch screen	Touchscreen-Bildschirm
	towel	Handtuch
	towel rail	Handtuchhalter
	town planner	Stadtplaner
	townhouse	Stadthaus
	trade chain	Handelskette
	trade fair	Handelsmesse
	traffic connections	Verkehrsverbindungen
	trash removal	Müllabfuhr
	tree	Baum
	trim (verb)	verputzen
	triplex	Dreifamilienhaus
	trunk road network	Fernstraßennetz
	truss	Dachstuhl
	trust	Vertrauen
	tumble-drier	Wäschetrockner
	tunnel	Tunnel
	turning-point	Wende, Wendepunkt
	two-persons household	Zweipersonenhaushalt
	two-room apartment	Zweizimmerwohnung
U	underground parking	unterirdisches Parkhaus
	unexpected	unerwartet
	unfurnished	unmöbliert
	unit	Einheit
	unlawful	gesetzwidrig
	unpaid rent	Mietrückstand
	unsatisfied, dissatisfied	unzufrieden
	urban	städtisch, urban
	urban development, urban extension	Stadterweiterung
	urban planner	Stadtplaner
	urban regeneration	Stadterneuerung
	urban regeneration programme	Stadterneuerungsprogramm
	urge (verb)	drängen, dringend bitten
	urgent	dringend
	useful life	Nutzungsdauer
	utility bill	Betriebskostenabrechnung
	utility charges	Nebenkosten
	utility costs	Versorgungskosten für Strom, Wasser, Gas usw.
	utility provider	Versorgungsunternehmen
V	vacancy	Leerstand
	vacancy loss	Verlust aus Leerstand
	vacant apartment, flat, dwelling	leer stehende Wohnung
	vacate (verb)	räumen, überlassen
	value	Wert
	vandalism	Vandalismus
	variable service charges	variable Mietnebenkosten
	VAT (Value Added Tax)	Mehrwertsteuer
	vessel	Schiff
	vigilant action / vigilant justice	Selbstjustiz
	villa	freistehendes Einfamilienhaus, Villa
	vineyard	Weingut
	vinyl	Vinyl
	voluntary social commitment	freiwillige Sozialverpflichtung
	vulgar	abgeschmackt, geschmacklos, vulgär
W	walk-in (adj.)	begehbar
	walk-through	Begehung
	walkway	Fußweg
	wall	Wand
	wall / floor tiling	Fliesen legen, Fliesenbelag
	wall cladding	Fassade
	warehouse	Lagerhaus
	warranty	Garantie
	WASCs – water and sewerage companies	Wasserversorgungsunternehmen
	washbasin	Waschbecken
	waste	Abfall
	waste container	Abfallbehälter
	waste disposal	Abfallentsorgung
	wasteful practice	Verschwendung
	water consumption	Wasserverbrauch
	water pipe	Wasserrohr
	water pressure	Wasserdruck
	watertight	wasserdicht
	wealth	Wohlstand
	wealthy people	wohlhabende Menschen
	wear and tear	Abnutzung, Verschleiß
	wheelchair	Rollstuhl
	window	Fenster
	window frame	Fensterrahmen
	window sill	Fensterbank, Fensterbrett
	wire	Draht
	wiring	Verdrahtung, Verkabelung
	withhold rent payment (verb)	Miete mindern
	wooden floor	Holzfußboden
	word-processing	Textverarbeitung
	workforce	Arbeitskraft
	written communication	schriftliche Kommunikation
	wrought-iron	schmiedeeisern
X	x-axis	X-Achse
Y	yard	Hof, Yard (Längeneinheit)
	y-axis	Y-Achse
	yellow pages	Gelbe Seiten
Z	zoning ordinance *oder* land use plan	Flächennutzungsplan

Vokabeln Deutsch-Englisch

A	(ab-)fallen	drop (verb)
	(ab-)fallen	fall (verb)
	(ab-)stürzen	plummet (verb)
	(an-)steigen	rise (verb)
	(Außen-)Anlagen	grounds
	(fest-)binden, festzurren	tie (verb)
	(Unter-)Mieter	lodger
	Abdichtung gegen Luftzug	air sealing
	Abfall	refuse
	Abfall	rubbish
	Abfall	waste
	Abfallbehälter	waste container
	Abfalldeponie	landfill
	Abfallentsorgung	waste disposal
	Abfluss	drainage
	Abgaben, Gebühren, Rechte	dues
	abgehängte Decke	suspended ceiling
	abgeschmackt, geschmacklos, vulgär	vulgar
	abkürzen	abbreviate (verb)
	Abkürzung	abbreviation
	Ablaufdiagramm	flow chart
	abnehmen	decrease (verb)
	Abnutzung, Verfall, Wertverlust	deterioration
	Abnutzung, Verschleiß	wear and tear
	Abriss	demolition
	Absatz	paragraph
	abschaffen	abolish (verb)
	Abschaffung	abolition
	abschrecken, abhalten von	deter (verb)
	Absenken	subsidence
	absenken, absacken	sink (verb)
	Abwasser	sewage
	Abwasserrohre	drains
	Abwassersystem, Kanalisation	sewerage
	abwehrend, abschreckend	deterrent
	abziehen	deduct
	Akte, Datei	file
	Aktenkoffer	briefcase
	Aktionär	shareholder
	akustische Isolierung	noise insulation
	Alarmanlage	burglar alarm
	alarmieren	alert (verb)
	Alkohol	booze
	Allzeithoch / -tief	all-time high / low
	alternative Wohnversorgung	alternative residential accommodation
	Altlast	legacy
	an der Küste	seafront
	Anbau	attachment
	Anbau, Windfang, Terrasse hinter dem Haus	back porch
	anbauen, anbringen, anfügen	attach (verb)
	Anbauten	additions
	ändern, verändern	alter (verb)
	Änderungen, Umbauten	alterations
	Andrang, Verdichtung	congestion
	Anerkennung, Bestätigung	acknowledgement

anfertigen, aufstellen, entwerfen	draw up (verb)
Anforderung, Erfordernis	requirement
Anfrage	enquiry
Anfrage, Anforderung	request
Anfrage, Ersuchen	query
angebaut, angefügt	attached
Angebot	bid
Angebot	offer
Angebot	quote
Angebot auf eine Ausschreibung	tender
Angebot (und Nachfrage)	supply (and demand)
Angebotsmarkt	offer-driven market
Angel, Drehkreuz	hinge
Angestellter, Arbeitnehmer	employee
Angreifer, Straftäter	offender
angrenzend	adjacent
angrenzende Immobilie	adjacent property
Angriff, tätlicher Übergriff	assault
Anlagen	enclosures
annehmen, übernehmen, vermuten, unterstellen	assume (verb)
Anordnung, Verfügung	ordinance
Anreiz	incentive
Anrufbeantworter	answer phone
ans Elektrizitätsversorgungsnetz angebunden	grid-connected
Anschlüsse	fittings
Anspruch	claim
ansteckende Krankheit	contagious disease
ansteigen	climb (verb)
Anstrich, Belag	coating
Anteil	share
anwachsen	grow (verb)
Anwohner	resident
Arbeitgeber	employer
Arbeits- und Gesundheitsschutz	health and safety at work
Arbeitskraft	workforce
Arbeitsplatte	countertop
Architekt	architect
Arrangements	arrangements
Arztpraxis, Behandlungsraum	surgery
Asche	ash
Attika, Dachgeschoss	attic
auf dem neusten Stand	state-of-the-art
auf der grünen Wiese	greenfield
Auf-Putz-Installation	on-wall mounting
Aufrissplan	elevation plan
Aufstand	riot
Auftrag	order
Auftragnehmer	contractor
auftreten, passieren, geschehen	occur (verb)
Ausflugsziele	destination, place of excursions
Ausgabe, Kosten	expense
Ausgaben, Aufwand	expenditures
ausgeglichener Markt	balanced market
Auslaufen des Mietvertrags	lease expiration
auslaufen, zu Ende gehen	expire (verb)
Ausschluss	exclusion

Vokabeln Deutsch-Englisch

	Außen-	exterior
	außen liegendes Treppenhaus	outside staircase
	Außenanlagen	outdoor facilities
	Außenarbeiten, Außenwandgestaltung	exterior finish
	Außenbeleuchtung	outside lighting
	Außengebäude, Nebengebäude	outbuilding
	Außenstände	outstanding financial obligations
	Außenwände	exterior walls
	Ausstattung, Ausrüstung	equipment
	Ausstellungsraum	showroom
	ausziehbare Dachstuhltreppe	pull-down stairs
	Auszug	move-out
B	Bäckerei	bakery
	Badezimmer	bathroom
	Badezimmerwaschbecken	bathroom sink
	Balken, Träger	beam
	Balkendiagramm	bar chart
	Balkon	balcony
	Bambusboden	bamboo flooring
	Bank	bank
	barrierefrei	barrier-free
	Bau	construction
	Bauarbeiter	construction operative
	Bauaufsicht	building inspection
	Baubranche	construction sector
	bauen	construct (verb)
	Baufertigstellung	building completion
	Baugenehmigung	building permission
	Baugenehmigung	building permit
	Baugrundstück	building plot
	Bauherr	principal
	Bauherr, Bauunternehmer	builder
	Bauherr, Häuslebauer	home-builder
	Bauholz	lumber
	Bauholz, Balken	timber
	Bauingenieur	building engineer
	Bauingenieur, Statiker	structural engineer
	Bauingenieurwesen, Hoch- und Tiefbau	civil engineering
	Baum	tree
	Baumaterial	construction material
	Bauplan	house plan
	Bauplatz, Baustelle	lot
	Baustelle	property site
	Baustelle	site
	Bauunternehmer	contractor
	Bauvolumen	construction volume
	beachtlich	considerable
	Beamter, öffentlicher Angestellter	civil servant
	Becken	basin
	Beeinträchtigung	nuisance
	Beeinträchtigung, Belästigung	annoyance
	beenden, abschließen	terminate (verb)
	Beendigung des Mietvertrags	termination-of-lease procedure

befestigt	fixed
befristeter Mietvertrag	fixed-term tenancy agreement
befristeter Mietvertrag	short-term lets
begehbar	walk-in (adj.)
Begehung	walk-through
beginnen	commence (verb)
Begradigung, Stufung	grading
Begrüßung	salutation
Begünstigter	beneficiary
behindert	disabled
behindertengerechte Badezimmerausstattung	handicapped-equipped bathroom equipment
Behinderung	disability
Behörden	authorities
beifügen	enclose (verb)
Beitrittsländer	accession countries
Belästigung	harassment
Belästigung, Unbill	inconvenience
belegt, genutzt	occupied
Belegung	occupancy
Belegungsrate	occupancy rate
beleuchtetes Display	backlit display
Beleuchtungssystem	lighting system
benachrichtigen	notify (Verb)
Benchmarking, Maßstab, Bezugsgröße	benchmarking
Bepflanzung	plantings
Beratung, Ratschlag	advice
berechnen, in Rechnung stellen	charge (verb)
Berechnungsingenieur	CAD technician
Berichtsbogen, Scorecard	scorecard
Beschränkungen	restrictions
besitzen	own (verb)
Besitztümer, Hab und Gut	belongings
Bestand	stock
Bestätigung	confirmation
bestehen aus	consist of (verb)
bestehend	existing
bestimmen, festlegen	determine (verb)
Beton	concrete
Betonplatte	concrete slab
Betragen, Benimm, Verhaltensweisen	manners
Betreffzeile	subject line
Betriebskostenabrechnung	bill of utility costs
Betriebskostenabrechnung	utility bill
Betriebskostenermittlung basierend auf Verteilungsschlüssel	Ratio Utility Based Systems RUBS
Betriebsstörung	breakdown
Betriebssystem	operating system
Bettelei	begging
Bevölkerung	population
Bevölkerungsdichte	population density
bewegliches Gut	chattel
Bewegungsmelder	motion detector
Bezirk, Gemeinde	borough
biometrische Zugangskontrolle	biometric access control
BIP = Bruttoinlandsprodukt	GDP = gross domestic product

Vokabeln Deutsch-Englisch

Birne	light bulb
Blechverkleidung	lead sheeting
bleiben, verbleiben	remain (verb)
Blitzeinschlag	lightning
Blockbebauung	block of flats
Blockbebauung	building block for urbanism
Bodenanalysebericht	soil report
Bodenbelag	floor covering, flooring
Bodenbelag	flooring material
Bogen	bow
Brache, Rand-	fringe
Brand	fire
Brand bekämpfen	fight fire (verb)
brechen, verletzen, zuwiderhandeln	breach (verb)
Breitband-Internet	broadband internet
Brennwertkessel	condensing boiler
Brennwertkessel	condensing gas boiler
Brennwerttechnologie	condensing heating technology
Briefkasten	mailbox
Briefkopf	letter head
Briefmarke	stamp
Briefpapier	stationery
Broschüre, Prospekt	brochure
Bruch	breach
Bruchteil	fraction
Brücke	bridge
Buchhaltung, Bilanzbuchhaltung	accounting
Bungalow	bungalow
Bürgerkrieg	civil commotion
Bürgerrechtler	civil rights campaigner
C Campingplatz, Stellplatz für ein Zelt	campsite
Chart, Diagramm	chart
Chef, Leiter	head of
Clubhaus	clubhouse
computergesteuert	computerised
D Dach	roof
Dachdecker	roof slater / tiler
Dachdecker	roofer
Dacheindeckung	roofing
Dachgarten	roof garden, roof-top garden
Dachluke, Dachfenster, Oberlicht	skylights
Dachneigung	roof pitch
Dachplan	roof plan
Dachrinne	gutter
Dachschiefer	slate
Dachstuhl	truss
Dachterrasse	deck
Dachziegel	roof tile
Dachziegel	tile
Darlehen, Baudarlehen	loan
Datenbank	database
Datenschutzgesetz	data protection act
Datenträger	data carrier
Deckung bei Schäden in Folge von terroristischen Anschlägen	terrorism cover

Dekorateur	decorator
Deutscher Mieterschutzbund	German Tenants' Protection Association
dezentralisiert	decentralised
Diagramm	diagram
Dicke	thickness
Diebstahl	theft
Diebstahlfolgeschäden	damage following theft
Dienstleistungsbetrieb	service enterprise
Display	display
Disziplinarmaßnahme	disciplinary action
Doppelverglasung	double glazed windows
Dossier	dossier
Draht	wire
dramatisch	dramatic
drängen, dringend bitten	urge (verb)
drastisch	drastic
Dreifamilienhaus	triplex
dringend	urgent
drogenbezogen	drug-related
durcheinander, ungeordnet	jumbled
durchgängige Rollläden	rolling grill
Durchschnitt, durchschnittlich	average
Dusche	shower
Duschkopf	shower head
Duschvorhang	shower curtain
E Ehestand	marital status
Eigenanteil	deductible
Eigenheimzulage	first-home buyer allowance
Eigentum	property
Eigentümergemeinschaft	community association
Eigentumswohnung	condominium
ein wenig	slightly
Einbauküche	fitted kitchen
Einbauschrank	built-in cupboard
Einbrecher	burglar
Einbruchdiebstahl	burglary
eine Konferenz abhalten	hold a conference (verb)
einen Anspruch haben auf	be eligible for (verb)
Einfamilienhaus	single family home
eingebaut	fitted
Eingemeindung, Gesellschaft (Unternehmensform)	incorporation
eingezäunt	fenced
Einheit	unit
Einigung, Vertrag	agreement
Einkaufspark	shopping park
Einkaufszentrum	shopping centre
Einkaufszentrum, Promenade	mall
Einkommen schaffend	income-producing
Einkommen, Ertrag	revenue
Einkommensgrenze	income limit
einräumen, gewähren	grant (verb)
Einrichtungshaus	furnishing house
Einschüchterung	intimidation
einseitig angebaut	semi-detached
Einstellplatz	car parking space, car port

Vokabeln Deutsch-Englisch

einstweilige Anordnung wegen antisozialen Verhaltens	Asbo
einträglich, profitabel	profitable
Eintreiben der Miete	rent recovery
Einwohner	inhabitant
Einzelhandelsgeschäft	retail shop
einzeln ablesen (Energieverbrauch o. Ä.)	sub-meter (verb)
Einzug	move-in
Elektriker	electrician
Elektrizität	electricity
Elektrogeräte	electrical appliances
Elektroplan	electrical plan
Empfänger (bei Geschäftskorrespondenz)	receiver
empfehlen	recommend (verb)
Endabnahme	final inspection
Endreihenhaus	end unit
Energieeinsparungen	energy savings
Energieversorger	energy provider
Entfernen von Wespen- und Bienennestern	removal of wasps and bees nests
Entität, Einheit	entity
entschädigen	compensate (verb)
entschädigen	indemnify (verb)
Entschädigung, Wiedergutmachung	compensation
entschuldigen	apologise (verb)
Entwässerungsrohre	drain pipes
entwickeln	develop (verb)
Entwicklung	development
Erdarbeiten	earthwork
Erdbeben	earthquake
Erdgeschoss	ground floor
Erhaltung, Naturschutz, Einsparung	conservation
Erhebung, Gutachten, Studie	survey
Erholungsanlage	recreation park
erreichen, erzielen	achieve (verb)
errichten	erect (verb)
Ersatzschlüssel	spare key
erschwinglich, bezahlbar	affordable
Ersparnisse	savings
Erweiterung, Zusatz, Zugabe	add on
Erwerb	acquisition
erwerben	acquire (verb)
Erwerber, Käufer	buyer
Esszimmer	dining room
Etagenheizung	self-contained central heating
Etikette, Benimmregeln	etiquette
EU-Mitgliedsstaaten	EU member states
explodieren	explode (verb)
Explosion	explosion
F Fachmann, -frau, Spezialist	specialist
Facility, Einrichtung	facility
Fahrradständer	bicycle stand, kick stand
Fahrstuhl	lift
Fällen und Zurückschneiden von Bäumen	felling and lopping of trees
fällig	due
Faser-	fibrous
Fassade	wall cladding
Fassadenverkleidung	cladding
fegen	sweep (verb)
fehlerhaft, defekt	faulty
Feindlichkeit	hostility
Fenster	window
Fenster-, Türsturz	lintel
Fensterbank, Fensterbrett	window sill
Fensterrahmen	window frame
Ferienpark	holiday park
Fernsehgesellschaft	television company
Fernstraßennetz	trunk road network
Fertighaus	prefabricated house
fest eingebaute Armatur	fixture
fester Brennstoff	solid fuel
festsetzen, niederlegen, vereinbaren, vorschreiben	stipulate (verb)
Feuchtigkeit	humidity
Feuerlöscher	fire extinguisher
Feuerwehr	fire brigade
finanzielle Transaktion	financial operation
Finanzierung	financing
Finanzierung	funding
Flachbettscanner	flat-bed scanner
Flachbildschirm	flat-screen monitor
Flachdach	flat roof
Fläche von 4.047 m^2	acre
Flächennutzungsplan	zoning ordinance *oder* land use plan
Fleischerei, Metzger	butchery, butcher's
Fliese	tile
Fliesen legen, Fliesenbelag	wall / floor tiling
Fliesenleger	tiler
Fliesenboden	tiled floor
Flugfeld, Flugplatz	airfield
Flughafen	airport
Fokus, Hauptaugenmerk	focus (verb)
fördern	promote (verb)
fossiler Brennstoff	fossil fuel
Fotogeschäft	photo shop
Fotovoltaiktechnologie	photovoltaic technology
Fracht	cargo
frei stehendes Einfamilienhaus, Villa	villa
frei stehendes Haus	detached house
freiwillige Sozialverpflichtung	voluntary social commitment
Freizeit	leisure
führend	leading
Führung, Steuerung	governance
Führungskraft	executive
Fundament	foundation
Fundamentplan	foundation plan
Fußbodenausbau	flooring
Fußbodenheizung	floor heating
Fußmatte	door mat
Fußweg	walkway
G gängig, aktuell	current
Garage	garage

Vokabeln Deutsch-Englisch

Garantie	warranty
garantieren, gewährleisten	guarantee
Gartenabfälle	green prunings
Gartenpflege	garden upkeep
Gärtner	gardener
Gas	gas
Gasgeruch	odour of gas
Gasgeruch	smell of gas
Gasheizung	gas heating
Gäste-WC	guest toilet
Gasuhr	gas meter
Gasversorger	gas provider
Gaszähler	gas meter box
Gaszentralheizung	central gas heating
Gebäudehaftpflichtgesetz	defective premises act
Gebäudehaftpflichtversicherung	property damage insurance
geeignet	appropriate
gefliest	tiled
gegenseitig	mutual
Gegensprechanlage	intercom
Gegensprechanlage	intercom system, interphone
Gegenstand von etw. sein	be subject to (verb)
gegenüber	face-to-face
Gehaltsliste	payroll
Gelbe Seiten	yellow pages
gelegen	located
gemeinnützige Wohnungsbaugesellschaft (britische Form)	housing association
gemeinschaftlich	common
Gemeinschaftsanlagen	common areas
Gemeinschaftseigentum	common property
genau, präzise	exactly (adv.)
Genehmigung	approval
Genehmigung	permission
Genossenschaft	cooperative
Gerät	appliance
Gericht	court
gerichtliche Anordnung	court possession order
Gerichtsentscheidung, gerichtliche Mahnung	court order
Gerichtsverfahren	legal action
Gerüst	scaffold
Gerüstbauer	scaffolder
gesamt	entire
Geschäftsaktivität, Geschäftssegment	line of business
Geschäftsbedingungen AGB	terms and conditions
Geschäftsbericht	financial statement
Geschäftsreise	business trip
Geschirrspülmaschine	dishwasher
geschlossener Kreislauf	closed-loop
geschmeidig, glatt	sleek
Gesellschaft mit beschränkter Haftung; GmbH	limited liability company
Gesetz	law
gesetzwidrig	unlawful
Gesichtsausdruck	facial expression
gestärkter Kragen	starched collar
Geste, Gebärde	gesture
gewährleisten, sicherstellen	ensure (verb)
Gewerbegebiet	business park, commercial area
Gewerbeimmobilie	commercial (real estate) property
Gewerbemiete	commercial rent
gewerblich	commercial
Gewerk	craft
Gewölbedecke	cathedral ceiling
Gips	gypsum
Gipsputz	plaster
Gitter, Fenstergitter, Gittertür	grille
Glasscheibe	pane
gleichmäßig, beständig, dauerhaft	steady
Glühbirne	bulb
Gras	grass
Grill	barbecue
grob	rude
Größe	size
große Anzahl an Menschen	crowd
Grund und Boden	land
gründen, begründen	found (verb)
Grundriss	floor plan, layout
Grundsteuer	property tax
Grundsteuer	real estate tax, tax on land and buildings
Grundstück	plot
Grundstücksplan, Lageplan	site plan
Grußformel	complimentary clause
günstig	favourable
Gussasphalt	mastic asphalt
Gutachter, Sachverständiger	surveyor
H Haftpflichtversicherung	liability insurance
Haftung	liability
halb	half
halbieren	halve (verb)
Handelskette	chain store
Handelskette	trade chain
Handelsmesse	trade fair
handhaben	handle (verb)
Handlauf, Geländer	handrail
Handtuch	towel
Handtuchhalter	towel rail
Handwerker	craftsman
Handwerkerschaft	craftspeople
Handy	cell phone
Hangar	hangar
Haupt-	key (adj.)
Hauptsitz	headquarter
Hausbesitzer, Eigentümer	homeowner
Häuserreihe, Terrasse	terrace
Haushalt	household
Haushalt, Budget	budget
häusliche Gewalt	domestic violence
Hauslicht	hallway light
Hausmeister, Hauswart	caretaker
hausmeisterlich	janitorial
Haustier	pet
Hausverkäufer	home-seller
Hefter	stapler

Vokabeln Deutsch-Englisch

Heizkosten	heating costs
Heiztechnologie	heating technology
Heizung	heating
Heizung	heating system
Heizung, Lüftung, Klimatechnik	HVAC = heating, ventilation, air conditioning
Heizungskeller	boiler room
Heizwasserkreislauf	heating circuit water
Herausforderung	challenge
Herrenhaus, Schloss	manor house
herrschaftliches Wohnhaus	mansion
Hersteller	manufacturer
Heu	hay
höchst, überragend, vorrangig, Haupt-	paramount
Höchstwert, Höchststand	peak
Hof, Yard (Längeneinheit)	yard
höflich, zuvorkommend	courteous
Höhe	height
höhenverstellbar	height adjustable
Höhepunkt	climax
Holzfußboden	wooden floor
Hypothek	mortgage
Hypothekenbank	mortgage bank
II. Deutsches Wohnungsbaugesetz von 1956	German housing act of 1956
I illegales Müllabladen	fly-tip (verb)
Immobilieneigentum	real estate property
Immobilienexposé	property description
Immobilieninvestition	real estate investment
Immobilienmakler	estate agent
Immobilienmakler (Vermietung)	letting agent
Immobiliensektor	real estate industry
in die Lage bringen, befähigen	enable (verb)
in Gemeinschaftsbesitz	community-owned
in Kraft setzen, durchsetzen	enforce (verb)
indexiert (mit Inflationsanpassung)	index linking
Industrie- und Handelskammer	chamber of commerce and industry
Industriebrache, Altlast	brownfield
Industriegebiet	industrial park
Infektionskrankheit	infectious disease
Infrastruktur	infrastructure
Innenausbau	interior finish
Inneneinrichter	shop fitter
Innenhof	inner courtyard, patio
Installateurarbeit	plumbing
instand gehalten	maintained
Instandsetzung, Reparatur	repair
Interpunktion	punctuation
Investitionsmöglichkeit	investment opportunity
Isolierung	insulation
IT-Markt	dotcom market
J Jahrhundert	century
Jahrzehnt	decade
jmd. bitten, auffordern	solicit (verb)
K Kabelfernsehen	cable TV
Kalkulationsblatt, Tabellenkalkulation	spreadsheet
Kaltmiete	rent excluding service charges
Kamin, Schornstein	chimney
Kammerjäger	pest-control
Kataster	land registry
kataster-	cadastral
Kauf- / Prospektprüfung	due diligence
kaufen, erwerben	purchase (verb)
Kaufhaus, Warenhaus	department store
kaufmännisch	mercantile
kaufmännischer Geschäftsführer	commercial manager
Kaufvertrag	sales agreement
Kaution	deposit / security deposit
Kaution, Anzahlung	deposit
Keller	basement
Keller	cellar
Kerngeschäft	core business
Kinderspielplatz	playground
Kinderzimmer	children's room
Klassifizierung	ranking
Kleiderordnung	dress code
Kleidung	attire
Kleingewerbe	small business enterprise
Klempner, Installateur	plumber
Klimaanlage	air conditioning
Klobrille	toilet seat
Knigge	grooming guide
Knoblauch	garlic
Kochnische	kitchenette
Kohle	coal
Kollegin, Kollege	colleague
kommunal	municipal
Kommunalbehörde	local authority
kommunaler Haushalt	local budget
Kommunalverwaltung	municipality
Konferenzzentrum	conference centre
konkurrieren	compete (verb)
konsolidieren	consolidate (verb)
Konto	account
Korkboden	cork flooring
Kostenauswertung	cost evaluation
Kostenmanagement	cost control
Kostenvoranschlag	estimate
Kot	faeces
Krawatte	tie
Kreislauf, Schaltkreis, Schaltschema	circuitry
Kubik-	cubic
Küche	kitchen
Kuchendiagramm	pie chart
Kühlschrank	refrigerator, fridge
Kunde	customer
Kündigung durch Vermieter	notice to quit
Kupfer	copper
Kupferrohr	copper pipe
kurzfristig	short-term
L Laden an der Ecke, Tante-Emma-Laden	corner shop
Ladenlokal	shop
Lage, Ort	location

Vokabeln Deutsch-Englisch

	Lagerhaus	warehouse
	Lagerraum	storage space
	Lagerräume	storage facilities
	Laminat	laminate
	Lampeninstallation	light fixture
	ländlich	rural
	Landschafts- und Gartengestaltung	landscaping
	Landschaftsbau	landscaping
	Länge	length
	Länge, Gesamtlänge	footage
	langfristige, strategische Finanzplanung	long-term strategic financial planning
	Lärmbelästigung	noise pollution
	laufende Toilette	leaking toilet
	laut, lärmend	noisy
	Lebensstandard	living standard
	Leck in der Gasleitung	gas leak
	Leckage	leak
	leer stehende Wohnung	vacant apartment, flat, dwelling
	Leerstand	vacancy
	Leistung	performance
	Leumund, Ruf, Reputation	reputation
	Licht	light
	Lieferant	supplier
	Lieferengpass	supply shortage
	liefern	supply
	Lieferung	delivery
	Lieferungen, Zubehör, Betriebsstoffe	supplies
	Liniendiagramm	line graph
	Linoleum	linoleum
	Liquiditätsreserve	cash reserve
	Loch	hole
	Loft, Wohnung über zwei Etagen	loft
	Lokal mit Speisen zum Mitnehmen	takeaway bar
	lösen, beschließen	resolve (verb)
	Lottoannahmestelle	lottery license shop
	Lücke, Kältebrücke	gap
	lüften	air (verb)
M	Mahnung	reminder
	Makler	agent
	Maler	painter
	Malerausbesserungsarbeiten	paint touch-ups
	managen, Geschäft führen	manage (verb)
	Mangel, Fehler	defect
	Marktführer	market leader
	Marktnische	market niche
	Marktstellung	market position
	Marmor	marble
	Maurer	bricklayer
	Maurer	stonemason
	Mehrfamilien-	multi-family
	Mehrfamilienhaus	multi-family house
	mehrgeschossig	multi-storey
	Mehrwertsteuer	VAT (Value Added Tax)
	menügesteuert	menu-driven
	Messing	brass
	Miet-	rental

	Miet- / Pachtverhältnis	tenure
	Miet-, Pachtvertrag	lease agreement
	Miete	rent
	Miete mindern (verb)	withhold rent payment
	Mieter	tenant
	Mieterakten	tenant files
	Mieterbeteiligung	tenants' involvement
	Mieterbund	tenants' association
	Mieterhöhung	rent increase
	mieternahe Dienstleistung	affiliated service
	Mietrückstand	unpaid rent
	Mietrückstände	rent arrears
	Mietvertrag	tenancy agreement
	Migration	migration
	Mikrowelle	microwave
	Missbrauch	misuse
	missbräuchlich, beleidigend	abusive
	Mittel (um etwas zu tun)	means
	mittelgroß	medium-sized
	Möbel	furniture
	mobil, Mobiltelefon	mobile, mobile phone
	möbliert	furnished
	Modeboutique	fashion boutique
	Modernisierung	refurbishment
	möglicher Mieter	prospective tenant
	Monats- / Quartalsbericht	periodical report
	Mörtel, Speis	mortar
	Müll	garbage
	Müllabfuhr	refuse collection
	Müllabfuhr	trash removal
	Müllbeutel	bin liner
	Mülleimer	garbage can
	Müllwagen	garbage truck
	mündliche Kommunikation	oral communication
	Muster	sample
N	Nachbarschaft, Wohnviertel	neighbourhood
	nachforschen	investigate (verb)
	Nachfragemarkt	demand-driven market
	nachfragen, fordern	request (verb)
	nachhaltig	sustainable
	nachhaltige Stadtentwicklung, Stadtumbau	sustainable urban development
	nachverfolgen	follow-up
	nachverfolgen, ablegen	file (verb)
	natürliche Ressourcen	natural resources
	Nebenkosten	service charges
	Nebenkosten	utility charges
	Nebenkostenvorauszahlung	advance payment for service charges
	Nettoeinkommen	net income
	Netzwerk	network
	Neuwertversicherung	day one reinstatement
	nicht zusammenpassen	mismatch (verb)
	Niederlassung	branch
	niedrige Miete	low rent
	Niedrigenergiehaus	low-energy house
	Not, Mangel	shortage
	Notar	notary
	Notfall	emergency
	Nutzungsdauer	useful life
O	Ofen	furnace
	öffentliche Interessengruppen	public interest group

Vokabeln Deutsch-Englisch

	öffentlicher Abfallkorb	street litter bin
	öffentlicher Dienst	civil service
	öffentliches Unternehmen	public-sector corporation
	Örtlichkeiten, Grundstück	premises
	Overall, Trainingsanzug	jump suit
P	Parkett	parquet
	Parkettfußboden	parquet flooring
	Parkhaus	multi-storey car park
	passen, taugen, übereinstimmen	suit
	Patio, Innenhof	patio
	Pauschale	lump sum
	periodisch	periodically
	Peripherie, Stadtrand	periphery
	Personal	personnel
	Personal	staff
	Personalkosten	personnel costs
	Pfand, Sicherheit	collateral
	Pfeiler	pier
	Pilotvorhaben	pilot scheme
	Pkw-Einstellplatz	parking-space
	Pkw-Stellplatz	parking
	Planwirtschaft	command economy
	Platte, Decke (Rohbau)	slab
	Plattenbau	industrialized building / apartment block
	plötzlich	sudden
	Polizei	police
	Portal, Veranda, Vorbau, Wintergarten	porch
	Postangestellter	postal worker
	Postausgangskorb	out-tray
	Posteingangskorb	in-tray
	Potenzial	potential
	Präambel	preamble
	Prämie	premium
	präventiv	preventive
	Preisliste	price list
	privates Wohnungsunternehmen	private housing company
	privatisieren	privatise (verb)
	Privatisierung	privatisation
	Privatsphäre	privacy
	Produktpalette, Bestand, Portfolio	portfolio
	Produktportfolio	range of products
	Projektleiter / Bauleiter	project manager
	proportional	proportionate
	provisorisch, vorläufig	tentative
	Prozentsatz	percentage
	pünktlich	on time
	Pünktlichkeit	punctuality
	PVC-Rohr	PVC pipe
Q	Quadratmeter	square metre
	Quartiersentwicklungsprojekt	community development project
R	Rabatt	discount
	Rahmen	frame
	Rasen	lawn
	Rasse	race
	rassistisch	racist
	Rauchmelder	smoke detector
	räumen, überlassen	vacate (verb)
	Räumung	eviction
	Rechnung für Wartung / Instandhaltung	maintenance bill
	Rechte und Pflichten	rights and obligations
	rechtliche Anforderungen	legal requirements
	Rechtsangelegenheit	legal matter
	Rechtsanwalt	lawyer
	Rechtsberatung	legal advice
	Rechtsschutzversicherung	legal expenses insurance
	Rechtsprechung	jurisdiction
	rechtsverbindlich	legally binding
	rechtwinklig	rectangular
	rechtzeitig	timely
	recyclen	recycle (verb)
	Regal(e)	shelf, shelves
	Regalbau	shelving
	Regelung, Rechtsvorschrift	regulation
	Reihenhaus	terraced house
	Reinigung	dry cleaning
	Reinigung und Pflege von Außenanlagen	groundskeeping
	Reinigungsdienst	cleaning service
	Reinigungsmittel	detergent
	Reklamation, Klage	complaint
	Renovierungspotenzial	renovation potential
	Reparaturarbeiten	repair jobs
	repräsentativ	representative (adj.)
	Rigipsplatte	plasterboard
	Risikobeurteilung	risk assessment
	Rohbau	framing, brickwork
	Rohr(-leitung)	pipe
	Rohrbruch	burst pipe
	Rollstuhl	wheelchair
	Routine	routine
	routinemäßig	routinely
	Rückenlehne	backrest
	rückerstatten	refund (verb)
	Rückstände	arrears
	Ruß	soot
S	Sackgasse	cul-de-sac
	Sägespäne	sawdust
	sanieren	refurbish (verb)
	Sanitär-	sanitary
	Sanitärinstallationen	sanitary system
	Sanitärinstallationsarbeiten	plumbing
	Sauberkeit	cleanliness
	Säule, Kolonne, Rubrik	column
	Schaden, Beschädigung	damage
	Schalter	switch
	Schalung	formwork
	Scheidung	divorce
	Schicht, Farbanstrich	coat
	Schiff	vessel
	Schimmel	mould, mold (AE)
	Schlafzimmer	bedroom
	schlecht, fehlerhaft	default
	Schlingel, Spitzbub	rogue
	Schloss	lock
	Schlosserarbeiten	mechanicals
	schmiedeeisern	wrought-iron

Vokabeln Deutsch-Englisch

schnörkelig, schrullig, schrill, sonderbar	quirky
Schornsteinfeger	chimney sweeper
Schreiner	carpenter
schriftliche Kommunikation	written communication
Schuppen, Lagerhaus	shed
Schuttentfernung	removal of debris
schwimmende Stadt	floating city
schwimmender Estrich	floating floor
Schwimmer	float-ball
Segment, Abschnitt	segment
selbst genutztes Wohneigentum	owner-occupied house
Selbstachtung, Selbstwertgefühl	self-esteem
Selbstjustiz	vigilant action / vigilant justice
sich der Länge nach hinstrecken / ausdehnen	sprawling
Sicherheit	safety
Sicherheit	security
Sicherung	fuse
Skelett	skeleton
solide	solid
Sonnen- / Solarenergie	solar energy
Sonnenblenden	sun blinds
sorgfältig	thorough
Souterrain	crawl space
Sozialamt	social services department
soziale, kulturelle, wirtschaftliche, ethnische Durchmischung	social, cultural, economic, ethnic mix
Sozialengagement	social commitment
sozialer Wohnungsbau	social housing
Sozialwohnung	social housing, council housing, RSL housing
Sozialwohnungsbau	low-income housing
Sozialwohnungsunternehmen in Großbritannien	RSL = Registered Social Landlord
speichern	store (verb)
Sperrholz, Schalungsplatte	plywood
Spiegel	mirror
spionieren	spy (verb)
Spitze, höchster Punkt	high
sprengen	bust (verb)
staatlich gefördert	government-funded
Stadt-, Gemeinderat	local government
Stadterneuerung	urban regeneration
Stadterneuerungsprogramm	urban regeneration programme
Stadterweiterung	urban development, urban extension
Stadthaus	townhouse
städtisch, urban	urban
Stadtplaner	town planner
Stadtplaner	urban planner
Stadtrand	outskirt
Stadtrat	city council
Stadtteil mit besonderem Entwicklungsbedarf, sozialer Brennpunkt, benachteiligtes Quartier	deprived area
Stadtwerke	public utility company
Stagnation, Stillstand	stagnation
stagnieren, stillstehen	stagnate (verb)
Stahlbauer	steel erector
Stahlträger	steel beam
Stalking	stalking
Standardversicherungssumme	standard limit of indemnity
Steckdose	outlet
Steckdose	socket
steif, starr	rigid
Steigerung	increase
Steigung	pitch
Steildach	pitched roof
Steuern, Abgaben	tax
Stockwerk	floor
Stockwerk, Geschoss	storey
Stopp	stop
Störung durch (Haus-)Tiere	disturbance caused by animals
Straße	road
Straßenrand, am Bürgersteig	kerbside
Straßenreinigung	street cleaning
Strauch, Bodendecker	shrub
Stroh	straw
Stromausfall	power-cut
Stromnetz	electricity grid
Stromversorgung	power-supply
Stromzähler	electric meter box
Stromzähler	electricity meter
stückchenweise, allmählich, nach und nach	piecemeal
Studentenwohnheim	student hostel
Sturm	storm
Swimmingpool	pool
Symbol	icon
T Tabakwaren	tobacco products
Tabelle	table
Tagesgeschäft	day-to-day operation
Teeküche	tea kitchen
Teer	bitumen
Telefonanschlussdose	telephone wall jack
Telefongesellschaft	telephone company
Temperaturfühler	temperature sensor
Tennisplatz	tennis court
Teppichboden	carpet, carpeted floor
Teppichbodenbelag	carpet flooring
Termin	deadline
teuer	costly
Textverarbeitung	word-processing
Thema	issue
Thermostat	thermostat
Tiefpunkt	low
Tilgung	amortisation
Tischler	bench joiner
Toilette, Wandschrank	closet
Toilettenschüssel	toilet bowl
Tor	gate
Touchscreen-Bildschirm	touch screen
tragende Wand	retaining wall load-bearing wall
Transaktion, Operation	operation

Vokabeln Deutsch-Englisch

	Trennwand	partition wall
	Treppen	stairs
	Treppenhaus	stairwell, staircase
	Trockenausbau	drywall
	tropfen	drip (verb)
	tropfend	dripping
	Tunnel	tunnel
	Türkette	door chain
	Türöffner	door-opener
	Türspion	door viewer
U	U-Bahn	subway
	Überangebot	oversupply
	Überbelegung	overcrowding
	überbewerten	overemphasize
	überblicken	oversee (verb)
	übereinstimmen mit	comply (verb)
	Überflutung	flood
	Überlastung	overload
	überprüfen, nachverfolgen	monitor (verb)
	überwachen, überprüfen	supervise (verb)
	Umfang	scope
	Umgebung / Umwelt	environment
	Umschlag	envelope
	Umwälzpumpe	circulating pump
	umweltfreundlich	environmentally friendly
	Umwidmung, Umwandlung	conversion
	unausweichlich	inevitable
	unbefristet	perpetual, for an unlimited period
	unbefristeter Mietvertrag	open-ended lease
	unbefristeter Mietvertrag	periodic tenancy agreement
	undichtes Dach	leaking roof
	unerlässlich	indispensable
	unerwartet	unexpected
	ungefähr, zirka	roughly
	unmöbliert	unfurnished
	Unterabteilung	subdivision
	Unterbringung	accommodation
	unterhalten, beibehalten, instand halten, warten	maintain (verb)
	unterirdisches Parkhaus	underground parking
	unterlassen	refrain
	Unternehmen	enterprise
	Unternehmens-	corporate
	Unternehmer	entrepreneur
	unternehmerisch	entrepreneurial
	unter Putz	flush mounted
	Unterschrift	signature
	untersuchen	examine (verb)
	untervermieten	sublet (verb)
	unterzeichnen	sign (verb)
	unzufrieden	unsatisfied, dissatisfied
	Urkunde	deed
V	Vandalismus	vandalism
	variable Mietneben-kosten	variable service charges
	Ventilator	fan
	Verabredung	appointment
	verantwortlich, zuständig	in charge
	Verantwortung	responsibility
	Veräußerung	disposition

verbessern	improve (verb)
Verbindung, Verhältnis	rapport
Verbrauch	consumption
Verbraucherschutz- und Lebensmittel-reinheitsgesetz	consumer protection and food safety acts
Verbrauchsgut	commodity
Verbrauchsgüter	consumption goods
Verbrennung	incineration
verdächtig, suspekt	suspicious
Verdienstausfallregulierung für Zeugenaussagen bei Gericht	court attendance compensation
verdoppeln	duplicate (verb)
Verdrahtung, Verkabelung	wiring
vereinnahmen	cash in (verb)
Vereinnahmung der Miete	rent collection
Verfahren bei Auszug / Einzug	move-in and move-out procedure
verfügbar	available
Verfügbarkeit	availability
vergittertes Fenster	metal-grilled window
Verglasung	glazing
verhandeln	negotiate (verb)
Verhandlung	negotiation
Verkaufsfläche	sales floor, sales area
Verkaufsprospekt	sales literature
Verkehrsverbindungen	traffic connections
verletzen	infringe (verb)
Verlobte(r)	fiancé(e)
Verlust aus Leerstand	vacancy loss
vermieten	let (verb)
Vermieter	landlord
Vermieterrechtsschutz-versicherung	commercial tenancy disputes insurance
verneinen, verleugnen, bestreiten, dementieren	deny (verb)
verpachten	lease (verb)
verpflichtend, vorgeschrieben	compulsory
verputzen	plaster (verb)
verputzen	trim (verb)
Verringerung, Reduktion	reduction
Verrohrung	ductwork
Verrohrung	pipework
versammeln	gather (verb)
Verschwendung	wasteful practice
versichert	insured
Versicherung	insurance
Versicherungsnehmer	insurer
Versicherungsprämie	insurance premium
Versicherungsunternehmen	insurance company
versorgen, bereitstellen	provide (verb)
Versorgungskosten für Strom, Wasser, Gas usw.	utility costs
Versorgungsrohr	supply pipe
Versorgungsunternehmen	utility provider
verstärken	reinforce (verb)
vertragliche Haftung	contractual liability
Vertrauen	trust
Vertreter	representative
verwohnt, abgewirtschaftet, heruntergekommen	rundown

Vokabeln Deutsch-Englisch

Vinyl	vinyl
Vorderfenster	front window
vorherige Benachrichtigung	prior notice
Vorkaufsrecht	option-to-buy
Vorkehrung	precaution
vorlegen	submit (verb)
Vorort	suburb
Vorort-	suburban
Vorzüge, Annehmlichkeiten, Ausstattungsmerkmale	amenities
W wachsen, anwachsen, steigern, ansteigen	increase (verb)
Wachstum	growth
wahllos, willkürlich	haphazard
Wand	wall
wandern, abwandern, ziehen, migrieren	migrate (verb)
Wandschrank	cabinet
Wärmeisolierung	thermal insulation
Warmwasseraufbereiter	boiler
Wartung und Instandsetzung	maintenance and repair
Wartung, Instandhaltung	maintenance
wartungsfrei	maintenance-free
Wartungskosten	maintenance cost
Waschbecken	washbasin
Wäschetrockner	tumble-drier
Waschküche mit Waschmaschine	laundry facilities
Waschküche, Wäschezimmer	laundry room
wasserdicht	watertight
Wasserdruck	water pressure
Wasserkran	faucet
Wasserkran	tap
Wasserrohr	water pipe
Wasserverbrauch	water consumption
Wasserversorgungsunternehmen	WASCs – water and sewerage companies
WEG-Verwaltung	service of condominium
Weingut	vineyard
Wende, Wendepunkt	turning-point
werben, Anzeigen schalten	advertise (verb)
Werbung	advertisement
Werkstatt	garage
Werkzeug	tool
Werkzeugkasten	toolbox
Wert	value
Wettbewerb, Konkurrenz	competition
wettbewerbsfähig	competitive
WGG, Wohnungsgemeinnützigkeitsgesetz	German non-profit housing act
wichtig	crucial
wichtig, wesentlich	essential
wiederherstellen, wiedereinstellen	reinstate (verb)
Wiederverkaufswert	re-sale value
Windel	nappy
Wintergarten, Gewächshaus	conservatory
Wirtschaft	economy
wohlhabende Menschen	wealthy people
Wohlstand	wealth
wohn-	residential
Wohnfläche	open-plan living area
Wohngebiet	estate, housing estate
Wohngebiet	residential area
Wohngeld	housing benefit
Wohngeld (für Eigentumswohnungen)	condo fee
Wohnheim, Herberge	hostel
Wohnimmobilie	residential (real-estate) property
Wohnimmobilie, Geschosswohnungsbau	apartment complex
Wohnküche	eat-in kitchen
Wohnraum	living space
Wohnung	dwelling
Wohnungsbaugenossenschaft	housing cooperative
Wohnungsbestand	dwelling stock
Wohnungsmarkt	housing market
Wohnungsübergabeprotokoll	move-out check list
Wohnungsübernahmeprotokoll	move-in check list
Wohnungsunternehmen	professional housing provider
Wohnungswesen	housing
Wohnversorgung	housing supply
Wohnwagen, Campingmobil	RV (Recreational Vehicle)
Wohnzimmer	living room
Wolkenkratzer	skyscraper
X X-Achse	x-axis
Y Y-Achse	y-axis
Z Zähler	register
Zaun	fence
Zeitschaltung	time switch
Zement	cement
Zentralheizung	central heating
Zentralheizung	central heating system
zentralisiert	centralised
zerkratzt	scratched
Zertifizierung	certification
Ziel	target
Ziel, Zweck	purpose
Zielgruppe	target group
Zimmer, möbliertes Zimmer	bed-sit
Zimmerdecke	ceiling
Zinsen	interests
Zinssatz	interest rate
zögern	hesitate (verb)
Zufahrt, Auffahrt	driveway
zufrieden	satisfied
Zusammenschaltung, Anschluss	hook-up
zuverlässig	reliable
Zuverlässigkeit	reliability
zuweisen	allocate (verb)
Zweifamilienhaus	duplex
Zweipersonenhaushalt	two-person household
Zweizimmerwohnung	two-room apartment